# The M.A.K. Halliday Library Functional Linguistics Series

This series focuses on studies concerning the theory and application of Systemic Functional Linguistics. It bears the name of Professor M.A.K. Halliday, as he is generally regarded as the founder of this school of linguistic thought. The series covers studies on language and context, functional grammar, semantic variation, discourse analysis, multimodality, register and genre analysis, educational linguistics and other areas. Systemic Functional Linguistics is a functional model of language inspired by the work of linguists such as Saussure, Hjelmslev, Whorf, and Firth. The theory was initially developed by Professor M.A.K. Halliday and his colleagues in London during the 1960s, and since 1974 it has held an international congress every year at various continents around the world. It is well-known for its application in a variety of fields, including education, translation, computational linguistics, multimodal studies, and healthcare, and scholars are always exploring new areas of application.

Man Guo · Qingshun He

# A Corpus-Based Study of Projection in English from the Systemic Functional Perspective

Springer

Man Guo
School of Foreign Languages
Sun Yat-sen University
Guangzhou, China

Qingshun He
School of Foreign Languages
Sun Yat-sen University
Guangzhou, China

ISSN 2198-9869 ISSN 2198-9877 (electronic)
The M.A.K. Halliday Library Functional Linguistics Series
ISBN 978-981-97-5093-1 ISBN 978-981-97-5094-8 (eBook)
https://doi.org/10.1007/978-981-97-5094-8



This Springer imprint is published by the registered company Springer Nature Singapore Pte Ltd.
The registered company address is: 152 Beach Road, #21-01/04 Gateway East, Singapore 189721, Singapore

# Acknowledgments

This book could not have been completed without the invaluable assistance and support of many colleagues, friends, and institutions. We are particularly grateful to Professor Guowen Huang at City University of Macao. Professors Chenguang Chang, Bingjun Yang, Yong Wang and Lei Zeng at Sun Yat-sen University have generally supported us in many ways during the writing and revising of the manuscript. Many thanks also to Rebecca Zhu, Sivananth S. Siva Chandran and Umamagesh A. Perumal from Springer Nature for their professional assistance and support in the publication process. This research is supported by the National Social Science Foundation of China (21BYY043).

Man Guo

# Contents

# Abbreviations

| | |
|---|---|
| ACAD | Academic |
| ADJ | Adjective |
| COCA | The Corpus of Contemporary American English |
| COHA | The Corpus of Historical American English |
| EFL | English as a Foreign Language |
| FIC | Fiction |
| MAG | Popular Magazines |
| NEWS | Newspapers |
| Phil | Philosophy |
| Rel | Religion |
| SFL | Systemic Functional Linguistics |
| SPOK | Spoken |
| TV | TV/Movies subtitles |
| Web | Web pages |

# List of Figures

# List of Tables

# Chapter 1
# Introduction

## 1.1 Research Background

Traditional grammar (e.g., Jespersen 1933; Quirk et al. 1985) refers to the subordinate clauses as in 1.1 as the objects of the main verbs of the matrix clauses from the perspective of constituent analysis. However, traditional grammar does not explain why the subordinate clause in 1.1a cannot be introduced by the complementizer *that* nor why the main verb *thinks* in 1.1b cannot be passivized:

1.1 a. He said, "We're talking about hiring a coach." (BNC_FIC)

b. She thinks that all soldiers are sluts. (COCA_FIC)

The relationship between the matrix clause and the subordinate clause in complementation has been studied in different schools of linguistics. Cognitive linguistics (e.g., Langacker 1991; Thompson 2002; Vandelanotte 2009; Verhagen 2005) specifies this relationship between the two clauses as conceptual subordination, and this relationship is determined by the prominence assigned to the two clauses. Pragmatic studies (e.g., Heine 2013; Holmes 1984; Myers 1989; Prince et al. 1982; Skelton 1997) of complementation are mainly about the role the reporting clause plays in performing speech acts, highlighting the grammaticalization process of reporting clauses as discourse markers.

The constructions in 1.1 are categorized into clause complexes of the projection type in systemic functional linguistics (SFL) (Halliday 1985, 1994, 2014; Halliday & Matthiessen 2004), the main clauses projecting and the subordinate clauses projected. Halliday (1977) first uses the term projection to refer to the logico-semantic relation between two grammatical units in SFL. The logico-semantic relation between two clauses can be either expansion or projection. Mental and verbal verbs can project. Halliday and Matthiessen (2014: 509–511) classify projection in terms of three systems: (1) level of projection, (2) mode of projection, and (3) speech function of projection. It is a source to enable human beings to talk about not just the first-order

 
M. Guo and Q. He, *A Corpus-Based Study of Projection in English from the Systemic Functional Perspective*, The M.A.K. Halliday Library Functional Linguistics Series,
https://doi.org/10.1007/978-981-97-5094-8_1

reality around them but also the second-order reality inside their consciousness. For example:

1.2 a. Ben said, "Why are you dressed like that?" (COCA_FIC).

b. Ben said he was working on the ninth of the twelve steps. (COCA_FIC)

In 1.2a, the level of projection is locution, the mode of projection is quoting and the speech function is statement. In 1.2b, the level of projection is idea, the mode of projection is reporting and the speech function is statement.

Projecting clauses that explicitly indicate modality (e.g., *I think*, *I expect*) are resources for enacting interpersonal meaning (Thompson 1996). Some projecting clauses (e.g., *I mean*) can also function as conjunctive expressions to construe the internal relation in organizing text (Halliday & Hasan 1976). Many studies of projection have been done in various areas, including refining the system network of projection (e.g., Ding 2000; Zeng & Yu 2005), exploring the metafunctions (e.g., Halliday & Matthiessen 2014; Xin & Huang 2010; Yang 2019; Zeng & Yu 2005) and grammatical metaphors (e.g., Dong et al. 2020; He 2021; Taverniers 2018; Yang 2019) realized in projection.

SFL's emphasis on language-in-use leads to its natural link with the corpus-based approach. Some studies on projection are conducted with empirical evidence from corpora (e.g., Dong & Fang 2021; He 2019a, 2021; Liardét 2016, 2018). These studies focus on the variation and development of projection. The user variation in employing projecting verbs indicates that the integration of projecting verbs with the authorial stance is an indicator of expertise in academic writing (Liardét & Black 2019). The genre and discipline variations are revealed by corpus-based studies from perspectives such as clause combining (He 2019a), ideational metaphor (Dong et al. 2020; Fang & Dong 2021) and interpersonal metaphor (He 2021; Liardét 2018).

A few studies (e.g., Dong et al. 2020; Fang & Dong 2021) investigate embedding projection as appositive, revealing that the finiteness of embedded projected clause demonstrates discipline variation and the types of projection and fact nouns demonstrate mode variation. Studies (e.g., Chen & He 2024; He 2021) from the perspective of interpersonal metaphor suggest that projecting clauses as interpersonal metaphor manifest less text technicality. These studies on the variation of projection provide insights that the use of projection is determined by a number of variables (e.g., projecting verbs, projection nouns and syntactic statuses) rather than by a singular variable. This calls for further investigation into the mode, genre, and discipline distributions of all types of projection.

The corpus-based diachronic research on projection has not yet been intensively conducted, but some findings have provided evidence on the development of projection from the perspective of clause combining (He 2019a). Some projections of embedding are regarded as the nominalization of clause complexes of projection (Halliday & Matthiessen 2004). However, the correlation between the development of the projection of interdependency and that of embedding is yet to be explored. The research on interpersonal metaphor indicates that the frequency of projecting clauses as explicit modality is increasing over time (He 2021), but projecting clauses as textual metaphor (e.g., *I mean*) have not been examined either. In addition, the function shift of projecting clauses (e.g., from the ideational domain to the interpersonal domain) also needs to be explored.

Grammatical metaphor in the Hallidayan sense arises from the semogenic rank-shift or transcategorization (e.g., He & Yang 2014; Yang 2019). The creation of grammatical metaphor across semantic domains is preliminarily discussed from the perspective of transcategorization from the ideational domain to the interpersonal domain and finally to the textual domain in nominal groups (He 2019b). These corpus-based diachronic studies suggest that grammatical metaphor can help identify the historical changes of projection in English.

## 1.2 Purpose of the Study

The purpose of this study is to investigate the text technicality of the different types of projection in real language use and to explore the evolution patterns of projection. For the investigation of text technicality, we will conduct a corpus-based synchronic study of the distribution patterns of projection in written and spoken texts with regard to mode, in non-academic and academic texts with regard to genre, and in soft and hard science texts with regard to discipline. For the exploration of evolution, we will conduct a corpus-based diachronic study of the shifts in projection from the perspective of metaphorization based on the notion of cline.

Theoretically, this study will deepen the understanding of the characteristics of projections in authentic language use and contribute to the theory of functional syntax. Practically, this study will provide insights into discourse analysis and pedagogical practice.

## 1.3 Organization of the Book

This book consists of eight chapters. Chapter 1 introduces the research background, the purpose of the study, and the layout of the research. Chapter 2 reviews the studies of projection in literature. Chapter 3 presents the theoretical framework. A systemic functional approach is taken to projection, and the notion of cline is adopted to explain indeterminacies in linguistic categorization. Chapter 4 describes the research design. The research questions, research methods, data collection and data processing are presented in this chapter. The next two chapters are corpus-based quantitative analyses. Chapter 5 is a COCA-based synchronic analysis of the mode, genre and discipline distributions of projection. Chapter 6 is a COHA-based diachronic analysis of the evolution patterns of projection. Chapter 7 is devoted to the discussion of the findings of the quantitative study. Chapter 8 concludes the research and points out the limitations and suggestions for future research.

## References

Chen C, He Q (2024) A corpus-based study of metaphor of modalization in English academic writing. SAGE Open 14(1): 1–15
Ding J (2000) A systemic study of project ion in English clause complexes. Mod Foreign Lang 23(1):45–57
Dong M, Fang AC (2021) Shell nouns as grammatical metaphor revealing disparate construals: Investigating the differences between British English and China English based on a comparable corpus. Corpus Linguist Linguist Theory 17(3):743–779
Dong M, Fang AC, Qiu X (2020) Shell nouns as grammatical metaphor in knowledge construal: Variation across science and engineering discourse. Lingua 248:1–25
Fang AC, Dong M (2021) Shell nouns as register-specific discourse devices. Int J Corpus Linguist 26(2):219–247
Halliday MAK (1977) Text as semantic choice in social contexts. In: van Dijk TA, János SP (eds) Grammars and descriptions: Studies in text theory and text analysis. De Gruyter, Berlin, pp 176–225
Halliday MAK (1985) An introduction to functional grammar. Arnold, London
Halliday MAK (1994) An introduction to functional grammar, 2nd edn. Arnold, London
Halliday MAK, Hasan R (1976) Cohesion in English. Longman, London
Halliday MAK, Matthiessen CMIM (2004) An introduction to functional grammar, 3rd edn. Arnold, London
Halliday MAK, Matthiessen CMIM (2014) An introduction to functional grammar, 4th edn. Routledge, London/New York
He Q (2019a) A corpus-based approach to clause combining in English from the systemic functional perspective. Springer, Singapore
He Q (2019b) A corpus-based study of transfers in English nominal groups. Glottotheory 10(1–2):57–84
He Q (2021) A corpus-based study of interpersonal metaphors of modality in English. Stud Neophilol 93(1):50–71
He Q, Yang B (2014) A study of transfer directions in grammatical metaphor. Aust J Linguist 34(3):345–360
Heine B (2013) On discourse markers: Grammaticalization, pragmaticalization, or something else? Linguistics 51(6):1205–1247
Holmes J (1984) Modifying illocutionary force. J Pragmat 8(3):345–365
Jespersen O (1933) Essentials of English grammar. George Allen & Unwin, London
Langacker RW (1991/2004) Foundation of coginitive grammar, vol. 2: Descriptive application. Stanford University Press, Stanford, Peking University Press, Beijing
Liardét CL (2016) Nominalization and grammatical metaphor: Elaborating the theory. Engl Specif Purp 44:16–29
Liardét CL (2018) "As we all know": Examining Chinese EFL learners' use of interpersonal grammatical metaphor in academic writing. Engl Specif Purp 50:64–80
Liardét CL, Black S (2019) "So and so" says, states and argues: A corpus-assisted engagement analysis of reporting verbs. J Second Lang Writ 44:37–50
Myers G (1989) The pragmatics of politeness in scientific articles. Appl Linguis 10(1):1–35
Prince EF, Frader J, Bosk C (1982) On hedging in physician-physician discourse. Linguist Prof 8(1):83–97
Quirk R, Sidney G, Geoffrey L, Svartvik J (1985) A comprehensive grammar of the English language. Longman, London
Skelton J (1997) How to tell the truth in the British medical journal: Patterns of judgement in the 19th and 20th centuries. In: Markkanen R, Hartmut H (eds) Hedging and discourse. Walter de Gruyter, Berlin, pp 42–63
Taverniers M (2018) Grammatical metaphor and grammaticalization: The case of metaphors of modality. Funct Lang 25(1):164–204

Thompson G (1996) Introducing functional grammar. Edward Arnold, London

Thompson SA (2002) "Object complements" and conversation towards a realistic account. Stud Lang 26(1):125–163

Vandelanotte L (2009) Speech and thought representation in English. Mouton de Gruyter, Berlin

Verhagen A (2005) Constructions of intersubjectivity: Discourse, syntax, and cognition. Oxford University Press, Oxford

Xin Z, Huang G (2010) Trigger mechanisms for the dynamic manifestation of projection across ideational and interpersonal metafunctions. Comput-Assist Foreign Lang Educ 8(1):44–50

Yang B (2019) Interpersonal metaphor revisited: Identification, categorization, and syndrome. Soc Semiot 29(2):186–203

Zeng L, Yu H (2005) Interpersonal meaning of projecting signal and its scale. Foreign Lang Educ 26(6):25–29

# Chapter 2
# Literature Review

The construction of projection has been discussed under different terms such as direct and indirect speech (Jespersen 1933), quotation (e.g., Bell 1991), citation (Swales 1986), reporting (Charles 2006), speech and thought representation (Quirk et al. 1985), speech reporting (Collins 2001) and many others. It has been an issue of central concern in a variety of approaches, such as philosophical approach, literary approach and linguistic approach. The literature review will focus on the linguistic approach, especially the syntactic and pragmatic analyses. The research in traditional grammar, cognitive linguistics, pragmatics and SFL will be reviewed.

## 2.1 Projection in Traditional Grammar

The projected clause is referred to as the content clause in Jespersen's (1933) term. A content clause contains a statement that does not exist by itself and should be treated as a whole to serve as the subject or object of a verb or preposition. It can be introduced with or without the complementizer *that*. See example 2.1 quoted from Jespersen (1933: 286):

2.1 a. I believe *that* he is dead.
b. I believe he is dead.

The content clause is "not a sentence by itself, but is made part of a sentence" (Jespersen 1933: 286). The complementizer *that* is desirable to expressively indicate subordination, but it is weakened and may not be preferred in colloquial language to enhance directness and straightforwardness. Jespersen (1933) observes the syntactic relationship between the matrix clause and the content clause from the constituent perspective, considering the content clause as the object of the main verb. Quirk et al. (1985) use the term reporting clause to refer to the speaker and the act of communication, and the term reported clause to refer to the report of the communication


M. Guo and Q. He, *A Corpus-Based Study of Projection in English from the Systemic Functional Perspective*, The M.A.K. Halliday Library Functional Linguistics Series,
https://doi.org/10.1007/978-981-97-5094-8_2

introduced by the reporting clause. The reported clause may take the form of direct speech, indirect speech, free direct speech or free indirect speech. For example, the reported clause in 2.2a is the direct speech, and that in 2.2b is the indirect speech, both functioning as the direct object of the main verb *said*:

2.2 a. Dorothy said, "My mother's on the plane." (1985: 1022)
b. Dorothy said that her mother was on the plane.

The matrix clause can also be viewed "as subordinate, functioning as an adverbial" in that it can be positioned variously and can sometimes be omitted (Quirk et al. 1985: 1023). For example, the reporting clause *they alleged* in 2.3a is positioned in the middle of the direct speech clause. It resembles the adverb *allegedly* functioning as a disjunct in 2.3b:

2.3 a. "Generals," they alleged, "never retire; they merely fade away."
b. Generals, allegedly, never retire; they merely fade away.

Disjuncts can be classified into style disjuncts and content disjuncts. Style disjuncts show the speaker's comment on the style and form of what he is saying. For example, *frankly* in *Frankly, I am tired* can be expressed as *I say frankly* or *I tell you frankly*. A series of longer disjuncts can be illustrated in as example 2.4 quoted from Quirk et al. (1985: 616):

2.4 a. *In short*, he is mad but happy.
b. *Putting it bluntly*, he has little market value.
c. *As a rough approximation*, you can expect a group of fifteen.
d. *Strictly speaking* she was out of order.
e. *If I may say so*, one of you is competent to make the legal judgment required.

Content disjuncts, also known as attitudinal disjuncts, concern the speaker's value judgment on the content. See example 2.5 quoted from Quirk et al. (1985: 622–623):

2.5 a. *Evidently*, he doesn't object.
b. *To my regret*, he did not accept our offer.
c. It is evident that he doesn't object.
d. That he doesn't object *is evident*.

## 2.2 Projection in Cognitive Linguistics

In cognitive linguistics, the relationship between the main clause and the subordinate clause can be divided by the prominence assigned to the two clauses. According to Langacker (1991/2004), the main clause and the subordinate clause differ from each other with respect to profiling. The main clause functions as the head at a particular level of organization, and the profile of the subordinate clause is overridden by that of the main clause. For example, in 2.6, *I know* is the profile determinant, and the whole sentence designates the process of knowing not of leaving:

2.6 I know she left.

Langacker (1991/2004) further specifies the relationship between the main clause and the subordinate clause as conceptual subordination. By conceptual subordination, he highlights the main clause's onstage role to frame the subordinate clause. The subordinate clause is not an independent object of the main verb but primarily plays a role within the relationship of subordination. Some studies (e.g., Diessel & Tomasello 2001; Thompson 2002; Verhagen 2005) argue that the main clause and the subordinate clause are equal in prominence but they support Langacker (1991/2004) that the subordinate clause is not the direct object of the main verb as proposed by Quirk et al. (1985). The reason is that subordinate clauses are not possible to be replaced by nouns and vice versa (Verhagen 2005) and that transitive verbs introducing noun objects can be passivized but clause objects cannot. For example:

2.7 a. I thought that he was too old. (COCA_MAG)
b. I thought oldness.
c. That he was too old was thought by me.

These reasons lead to different understandings of this construction. Diessel and Tomasello (2001) examine the development of object clauses in natural speech, finding that finite object clauses are some of the children's earliest complex expressions and the main clauses are propositionally empty functioning as epistemic markers, attention getters, or markers of illocutionary force. According to Limber (1973) and Shatz et al. (1983), *think* and other mental verbs are not used for mental reference in children's speech but rather for conversational functions. See examples quoted from Diessel and Tomasello (2001: 102, 111–114):

2.8 a. Peter remembered clearly that he had seen this guy before.
b. Peter told Mary that he would not come to the party.
c. Peter saw that Mary was coming.

2.9 a. I think I'm going in here.
b. I guess I better come.
c. I bet the other one's Shaggy.

The three sentences in 2.8 describe a cognitive activity (2.8a), a communicative act (2.8b) and the perception of an activity (2.8c) respectively, and the main clauses in these three sentences have propositional content. The three sentences in 2.9 are from children's speech. The subjects of the main clauses in these sentences are the first-person pronoun *I*. The main clauses represent the speakers' comments on the propositional content of the object clauses, and the main clauses themselves have no propositional content. Diessel and Tomasello (2001) propose that early complex constructions in children's speech are learned early and stored separately and have specific properties of their own.

Thompson (2002) also analyzes the data in conversation, proposing that object clauses should not be regarded as being subordinate to the main clauses but should be treated as having the same degree of prominence as the main clauses. The main clauses such as *I think* and *I guess* provide a certain perspective or stance toward the actions, e.g., assessment, claim, counterclaim and proposal, in the object clauses. See example 2.10 quoted from Thompson (2002: 132):

2.10 (at a birthday party, after Kevin was discovered to have lettuce on his tooth, everyone has jokingly commented on it, and Kendra has asked for a toothpick)
WENDY: everybody's getting uh,
Tooth obsessed.
KEN: I guess we a = re.

In this example, it is *we are* that aligns Ken's speech with Wendy's speech. The object clause is hence prominent in the interactional sense. The main clause serves as the stance frame for the succeeding object clause. Such a stance is usually epistemic, evidential and/or evaluative. Thompson (2002)'s viewpoint is shared by Biber et al. (1999) in their discussion of complement clauses. According to Biber et al. (1999), speech and mental verbs indicate the degree of certainty and express stance associated with the reported information. Semantically, the stance can be further categorized into three types, i.e., epistemic, attitudinal and style of speaking. Their corpus-based analysis shows that the main clauses with personal nouns tend to occur more in conversation and rarely in academic prose. Though Biber et al. (1999) do not highlight the prominence of the main clauses and that of the object clauses, they also consider the primary function of the main clauses as a frame of stance for the propositional information in the object clauses. Biber et al. (1999) term such main clauses as comment clauses. Seen from this perspective, the main clauses are not as prominent as the object clauses that contain propositional information.

Verhagen (2005) refers to the complementation construction as the complement construction, the main clause as the complement-taking clause and the object clause as the complement clause. His analysis is communication-oriented rather than ideation-oriented. According to Verhagen (2005), language is a system for mutually influencing which is achieved by intersubjective coordination. A language user can on the one hand subjectively keep relevant with the addressee and on the other hand objectively send information to the addressee. A construal configuration about intersubjectivity is illustrated in Fig. 2.1.

The whole complementation construction is a grammaticalized expression "for intersubjective coordination" (Verhagen 2005: 98). The main clause locates at the S level, and its primary function is to direct the addressee to adopt a certain perspective

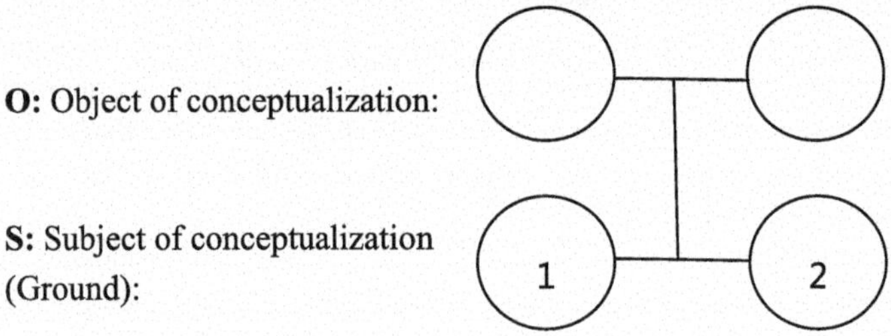


**Fig. 2.1** Construal of configuration and its basic elements (Verhagen 2005:7)

to perceive the upcoming proposition. The object clause locates at the O level and functions to convey a description of the event or situation. For example (Verhagen 2005: 105):

2.11 a: Will we be in time for the launch?
b1: It was scheduled for 4 p.m.
b2: I think it was scheduled for 4 p.m.
b3: Someone said that it was scheduled for 4 p.m.

In 2.11, the three responses can be regarded as different ways to invite the inference that the answer is "yes, we will probably be in time". The object clause contains the issue or claim being discussed and the main clauses *I think* and *someone said* show the speakers' stance toward the issue. The issue can stand on its own as in 2.11b1, which is labeled as "non-perspectivized utterance". 2.11b2 and 2.11b3 are labeled as "perspectivized utterance" (Verhagen 2005: 106). Their construal configurations are illustrated in Figs. 2.2 and 2.3.

In 2.11b2, there is an *I* that is an explicit conceptualizer to direct the perspective to be adopted, whereas in 2.11b1 there is no such "onstage conceptualizer" (Verhagen 2005: 106). Verhagen (2005) hereby concludes that the primary function of the perspectivized utterance is to coordinate cognitively with the addressee with the perspective specified by the main clause. The two-level analysis seems to be an explanation for why traditional constituency analysis fails to be applied to analyze the status of the construction. Verhagen (2005) further identifies personal and impersonal complementation. The onstage conceptualizer of the first-person complementation has the maximum argumentative force because the cognitive coordination is

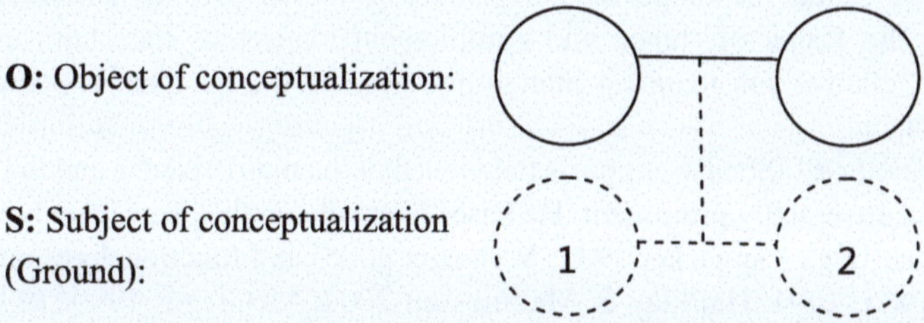


**Fig. 2.2** Construal configuration for non-perspectivized utterance (b1) (Verhagen 2005:106)

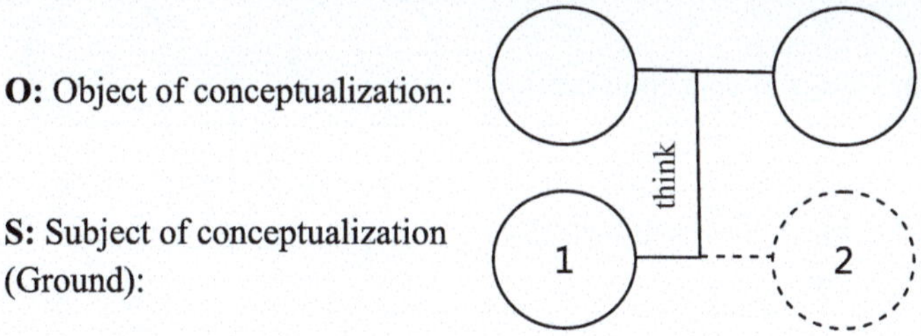


**Fig. 2.3** Construal configuration for first-person perspective (b2) (Verhagen 2005:106)

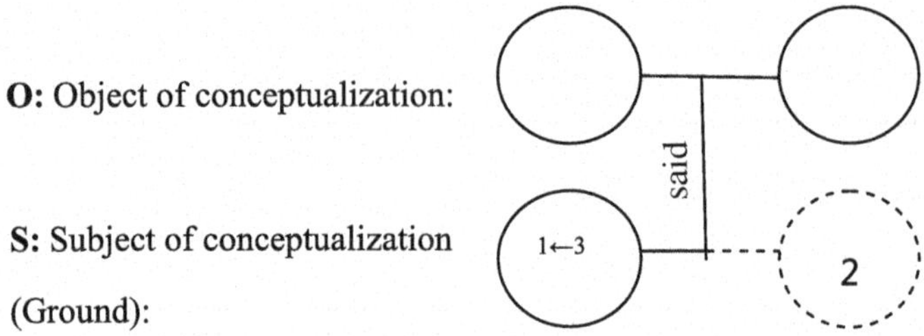


**Fig. 2.4** Construal configuration for third-person perspective (b3) (Verhagen 2005:106)

direct and explicit. It shoulders the responsibility and commitment for the succeeding claim. The addressee can directly ascribe the responsibility to the speaker. However, the onstage conceptualizer of a third-person complementation temporarily adopts a perspective from others and hereby the invitation to coordinate is indirect. See Fig. 2.4.

This makes its argumentative strength weaker than that of a first-person complementation. Verhagen (2005) considers extraposed *that-* clauses (e.g., *it is clear that…*) proposed by Biber et al. (1999: 672) as impersonal complementation. The construal configuration of such constructions is illustrated in Fig. 2.5.

Normally, the addressee will ascribe the responsibility for the claim that something is clear to the speaker. As indicated in Fig. 2.5, the impersonal complementation has no reference to a person who is the source of the judgment, and the identification of the subject of the conceptualization remains unspecified and may be left open.

To sum up, Verhagen (2005) opposes the idea that the matrix clause is the direct complement. Rather, he adopts the perspective of intersubjectivity and treats matrix clauses as the frame of stance and complement clauses as the claim container. The matrix clauses can manifest intersubjectivity by the personal and impersonal conceptualizers.

Vandelanotte (2009) also supports the view that the matrix clause and the complement clause are equally prominent. He bases his study on the ideas from both cognitive grammar (e.g., Langacker 1987; Verhagen 2005) and functional grammar (e.g., Halliday 1985, 1994; Halliday & Matthiessen 2004; McGregor 1990, 1994,1997), and interprets the relationship between the two clauses in the complementation

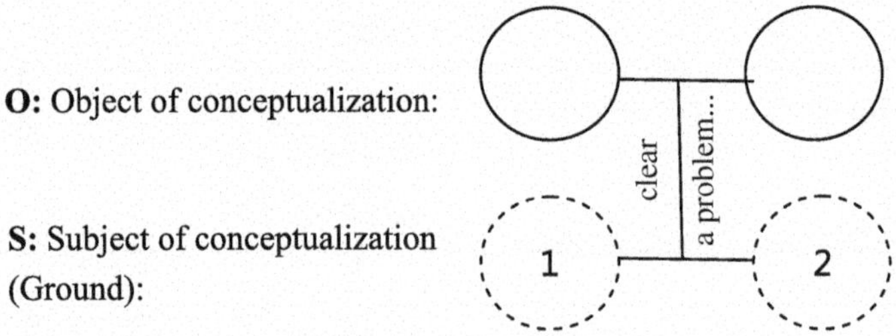


**Fig. 2.5** Construal configuration for impersonal perspective (Verhagen 2005:134)

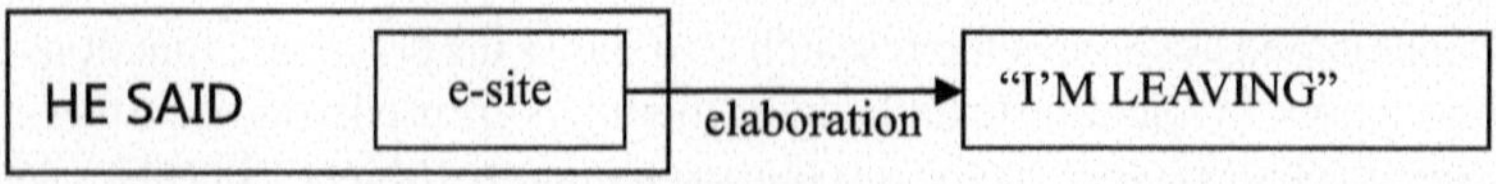


**Fig. 2.6** The conceptual dependence structure of direct speech or thought (Vandelanotte 2009:38)

construction from the perspective of intersubjectivity. Vandelanotte (2009: 38) proposes a new model to analyze the complementation construction. See Fig. 2.6.

Figure 2.6 shows that the complementation construction consists of two basic units. The matrix clause is semantically incomplete and hence is regarded as a conceptually dependent head. The object clause is conceptually a more autonomous complement (not a modifier) of the matrix clause as a whole (not of the main verb). Vandelanotte (2009) refers to the syntagmatic relation in free indirect speech and direct speech as juxtaposition, where the matrix clause can appear in different positions in the sentence, and the object clause does not need to have a complementizer. Meanwhile, he refers to the syntagmatic relation in indirect speech as a corporation, where the matrix clause can have a complementizer and is more tightly linked to the object clause.

## 2.3 Projection in Pragmatics

The research of the complementation construction from the perspective of pragmatics is mainly about the role the reporting clause plays in performing speech acts and social negotiation.

As for performing speech acts, the reporting clause can serve as a commitment modifier (Prince et al. 1982), modifier of illocutionary acts (Holmes 1984), hedging modifier (Myers 1989) and major truth judgment (Skelton 1997). The reporting clause as a modifying device can externally strengthen or soften the illocutionary force whose effects are unwelcome to the addressee (Fraser 1980: 342). See example 2.12 quoted from Holmes (1984: 347–348):

2.12 a. I guess it's probably a day-school. (teacher to student)
b. I solemnly promise I won't be late home today. (husband to wife)

In 2.12a, *I guess* can soften the illocutionary force. The information presented will be more acceptable and the addressee would have a stronger sense of being invited to engage in the discussion. In 2.12b, *I solemnly promise* can strengthen the illocutionary force to express a higher degree of intention of the speaker, reflecting the speaker's loyalty toward the addressee. Therefore, the degree of illocutionary force expressed by the reporting clause is not necessarily the speaker's judgment on the certainty of the reported proposition. Rather, it is a communicative strategy that is motivated by politeness in order to maintain the relation between the speaker and the addressee.

Evidence-based genre-specific research also shows the pragmatic functions of the reporting clauses. In scientific texts, hedging modifiers are used to indicate that certain claims are unacknowledged by the discourse community (Myers 1989: 12). Another study based on academic written texts by Myers (2010) includes reporting clauses into hedging speech acts and identifies three roles they play: (1) predicting a speech act of fact-threatening (e.g., *I would like*); (2) reducing and avoiding commitment to the proposition (e.g., *I suggest, it is hard to say*); (3) weakening illocutionary force of a claim (e.g., *be found, be identify*). The employment of hedging speech acts is also motivated by the norm and convention of the speech community. Likewise, reporting clauses can be understood as contributors to the indetermination, subjunctivization and depersonalization (Namsaraev 1997).

With respect to social negotiation, some reporting clauses are semantically understood as metadiscourses. Metadiscourse is sometimes referred to as metatext, or text about text (Hyland 2005; Kopple 1985; Moreno 2003). It is "the cover term for the self-reflective expressions used to negotiate interactional meanings in a text" (Hyland 2005: 37). Accordingly, metadiscourse is distinct from propositional meaning, embodies the writer-reader interaction and refers only to the internal relation of text. See Fig. 2.7 quoted from Hyland (2005: 44).

Reporting clauses can be regarded as a source of metadiscourse to help guide the reader through the text by indicating evidentiality (e.g., *Z states that*) and to involve the reader in the text by functioning as hedges (e.g., *I suppose*), boosters (e.g., *it is clear that, I'm sure that*), attitude markers (e.g., *I agree*), self-mentions (e.g., *I agree*) and engagement markers (e.g., *you can see that*) (Hyland 2005).

Another central concept in investigating the internal connection within a discourse is a discourse marker. Discourse markers are "sequentially dependent elements which bracket units of talk" (Schiffrin 1987: 31–41). Research (e.g., Brinton & Traugott 2005; Heine & Kaltenböck 2021; Thompson & Mulac 1991; Van Bogaert 2006, 2010) shows that some reporting clauses such as *I think* and *you know* function similarly to discourse markers such as *well* and *alright*. Such reporting clauses are not syntactically connected to the rest of the clause nor semantically referential. They can appear in flexible positions and are regarded as "parenthetical items of a clause

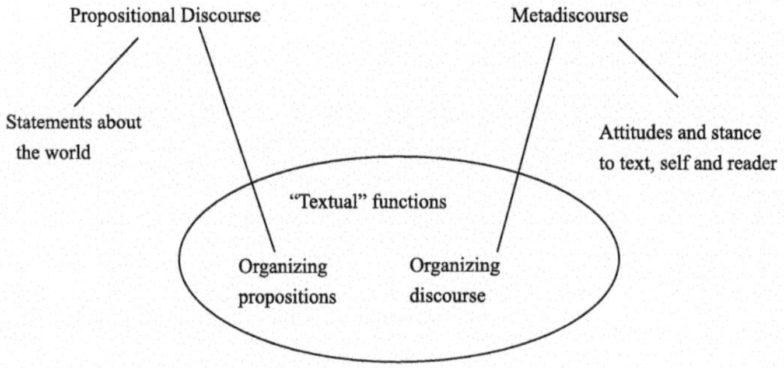


**Fig. 2.7** Types of textual functions (Hyland 2005:44)

nature" (Brinton 2008: 1). For example, the construction *I believe* in "*There were no other applicants, I believe, for that job*" occurs in the medial syntactic position, and it can also occur in the final syntactic position, as in "*There were no other applicants for that job, I think*" (Heine et al. 2021: 2).

Regarding reporting clauses such as those in 2.18 as discourse markers echoes Quirck et al.'s (1985) observation of content and style disjuncts, Hansen's (1998: 57–62) illustration about sentence adverbials, Rouchota (1998) and Huddleston and Pullum's (2002) discussion about parentheticals.

In the 1990s, the diachronic analysis started to emerge. Since then a large body of literature has focused on the development of reporting clauses into parenthetical-like markers.

One pathway to explain how parenthetical-like reporting clauses emerge is grammaticalization (e.g., Boye & Harder 2007; Brinton 1996; Brinton & Traugott 2005; Hopper 1991, Thompson & Mulac 1991; Van Bogaert 2006). Thompson and Mulac (1991) propose a matrix clause hypothesis based on their empirical study on reporting clauses such as *I think* and *I see.* They believe that the reporting clause was originally the matrix clause followed by the complementizer *that* and the subordinate clause. Later the complementizer *that* was gradually deleted and resulted in structural indeterminacy. The matrix clause is reinterpreted as an epistemic phrase expressing belief or attitude over the subordinate clause. Once becoming an epistemic phrase, this construction is free to float to various positions in the evaluated clause. Such positional mobility marks the emergence of epistemic parentheticals (Thompson & Mulac 1991: 326). The matrix clause hypothesis can be illustrated in example 2.13:

2.13 a. I think that the world is flat.
b. I think the world is flat.
c. The world is flat, I think.

This proposal is supported by the strong correlation between the frequency of *that* deletion and that of epistemic parentheticals (Thompson & Mulac 1991). The diachronic development of reporting clauses as pragmatic markers meets the five principles of grammaticalization proposed by Hopper (1991), i.e., layering, divergence, persistence, specialization and decategorialization.

The matrix clause hypothesis also received some criticism (e.g., Aijmer 1997; Brinton 1996; Rissanen 2008). Firstly, this hypothesis applies only to a few cases such as *I/you admit, I say* and *I see* and lacks applicability (Brinton 2006, 2007, 2008). Secondly, empirical studies on the diachronic change of more discourse markers show that the reanalysis of matrix clauses as parentheticals is not determined by *that* deletion or positional mobility. Although the diachronic pathway from matrix clauses to discourse markers remains controversial, it is popularly accepted that this diachronic development is non-prototypical grammaticalization (e.g., Brinton 1996; Brinton & Traugott 2005; Onodera 1995; Stenström 1998; Suzuki 1999; Traugott 1995).

Brinton (2008) applies parenthetical analyses to explain the process of change from reporting clauses to discourse markers, proposing that the change is not decategorialization but rather a shift from the narrow scope to the wide scope (from within the proposition scope to the scope over the proposition). The bond between the two clauses is getting loose, and this will lead to the reanalysis of the reporting clause as a syntactically independent element that is free to move. Unlike the matrix clause hypothesis, Brinton's (2008) hypothesis does not involve a reversal of syntactic hierarchy (matrix clause > parenthetical, subordinated > main clause), but the "deletion of an adverbial connective in cases where the logical connection of main and adverbial clause is contextually inferable" (Brinton et al. 2007: 160).

Boye and Harder (2007, 2012, 2021) provide an improved understanding of the grammaticalization of parenthetical reporting clauses. The diachronic change of parenthetical reporting clauses is a change from lexical clauses to grammatical clauses. The lexical and grammatical clauses can be either discursively primary or secondary. Grammaticalization consists in the conventionalization of the discursively secondary status. The final step of grammaticalization consists in the grammatical secondary clauses obtaining an adverbial distribution. Based on this account, all reporting clauses are structurally qualified to be grammaticalized.

Boye and Harder's (2007, 2012, 2021) proposal is compatible with Thompson and Mulac's (1991) matrix clause hypothesis and Brinton's (1996) account. However, challenges still remain in the decategorialization paradox and the lack of internal fixation.

Van Bogaert (2010, 2011) also adopts a usage-based emergent approach to redefine the diachronic development of *I think* as constructional grammaticalization, highlighting the schematicity and productivity that the reporting clause as a whole unit gains in the historical change. Constructional grammaticalization manifests degrees of grammaticalization. For example, *I think* is undergoing grammaticalization and hence explains why its decategorialization is incomplete. The grammaticalization of schematic constructions that are part of a wider taxonomy rather than isolated sequences explains why relative constructions lack internal fixation. Van Bogaert (2011) identifies a construction taxonomy of complement-taking mental predicates based on his research on *I think*.

The second pathway to explain the historical emergence of reporting clauses as pragmatic markers is pragmaticalization, a term defined as "a process of linguistic change in which a full lexical item or grammatical item changes category and status and becomes a pragmatic item" (Dostie 2009: 203). The outcome of pragmaticalization is a pragmatic marker which does not belong to any grammatical category. Some scholars (e.g., Aijmer 1997; Claridge & Arnovick 2010; Dostie 2004; Erman & Kotsinas 1993; Günthner & Mutz 2004; Waltereit 2002, 2006) hold that it is more appropriate to describe the shift from reporting clauses to discourse markers as a process of pragmaticalization. Their main argument is that pragmatic elements are optional in the sentence, not an obligatory part of the grammatical "core" (Aijmer 1996: 3).

In the case of pragmaticalization, a lexical item develops directly into a pragmatic marker without any intermediate stage of grammaticalization. The outcome markers mainly serve "as text structuring devices at [non-sentential] levels of discourse" (Erman & Kotsinas 1993: 79). One case of pragmaticalization is *you know* being seen as delexicalized without a trace of grammaticalization (Erman & Kotsinas 1993).

Another example is *I think* which develops meanings involving the speaker's attitude to the hearer or message (Aijmer 1997).

Waltereit (2002, 2006) insisted that the development of pragmatic markers is not a case of grammaticalization. Though he does not use the term pragmaticalization, his description of the process is close to the approach of pragmaticalization. Three stages are identified in the emergence of "historical relics of speakers' strategies for manipulating the structure of the discourse of the interaction" (Walterait 2006: 66). In the first stage, speakers recognize the potential inherent in certain forms for expressing textual interpersonal meaning and use ("abuse") them in contexts that are not justified by their primary meaning. In the second stage, such "abuse" gets more frequent, and speakers recognize that these forms are being overused or "abused" and they then reanalyze them as pragmatic markers in some contexts. The reanalysis leads to the semantic change while the conventional implicature is conventionalized. In the third stage, the pragmatic use can appear in additional contexts. Many pragmatic markers arise from words or constructions that "already have some properties typical for discourse markers" (Walterait 2006: 75).

As an explanatory concept for the rise of discourse markers, pragmaticalization has been the subject of debate. On the one hand, pragmaticalization shares a lot with grammaticalization in that they both result in functional words, dummy markers or clitics (Erman & Kotsinas 1993: 79), and both may adhere to Hopper's (1991) five criteria of grammaticalization. Some scholars (Brinton 2007; Prévost 2011; Traugott 1995) propose to include pragmaticalization as a subclass of grammaticalization.

The evolution of parenthetical reporting clauses is also studied in discourse grammar (e.g., Heine 2013; Heine et al. 2012; Kaltenböck 2011). Discourse grammar is composed of all linguistic resources that are available for constructing spoken or written texts. The linguistics resources can be further distinguished between sentence grammar and thetical grammar. See Fig. 2.8.

Sentence grammar is well documented in mainstream linguistics in terms of propositional concepts and clauses and their combination. Thetical grammar, on the other hand, comprises elements that are generally seen as being outside the confines of sentence grammar, the so-called theticals. Traditional grammar consists of a catalog of thetical formulae and constructions and the ability to coopt new theticals from sentence grammar for structuring discourse. Theticals are metatextual and relate to the immediate situation of discourse, mainly involving the following areas

**Fig. 2.8** A sketch of the architecture of Discourse Grammar (Heine et al. 2012:1217)

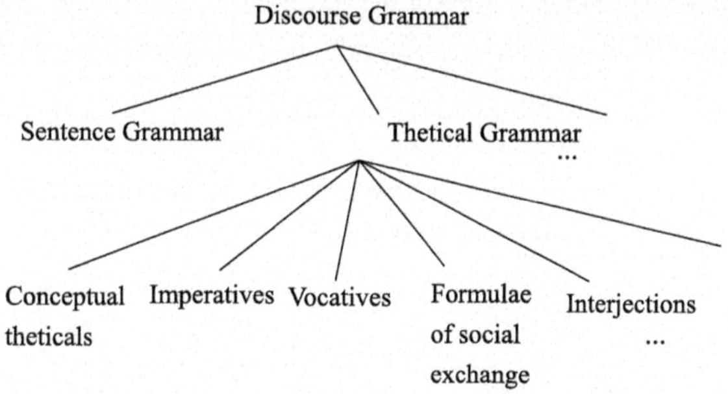

of discourse processing: text organization, speaker-hearer interaction and attitudes of the speaker (Heine & Kaltenböck 2021).

According to discourse grammar, cooptation is a ubiquitous operation whereby a chunk of sentence grammar like a clause, a phrase, a word, or any other unit is taken from sentence grammar and deployed for use as a thetical (Kaltenböck et al. 2011). Cooptation is by nature a cognitive operation whereby the existing material is exploited for a new function. In this sense, the reporting clause functioning as a discourse marker has also moved from the domain of sentence grammar to that of thetical grammar, and hence has undergone cooptation (Heine 2013). According to Heine and Kaltenböck (2021), the change of reporting clauses such as *I think* and *you know* from clause to discourse has involved both cooptation and grammaticalization (Heine & Kaltenböck 2021). Cooptation hence initially leads to semantically and syntactically free forms and then grammaticalization leads to internal integration and fixation.

These historical studies are largely qualitative and based on early documented instances of pragmatic markers in history. They highlight how reporting clauses initially started to play pragmatic roles and suggest a pertinent role that grammaticalization plays in the historical development of reporting clauses. The findings shed light on the subsequent development of complementation and call for quantitative research based on large-scale corpora.

## 2.4 Projection in Systemic Functional Linguistics

Halliday's discussion of projection starts from the identification of the relationship between clauses (Halliday 1985, 1994, 2014; Halliday & Matthiessen 2004). Projection is a type of logical semantic relation between the two clauses in a clause complex, in which a "clause comes to function not as a direct representation of (material) experience but as a representation of a (linguistic) representation" (Halliday 1994: 250).

Language serves three metafunctions, namely ideational function, interpersonal function and textual function (Halliday 1985). As a semantic domain, projection is manifested logically as clause nexus and experientially as circumstance within the ideational metafunction and interpersonally in the form of modal adjunct within the interpersonal metafunction (Halliday & Matthiessen 2004). See example 2.14 quoted from Halliday and Matthiessen (2004: 604–605):

2.14 a. The heavy storm has delayed the operation for a second straight day, said an officer. (logical)
b. A 12-year-old boy was in grave condition, according to witnesses and authorities. (experiential)
c. The ferry was reportedly carrying about 40 passengers when it capsized. (interpersonal)

**Fig. 2.9** Continuum of projection's manifestation

Projection is one of the two fundamental semantic domains that range over two or more grammatical domains, spanning two or more grammatical units (Halliday & Matthiessen 2014). Matthiessen (1995: 90) refers to the features of such categories that are "manifested in different ranking environments" as "FRACTAL".

Projection is believed to be one type of conjunction involving two dimensions: experiential and interpersonal (Thompson 2005). In experiential projection, the projecting clause is structurally the main clause and semantically the main proposition. In interpersonal projection, the projecting clause serves as a tag attached to the main proposition in the projected clause (Thompson 2014). Hereby, interpersonal projection is an important resource to construct intersubjectivity in discourse (Xin 2011). From the ideational perspective, the projecting clause construes the first-order phenomenon of the material world, and the projected clause is the second-order phenomenon of meaning and wording (Halliday & Matthiessen 1999; Thompson 2005). When there is a projecting clause, there is a projected clause. From the interpersonal perspective, some projecting clauses can be regarded as modal adjuncts (Halliday & Matthiessen 2004). The different interpretations of projecting clauses in the ideational domain and the interpersonal domain echo "fractal" features of projection (Matthiessen 1995: 90).

Xin and Huang (2010) propose a continuum of projection's manifestation across experiential and interpersonal metafunctions, with experiential projection on one pole and interpersonal projection on the other. See Fig. 2.9.

Hence, a projecting clause can be interpreted from either the experiential or the interpersonal pole. This is a dynamic and subtle interpretation. It is determined by various factors, including explicit factors such as first-person projector, tense and modality of projecting clause as well as implicit factors such as genre, cohesion, cultural background and so on. Accordingly, some strategies are introduced to facilitate judgment on whether a projection tends to be experiential or interpersonal. One common practice is by adding a tag question. See example 2–15 quoted from Xin and Huang (2010: 66):

2.15 a. Henry admits that this advice has been ignored by linguists.
b. Henry admits that this advice has been ignored by linguists, doesn't he?
c. I would say that this advice has been ignored by linguistics.
d. I would say that this advice has been ignored by linguistics, hasn't it?

Adding a tag question can help identify the intention of the speaker. As shown in 2.15a, if the speaker tends to experientially construe a verbal process, the choice of personal pronoun in the tag question will be consistent with the subject in the projecting clause. As illustrated by 2.15c, if the speaker tends to frame the projected clause with a personal judgment of the evidentiality and the projected clause is the main proposition being discussed, the choice of the personal pronoun in the tag question will be consistent with the subject in the projected clause.

Another strategy is to analyze whether the subject of the projecting clause is involved in the theme-rheme progression. See example 2.16 quoted from Thompson (2002: 132):

2.16 (talking about a photo collage on the wall)
TERRY: I think it's cool.
ABBIE: it i = s cool
MAUREEN: it i = s great.

In 2.16, the subject *I* in the projecting clause does not involve in the theme-rheme progression in the text. It indicates that *I think* is not the main proposition being discussed.

The projecting clause is also regarded as a metaphorical realization of interpersonal meaning (Davidse 1991/1999; Halliday & Matthiessen 2004; Martin 1992 ). When the interpersonal meaning is realized outside the clause, interpersonal metaphor is involved (Halliday & Matthiessen 2004). For example:

2.17 a. It is probably a dog. (COCA_BLOG)
b. I think it's a dog.

In 2.17b, the same modal meaning is explicitly realized as a separate clause, i.e., projecting clause or modal claused.

Two features of the projecting clause indicate that it is a modal assessment of the main proposition. The first is tag adding and the second is negation transferring. The following examples will help illustrate the two features:

2.18 a. I think it's going to rain.
b. I think it's going to rain, isn't it?
c. I don't think it's going to rain.

In 2.18b, a personal pronoun in the tag question corresponds with the subject in the projected clause rather than the projecting clause. The projecting clause constitutes the matrix clause in the dialogue. This is shown by the fact that it is the evaluated proposition that is being taken up by a question tag (Aijmer 1972; Halliday 1994; Nuyts 1990). Concerning negation transferring, when the proposition assessed is negative, the negation can either be expressed in the proposition itself or in the evaluating expression (Quirk et al. 1985). In 2.18c, the projecting clause can express the negation of the main proposition. Hence, the projecting clause fulfills the role of modal assessment and does the job of finite. As Thompson (2005) states, it is more common for the modal clause that is negated.

Halliday and Matthiessen (2004) distinguish two types of interpersonal metaphors of modality, namely explicit subjective modality and explicit objective modality. For example:

2.19 a. I expect that the right's heads will be exploding now. (COCA_WEB)
b. It is quite possible that the right's heads will be exploding now.

Both the projecting clauses in 2.19 are metaphor of modality 2.19a being subjective and 2.19b objective.

Nuyts (2000: 122–123) argues that the interpersonal meaning tends to have an operator-like status and stands apart from the rest of the clause representing a state of affair. Hereby, interpersonal expressions tend to be "free-wheeling" to take different positions in the clause. Halliday (1994: 197) holds a similar idea in his discussion of nominal groups and verbal groups that these types of groups begin with an "element that 'fixes' the group with relation to the speech exchange and end with an element that specifies the representational content".

Interpersonal metaphor can be discussed from the onomasiological perspective, i.e., a certain type of interpersonal meaning is taken as a starting point, which may be the congruent realization; and alternative of this meaning may be metaphorical. Taverniers (2008) then defines interpersonal metaphor as involving a doubling of semiosis: a doubling of scoping in its structural-realizational dimension, and a doubling of grounding in its semantic-functional dimension. For example, in *I think Andrea's put her finger on it*, to the grounded proposition (i.e., Andrea's put her finger on it), a second modal grounding (i.e., *I think*) is added, which embodies the speaker's evaluation of the validity of the proposition. The most grammaticalized realizations such as the expressions *I think* and *I suppose* receive a more independent status and thus acquire more flexible positioning (Taverniers 2008).

Interpersonal metaphor is also found to be mode sensitive and genre sensitive. The metaphor of modality is believed to be an important resource in the construction of academic texts (Liardét 2018). However, a more detailed investigation of modality specified by explicit/implicit and subjective/objective dimensions shows that subjective modal expressions dominate in fictional texts because they reinforce the existence of the speaker, while objective modal expressions dominate in academic texts (He 2021).

Halliday and Hasan (1976) categorize conjunction into internal and external conjunction. External relations are experiential relations oriented to what is going on outside the text. Internal relations encode the organization of text, functioning "in the unfolding of the speaker's communication role" (Halliday & Hasan 1976: 240). Take projecting clauses *I mean* as an example, it can serve as an internal conjunction to fulfill two types of cohesive relations: additive (exposition or exemplification) and adversative (of wording). The following examples illustrate how projecting clauses serve as an internal conjunction to indicate the relation between clauses. See the following example (Halliday & Hasan 1976: 254):

2.20 "What a beautiful belt you've got on!" Alice suddenly remarked… "At least," she corrected herself on second thoughts, "beautiful cravat, I should have said—no, a belt, I mean-…"

*I mean* in 2.20 indicates that the clause it belongs to is a correction of the wording of the preceding clause. Such a corrective relation ("not, but") is an adversative one between two language units within the text. Conjunctive elements do not directly connect discourse (Halliday & Hasan 1976: 226).

Martin (1992: 227) points out that "verbal processes are the most common way of explicitly constructing text as part of the world as it were". For example (Martin 1992: 226):

2.21 a. Ben came, *because* I spoke to him. (internal conjunction)
b. I spoke to Ben, so I'm telling you that he came.

2.21b is the paraphrase of 2.21a. If *because* construes internal conjunction, 2.21b is the correct paraphrasing. The paraphrase transforms the internal relation into an external one by "reconstructing the rhetorical structure of the text in the experiential world", and this is an instance of "the process of grammatical metaphor" (Martin 1992: 228). Martin (1992: 416) also proposes that discourse systems that can be used to construe text as "material" social reality are textual metaphors. Internal conjunction can be regarded as a type of textual metaphor because it is a text-organization pro-form. It should be noted that textual metaphor could be not only logically oriented but also interpersonally oriented (Martin 1992). It is a device used to express the speaker's attitude to the meanings being made.

Besides internal and external text organizations, textual metaphors are identified and defined from different perspectives, i.e., double transitivity (Thompson 2014), structural and unstructural organization of text (Lassen 2003a) and double functionality (He et al. 2015). Textual metaphors identified by double functionality are found to be genre sensitive and discipline sensitive (He 2021; He et al. 2015; He & Wen 2017).

## 2.5 Summary

This chapter reviews previous studies on projection, showing that projection is a widely investigated linguistic phenomenon in all grammatical traditions.

Traditional grammar (e.g., Jespersen 1933; Quirk et al. 1985) mainly adopts an approach of constituent analysis to analyze the form of the complementation construction. The subordinate clause is viewed as the direct object of the main verb. Cognitive linguistics focuses more on the syntactic relation between two clauses. Views vary on the status of the prominence of projecting and projected clauses (Diessel & Tomasello 2001; Langacker 1987; Thompson 2002; Verhagen 2005). The pragmatic studies of complementation show great interest in the pragmatic roles that reporting clauses play in social negotiation and discourse management (Heine et al. 2021; Holmes 1984; Hyland 2005; Myers 1989; Skelton 1997). The historical studies from the pragmatic perspective indicate that some reporting clauses may undergo a process of grammaticalization or pragmaticalization. However, the grammatical status of reporting clauses in complementation needs to be revisited and redefined.

SFL investigates projection in terms of clausal relation, metafunction and grammatical metaphor. Studies have been conducted on the synchronic (e.g., He 2021; He & Wen 2017; Liardiét 2018, 2022; Taverniers 2018) and diachronic (Halliday & Matthiessen 2004; He 2021) distributions of projection. However, no specific research has been done on the evolution of projection across different functional domains and the interplay between different types of grammatical metaphors. Therefore, a systematic study on projection can be further conducted with empirical evidence from large-scale corpora to elucidate the relationship between types of projection and text technicality, as well as the historical development of projection.

## References


Aijmer K (1972) Some aspects of psychological predicates in English. Almqvist & Wiksell, Stockholm

Aijmer K (1996) Conversational routines in English: Convention and creativity. Longman, London

Aijmer K (1997) I think — an English modal particle. In: Swan T, Westvik O (eds.) Modality in Germanic languages: Historical and comparative perspectives. De Gruyter Mouton, Berlin/New York, pp 1–48

Almutairi BAA (2021) Towards estimating global probabilities of evaluation in English based on automatic extraction of least delicate appraisal in large corpora. Lang Sci 88:1–19

Bell A (1991) The language of news media. Blackwell, Oxford

Biber D, Johansson S, Leech G, Conrad S, Finegan E (1999) Longman grammar of spoken and written English. Longman, London

Boye K, Harder P (2007) Complement-taking predicates: Usage and linguistic structure. Stud Lang 31(3):569–606

Boye K, Harder P (2012) A Usage-based theory of grammatical status and grammaticalization. Language 88(1):1–44

Boye K, Harder P (2021) Complement-taking predicates, parentheticals and grammaticalization. Lang Sci 88:1–19

Brinton LJ (1996) Pragmatic markers in English: Grammaticalization and discourse functions. Mouton de Gruyter, Berlin

Brinton L J (2006) Pathways in the development of pragmatic markers in English. In: van Kemenade A, Los B (eds.) The handbook of the history of English. Blackwell, Oxford, pp 307–334

Brinton LJ (2007) The development of I mean: Implications for the study of historical pragmatics. In: Fizmaurice SM, Taavitsainen I (eds) Methods in historical pragmatics. Mouton de Gruyter, Berlin, pp 37–80

Brinton LJ (2008) The comment clause in English. Cambridge University Press, Cambridge

Brinton LJ, Traugott EC (2005) Lexicalization and language change. Cambridge University Press, Cambridge

Charles M (2006) Phraseological patterns in reporting clauses used in citation: A corpus-based study of these in two discipline. J English Spec Purposes 25:310–331

Chen S, Xuan WW, Yu W (2022) Beyond reporting verbs: Exploring Chinese EFL learners' deployment of projection in summary writing. SAGE Open 12(2):1–12

Claridge C, Arnovick L (2010). Pragmaticalisation and discursisation. In: Jucker A H, Taavitsainen I (eds.) Historical pragmatics, Handbook of Pragmatics, vol. 8. Mouton de Gruyter, Berlin, pp 165–192

Collins DE (2001) Reanimated voices: Speech reporting in a historical-pragmatic perspective. Benjamins, Amsterdam.

Danis N (2022) A corpus analysis of disciplinary identity in evaluative journal articles: A systemic functional linguistics approach. Engl Specif Purp 68:87–101

Davidse K (1991/1999) Categories of experiential grammar. Clifton: Department of English and Media Studies. Nottingham Trent University

Diessel H, Tomasello M (2001) The acquisition of finite complement clauses in English: A corpus-based analysis. Cognit Linguist 12(2):97–141

Dong M, Fang AC (2021) Shell nouns as grammatical metaphor revealing disparate construals: Investigating the differences between British English and China English based on a comparable corpus. Corpus Linguist Linguist Theory 17(3):743–779

Dong M, Fang AC, Qiu X (2020) Shell nouns as grammatical metaphor in knowledge construal: Variation across science and engineering discourse. Lingua 248:1–25

Dostie G (2004) Pragmaticalisation et marqueurs discursifs: Analyse sémantique et traitement lexicographique. De Boeck & Larcier, Brussels

Dostie G (2009) Discourse markers and regional variation in French. Sociolinguistic Variation in Contemporary French 26:201

Erman B, Kotsinas UB (1993) Pragmaticalization: The case of ba'and you know. Studier i Modern Språkvetenskap 10:76–93

Fang AC, Dong M (2021) Shell nouns as register-specific discourse devices. Int J Corpus Linguist 26(2):219–247

Flowerdew L (1997) Interpersonal strategies: Investigating interlanguage corpora. RELC J 28(1):72–88

Flowerdew L (1998a) Concordancing on an expert and learner corpus for ESP. CALL J 8(3):3–7

Flowerdew L (1998b) Corpus linguistic techniques applied to textlinguistics. System 26(4):541–552

Fraser B (1980) Conversational mitigation. J Pragmat 4(4):341–350

Green C, Christopher E, Lam J, Mei K (2000) The incidence and effects on coherence of marked themes in interlanguage texts: A corpus-based enquiry. Engl Specif Purp 19(2):99–113

Günthner S, Mutz K (2004) Grammaticalization vs. pragmaticalization? The development of pragmatic markers in German and Italian. In: Bisang W, Himmclmann N, Wiemer B (eds.) What makes grammaticalization? A look from its fringes and its components. Mouton de Gruyter, Berlin, pp 77–107

Halliday MAK (1959) The language of the Chinese: Secret history of the mongols. Blackwell, Oxford

Halliday MAK (1985) An introduction to functional grammar. Arnold, London

Halliday MAK (1994) An introduction to functional grammar, 2nd edn. Arnold, London

Halliday MAK, Hasan R (1976) Cohesion in English. Longman, London

Halliday MAK, Matthiessen CMIM (1999) Construing experience through meaning: A language-based approach to cognition. Cassell, London

Halliday MAK, Matthiessen CMIM (2004) An introduction to functional grammar, 3rd edn. Arnold, London

Halliday MAK, Matthiessen CMIM (2014) An introduction to functional grammar, 4th edn. Routledge, London

Hansen MM (1998) The function of discourse particles: A study with special seference to spoken standard French. John Benjamins Publishing, Amsterdam

He Q (2019a) A corpus-based approach to clause combining in English from the systemic functional perspective. Springer, Singapore

He Q (2019b) A corpus-based study of transfers in English nominal groups. Glottotheory 10(1–2):57–84

He Q (2021) A corpus-based study of interpersonal metaphors of modality in English. Stud Neophilol 93(1):50–71

He Q (2022) A Corpus-based study of textual metaphor in English academic writing. Stud Linguist 76(2):381–405

He Q, Wen B (2017) A corpus-based study of textual metaphor in English. Australian J Linguist 37(3):265–285

He Q, Wen B (2018) A corpus-based study of the correlation between text technicality and ideational metaphor in English. Lingua 203:51–65

He Q, Yang B (2014) A study of transfer directions in grammatical metaphor. Australian J Linguist 34(3):345–360

He Q, Yang B, Wen B (2015) Textual metaphor from the perspective of relator. Australian J Linguist 35(4):334–350

Heine B (2013) On discourse markers: Grammaticalization, pragmaticalization, or something else? Linguistics 51(6):1205–1247
Heine B, Kaltenböck G (2021) From clause to discourse marker: On the development of comment clauses. Lang Sci 87:1–16
Heine B, Kaltenböck G, Kuteva T, Long H (2012) An outline of discourse grammar. In: Bischoff S, Jeny C (eds) Reflections on functionalism in linguistics. Mouton de Gruyter, Berlin, pp 155–206
Holmes J (1984) Modifying illocutionary force. J Pragmat 8(3):345–365
Hopper PJ (1991) On some principles of grammaticization. Approach Grammaticalizat 1:17–35
Huddleston R, Pullum G K (2002) The Cambridge grammar of the English language. Cambridge University Press, Cambridge
Hunston S, Francis G (2000) Pattern grammar: A corpus-driven approach to the lexical grammar of English. John Benjamins, Amsterdam
Hyland K (2005) Metadiscourse: Exploring interaction in writing. Continuum, London
Jespersen O (1933) Essentials of English grammar. George Allen & Unwin, London
Kaltenböck G (2011) Explaining diverging evidence. The case of initial *I think*. In Schönefeld D (ed) Converging evidence: Methodological and theoretical issues for linguistic research. Benjamins, Amsterdam, pp 81–112
Khany R, Hamzelou Z (2014) A systemic functional analysis of dictators speech: Toward a move-based model. Procedia Soc Behav Sci 98(1):917–924
Kopple WJV (1985) Some exploratory discourse on metadiscourse. Coll Composit Commun 36(1):82–93
Langacker RW (1987) Foundations of cognitive grammar, vol. 1: Theoretical prerequisites. Stanford University Press, Redwood
Langacker RW (1991/2004) Foundation of coginitive grammar, vol.2: Descriptive application. Stanford University Press, Stanford. Peking University Press, Beijing
Lassen IM (2003) Accessibility and acceptability in technical manuals: A survey of style and grammatical metaphor. John Benjamins, Amsterdam
Li Q, Zhang X (2021) An analysis of citations in Chinese English-major master's theses and doctoral dissertations. J Engl Acad Purp 51:1–14
Liardét CL (2016) Nominalization and grammatical metaphor: Elaborating the theory. Engl Specif Purp 44:16–29
Liardét CL (2018) "As we all know": Examining Chinese EFL learners' use of interpersonal grammatical metaphor in academic writing. Engl Specif Purp 50:64–80
Liardét CL, Black S (2019) "So and so" says, states and argues: A corpus-assisted engagement analysis of reporting verbs. J Second Lang Writ 44:37–50
Limber J (1973) The genesis of complex sentences. In: Moore TE (ed) Cognitive development and acquisition of language. Academic Press, Cambridge, pp 169–185
MaGrath D, Liardét C (2022) A corpus-assisted analysis of grammatical metaphors in successful student writing. J Engl Acad Purp 56:1–12
Martin JR (1992) English text: System and structure. John Benjamins, Philadelphia
Matthiessen CMIM (1995) Lexicogrammatical cartography. International Language Sciences Publishers, Tokyo
Matthiessen CMIM (1997) The relationship between grammar and discourse: An exploration based on computational tools. University of Macau, Paper presented at international conference on discourse analysis
McGregor WB (1990) The metafunctional hypothesis and syntagmatic relations. Occasion Pap System Linguist 4:5–50
McGregor WB (1994) The grammar of reported speech and thought in Gooniyandi. Australian J Linguist 14:63–92
McGregor WB (1997) Semiotic grammar. Clarendon Press, Oxford
McGregor WB (1990) A functional grammar of Gooniyandi. Benjamins, Amsterdam

Myers PG (2010) Hedging strategies in written academic discourse: Strengthening the argument by weakening the claim. In: Markkanen R, Hartmut H (eds) Hedging and discourse. Walter de Gruyter, Berlin, pp 21–41
Moreno AI (2003) Matching theoretical descriptions of discourse and practical applications to teaching: The case of causal metatext. Engl Specif Purp 22(3):265–295
Myers G (1989) The pragmatics of politeness in scientific articles. Appl Linguis 10(1):1–35
Namsaraev V (1997) Hedging in russian academic writing in sociological texts. In: Markkanen R, Schröder H (eds.) Hedging and discourse. De Gruyter, Berlin, pp 64–80
Nuyts J (1990) Negative-raising reconsidered: Arguments for a cognitive-pragmatic approach. J Pragmat 14:559–588
Nuyts J (2000) Tensions between discourse structure and conceptual semantics: The syntax of epistemic modal expressions. Stud Lang 24:103–135
Onodera NO (1995) Diachronic analysis of Japanese discourse markers. In: Jucker AH (ed) Historical pragmatics: Pragmatic development in the history of English. John Benjamins, Amsterdam, pp 393–438
Prévost S (2011) A propos from verbal complement to discourse marker: A case of grammaticalization? Linguistics 49(2):391–413
Prince EF, Frader J, Bosk C (1982) On hedging in physician-physician discourse. Linguist Profess 8(1):83–97
Quirk R, Sidney G, Geoffrey L, Svartvik J (1985) A comprehensive grammar of the English language. Longman, London
Rissanen M (2008) From 'quickly' to 'fairly': On the history of rather. Engl Lang Ling 12 (2):345–359
Rouchota V (1998) Procedural meaning and parenthetical discourse markers. In: Jucker AH, Ziv Y (eds) Discourse markers: Descriptions and theory. John Benjamins, Amsterdam, pp 97–126
Schiffrin D (1987) Discourse markers. Cambridge University Press, Cambridge
Shatz M, Wellman HM, Silber S (1983) The acquisition of mental verbs: A systematic investigation of the first reference to mental state. Cognition 14(3):301–321
Sinclair J (1991) Corpus, concordance and collocation. Oxford University Press, Oxford
Sinclair J (2003) Corpora for lexicography. In: Sterkenber PV (ed) A practical guide to lexicography. John Benjamins, Amsterdam, pp 167–178
Skelton J (1997) How to tell the truth in The British medical journal: Patterns of judgement in the 19th and 20th centuries. In: Markkanen R, Hartmut H (eds) Hedging and discourse. Walter de Gruyter, Berlin, pp 42–63
Stenström AB (1998) From sentence to discourse: Cos (because) in teenage talk. In: Jucker AH, Ziv Y (eds) Discourse markers: Descriptions and theory. John Benjamins, Amsterdam, pp 127–146
Suzuki S (1999) Marker of unexpected statements: An analysis of the quotative particle datte. J Assoc Teach Japanese 33(1):44–67
Swales JM (1986) Citation analysis and discourse analysis. Appl Linguis 7(1):39–55
Taverniers M (2008) Interpersonal grammatical metaphor as double scoping and double grounding. Word 59(1–2):83–109
Taverniers M (2018) Grammatical metaphor and grammaticalization: The case of metaphors of modality. Funct Lang 25(1):164–204
Thompson SA (2002) "Object complements" and conversation towards a realistic account. Stud Lang 26(1):125–163
Thompson G (2005) But me some buts: A multidimensional view of conjunction. Text 25(6):763–791
Thompson G (2014) Introducing Functional Grammar (3rd edition). Routledge, London/New York
Thompson SA, Mulac AA (1991) Quantitative perspective on the grammaticization of epistemic parentheticals in English. Approach Grammaticalizat 2:313–329
Thompson G, Hunston S (eds) (2007) System and corpus: Exploring connections. Equinox, Sheffield.

Traugott EC (1995) The role of the development of discourse markers in a theory of grammaticalization. In: Paper presented at the 12th innternational conference on historical linguistics, Manchester, UK

Van Bogaert J (2006) I guess, I suppose and I believe as pragmatic markers: Grammaticalization and functions. BELL-Belgian J English Lang Literat 4:129–149

Van Bogaert J (2010) A constructional taxonomy of I think and related expressions: Accounting for the variability of complement-taking mental predicates1. English Langu Linguist 14(3):399–427

Van Bogaert J (2011) I think and other complement-taking mental predicates: A case of and for constructional grammaticalization. Linguistics 49(2):295–332

Vandelanotte L (2009) Speech and thought representation in English. Mouton de Gruyter, Berlin

Verhagen A (2005) Constructions of intersubjectivity: Discourse, syntax, and cognition. Oxford University Press, Oxford

Waltereit R (2002) Imperatives, interruption in conversation, and the rise of discourse markers: A study of Italian guarda. Linguistics 40:987–1010

Waltereit R (2006) The rise of discourse markers in Italian: A specific type of language change. In: Fischer K (ed.) Approaches to discourse markers, Studies in Pragmatics, vol.1. Elsevier, Amsterdam, pp 61–76

Xin Z (2011) The projecting clause system for the construction of intersubjectivity: A corpus-based and text-type-oriented study. Foreign Lang China 3(1):44–50

Xin Z, Huang G (2010) Trigger mechanisms for the dynamic manifestation of projection across ideational and interpersonal metafunctions. Comput-Assist Foreign Lang Educat 8(1):44–50

Yang Y (2013) A corpus-based study of interpersonal grammatical metaphor in spoken Chinese. Lang Sci 38:1–21

Yang A, Zheng SY, Ge GC (2015) Epistemic modality in English-medium medical research articles: A systemic functional perspective. Engl Specif Purp 38:1–10

Yang B (2020) Interpersonal metaphor used in different discursive moves in reply posts of an online health forum. In: Yang B, Wen L (eds) Corpus-based approaches to grammar, media and health discourses: Systemic functional and other perspectives. Springer, Singapore, pp 377–396

# Chapter 3
# A Systemic Functional Approach to Projection in English

## 3.1 Introduction

The basic language unit of analysis in SFL is clause. Two clauses can be linked or bound together to form a clause complex. The logico-semantic relation between two clauses can be either expansion or projection. In expansion, one clause expands the meaning of the other clause, i.e., elaborating, extending and enhancing. In projection, one clause projects the other clause in the sense that the projected clause is a "second-order" use of language (Thompson 1996). In this chapter, the relation types of clause complexes of projection will be summarized. Then the characteristics of projection following the notion of cline will be discussed.

## 3.2 An Overview of Projection

A clause can be downgraded to function in another clause as a component of that clause or embedded in a constituent of another clause to function as a modifier of that constituent. Two clauses in a clause complex can be bound by structural devices. Accordingly, two clauses can realize two types of structural relations, including constituent relation of embedding within a clause and clausal relation of interdependency within a clause complex. For example:

3.1 a. The fact that it was some thousands of miles away troubled him not at all. (COCA_FIC)
b. She said that there was awful much talking. (COCA_FIC)

In 3.1a, the clause *it was some thousands of miles away* is embedded to serve as a modifier of the noun *fact* which is a constituent in the independent clause. 3.1a demonstrates the relation of embedding. The two clauses in 3.1b are linked by the



M. Guo and Q. He, *A Corpus-Based Study of Projection in English from the Systemic Functional Perspective*, The M.A.K. Halliday Library Functional Linguistics Series,
https://doi.org/10.1007/978-981-97-5094-8_3

complementizer *that* and form a clause complex, demonstrating a relationship of interdependency.

In embedding, the matrix clause is independent and the embedded clause is rank-shifted. Embedded clauses can stand on their own or serve as appositives of nominal groups. An embedded clause standing on its own or a nominal group with an embedded clause as appositive can realize participants in the clause being embedded into. For example:

3.2 a. That he has a leg up on new arrival Donald Penn isn't too shocking. (COCA_NEWS)
b. The reason is that the tax reform had serious limitations. (COCA_ACAD)
c. The idea that their birth certificates are filed away somewhere inside is a fantastical one. (COCA_MAG)
d. But I hated the idea that one day it might happen to me. (COCA_FIC)

The embedded clauses serve as the subject in 3.2a and as the complement in 3.2b, and they are known as the subject clause and complement clause in traditional grammar. The embedded clauses serve as the appositives of the nominal groups serving as the subject in 3.2c and as the a complement in 3.2d.

According to Halliday (1994), two clauses, i.e., the primary clause and the secondary clause, in a clause complex bear the relation of taxis. Taxis refers to the degree of interdependency, i.e., parataxis (equal status) and hypotaxis (unequal status). Hence, there is one initiating clause and one continuing clause in a paratactic clause complex, and there is one dominant clause and one dependent clause in a hypotactic clause complex. For example:

3.3 a. "It's everything I could have ever asked for," Littleton said, emotionally. (COCA_NEWS) (paratactic clause complex)
b. Littleton said, emotionally, "It's everything I could have ever asked for". (paratactic clause complex)
c. He thought that the students, both at Oxford and Cambridge were wealthy and arrogant. (COCA_ACAD) (hypotactic clause complex)

As shown in 3.3a and 3.33b, the first clause is the initial clause and the second clause is the continuing clause. They are equal in status and are reversible in positioning. Hence both 3.3a and 3.3b are acceptable. 3.3c demonstrates a hypotactic clause complex composed of a dominant clause and a dependent clause. They are not equal in status, and their syntactic positions are not reversible.

The clauses in a clause complex bear a logico-semantic relation, including expansion and projection. Expansion relates experiences of the same order of phenomenon while projection relates phenomena to phenomena of a higher order of experience. For example:

3.4 a. We were in the car when it happened. (COCA_NEWS) (expansion)
b. The manager said the city never removed any trash. (COCA_NEWS) (projection)

3.4a is a hypotactic clause complex of expansion. The dependent clause *when it happened* complements the meaning of the dominant clause *we were in the car* by extending the circumstance of time in the process of the dominant clause. 3.4b is a hypotactic clause complex of projection. The dependent clause *the city never removed any trash* is projected by the dominant clause *the manager said*. That means the projected clause "has already been said somewhere else" in prototypical cases (Thompson 1996: 200).

The two ways of structurally combining two clauses intersect with the logico-semantic relationship forming the system network of clausal relations in English (see Appendix A).

The current research will focus on projection. Accordingly, the basic types of projections can be identified. For example:

3.5 a. That he has a leg up on new arrival Donald Penn isn't too shocking. (COCA_NEWS) (embedding as subject)
b. Einstein came to regret that he had needlessly mutilated his original theory. (COCA_ACAD) (embedding projection as complement)
c. The chance that they would match up at every one of the fifteen to twenty sites is well beyond 1-in-1-trillion. (COCA_MAG) (embedding projection as appositive)
d. She said: " Do you think this will ever get easier? " (COCA_MAG) (paratactic projection)
e. She said that Democrats were trying to weaponize politics. (COCA_ SPOK) (hypotactic projection)

3.5a-c are embedding projections. In 3.5a and 3.5b, the projected clause directly serves as the subject and complement in the clause. In 3.5c, the projected clause functions as the post-modifier of the noun *chance* which serves as the subject of the matrix clause. 3.5d is a paratactic projection. The projected clause stands for the wording which is itself a representation. The projecting clause is a verbal process and the projected clause has a status of a wording. Paratactic projection reuses the original wording of other language events. 3.5e is hypotactic projection. The dominant clause basically precedes the dependent clause and the order is not reversible. The projecting clause is a verbal or mental process, and the projected clause represents meaning rather than wording. Unlike paratactic projection with an idealized function to represent exact wording, hypotactic projection has an idealized function to represent sense or gist. Hypotactic projection projects the meaning instead of the wording clause.

Clauses in the paratactic clause complex are both finite while the dependent clause in the hypotactic clause complex and the embedded projected clause can be non-finite. For example:

3.6 a. I want you *to watch something*. (COCA_FIC) (hypotactic projection)
b. He promised *to get his partners behind the financing and management*. (COCA_FIC) (hypotactic projection)

c. Truex isn't wrong when he highlights the need to collect whatever points he can accumulate over the next two weeks. (COCA_MAG) (embedding projection)

In 3.6a *to watch something* is the non-finite agnate clause of *you watch something.* In 3.6b, the non-finite clause is the agnate clause of *he will get his partners behind the financing and management*. In 3.6c, the non-finite clause succeeds the noun *need* and *the need* equates to the agnate clause of *people should collect whatever points he can accumulate over the next two weeks.*

Projection can be further categorized by the following three sub-systems: (1) level of projection, (2) mode of projection and (3) function of projection (Halliday & Matthiessen 2004). The level of projection helps distinguish two types of projections, including locutions and ideas. Locution refers to projection of the content of what is said and idea refers to that of what is thought. Mode of projection manifests the combination of projection with tactic interdependency and hence leads to two types: quote as paratactic projection and report as hypotactic projection. Paratactic quote is equivalent to direct speech, and hypotactic quote is equivalent to indirect speech in traditional grammar. It should be noted that there is one more environment for projection to occur in embedding. Embedding projection is equivalent to subject clause, appositive clause and complement clause in traditional grammar. The function of projection distinguishes whether the projection involves proposition (what is exchanged is information) or proposal (what is exchanged is goods and services) in enacting interpersonal relationships. Both quote and report allow for both proposition and proposal.

### *3.2.1 Parataxis*

The projection of locution and idea can both be paratactic. Since the two clauses are equal in status, both the initiating clause and the continuing clause can be finite. The projected clause can be either a major clause or a minor clause. Examples 3–7 are quoting propositions which include statements giving information and questions demanding information. Examples 3.8 are quoting proposals. For example:

3.7 a. "I wouldn't say I feel bad for him," Ayers said. (COCA_NEWS) (quoting locution: proposition-statement)
b. "What is this 'kingdom of God'? " he asked. (COCA_MAG) (quoting locution: proposition-question)
c. The rest we could imagine: the two chairs angled together, the feet bumping under the table, the smell of our mother's hair as she swished it from her face. (COCA_FIC) (quoting idea: proposition-statement)
d. Yes, filters are a necessary evil, but one has to wonder: Do they have to be so necessary? (COCA_ACAD) (quoting idea: proposition-question)

3.8 a. I promise: I'll listen to you complain. (COCA_FIC) (quoting locution: proposal-offer)
b. The waiter came along, and they ordered: roast beef for him and a small house salad for her. (COCA_FIC) (quoting locution: proposal-command)
c. I always come back from these walks thinking: "Okay, I'm ready to take on the next challenge." (COCA_MAG) (quoting idea: proposal-offer)
d. Andrew nods: He should have Medo hide the cameras. (COCA_FIC) (quoting idea: proposal-command)

### *3.2.2 Hypotaxis*

The projection of both locution and idea can occur in a hypotactic clause complex. The reported locution and idea can involve both proposition and proposal. Examples 3.9 are reported projections of proposition and examples 3.10 are reported proposals. For example:

3.9 a. He said the current situation is very dangerous and urged those traveling to be careful. (COCA_BLOG) (reporting locution: proposition-statement)
b. She asks if he's going to swim too. (COCA_FIC) (reporting locution: proposition-question)
c. We recognize that direct S-nitrosylation experiments shown in Fig. 6 are not conclusive. (COCA_ACAD) (reporting idea: proposition-statement)
d. I doubt if either would put themselves in that position. (COCA_NEWS) (reporting idea: proposition-question)

3.10 a. He promised that he would not raise taxes on anyone making less than $250,000 per year. (COCA_BLOG) (reporting locution: proposal-offer)
b. He ordered that all incidents with the United States must be avoided in the coming weeks. (COCA_MAG) (reporting locution: proposal-command)
c. He wished that his partner would come to that realization and then stop asking him. (COCA_FIC) (reporting idea: proposal-offer)
d. We hope that the revised form of our manuscript will be more comprehensible. (COCA_ACAD) (reporting idea: proposal-command)

Since the secondary is dependent on the primary clause, it allows the possibility of being non-finite. Projected propositions are realized as finite clauses, and projected proposals can be realized as finite or non-finite clauses. For example:

3.11 a. They promised to restart lower-level negotiations in two to three weeks. (COCA_SPOK) (non-finite reporting locution: proposal-offer)
b. She had commanded him to stay at home, and if he disobeyed her she would be very unhappy. (COCA_MAG) (non-finite reporting locution: proposal-command)
c. Later in the day, he planned to collect evergreen branches for the roof. (COCA_FIC) (non-finite reporting idea: proposal-offer)

d. They want you to tell them a certain thing and they want you to tell it to them in a certain way. (COCA_ACAD) (non-finite reporting idea: proposal-command)

Subjects in non-finite clauses of reported offer and command vary. The subject in the former one is in consistency with the subject of the primary clause, while that in the latter one is in consistency with the complement of the main verb in the primary clause.

### 3.2.3 Embedding

Projected clauses can be rank-shifted to be a constituent within a nominal group. The embedded clause does not bear direct relation with the matrix clause within which it is embedded. An embedded projected clause can serve as a post-modifier of the Head in a nominal group or prepositional phrase or as the Head of the nominal group. For example:

3.12 a. And I had the advantage that they had shut down the airport. (COCA_SPOK) (embedded attributive clause: post modifier in nominal group)
b. There is little or no stalking involved, but still abide by the rule that you should not press a subject. (COCA_ACAD) (embedded attributive clause: post modifier in prepositional group)
3.13 That he is considered a criminal is an obscenity. (COCA_NEWS) (embedded attributive as head of nominal group)

All three types of projections can be embedded, including reports, ideas and facts. For example:

3.14 a. I've been reading the statement that Bernie Sanders just put out about Nevada. (COCA_SPOK) (finite embedded locution)
b. This supports the assumption that this cell subset is the major site of TTV replication14, 15, 16 and suggests that TTV DNA load may behave as an immune system reconstitution marker. (COCA_ACAD) (finite embedded idea)
c. The fact that Blum was half Jewish made this even less funny. (COCA_FIC) (finite embedded fact as modifier)
d. That he's also half mortician is the secret he keeps to himself. (COCA_SPOK) (non-finite embedded fact as Head)

The nominal group in which the projected clauses are embedded can be used as subject, complement or as part of the adjunct.

3.15 a. The evidence that human and monkey stem cells are able to blossom into any cell type has been mostly circumstantial. (COCA_MAG) (embedded projection in subject)

b. These data support the idea that the natural variation in ER Ca2+ content across cells is a potential driver of synapse function via a feedback loop connecting ER Ca2+ and plasma membrane function. (COCA_ACAD) (embedded projection in complement)
c. We are, moreover, mesmerized by the promise that supercentralized controls will save the earth. (COCA_NEWS) (embedded projection in adjunct)

Embedding enables the projection nouns and the projected clauses to collectively function as participants in a process.

#### 3.2.3.1 Embedded Locution and Idea

Locution is projected by verbal process and idea is projected by mental clause. The Head noun that the embedded locution or idea modifies is the nominalization of the verbal group of projection (e.g., *statement* from *state*) or is derived from the verbal group of projection (e.g., *idea* from *think*). An embedded locution or idea must succeed a projection noun which serves as the Head of the nominal group. Embedded locution or idea cannot serve as the Head in a nominal group. Embedded locution and idea belong to restrictive attributive clauses in traditional grammar.

Embedded locution and idea can be divided into proposition and proposal in speech function. Proposition is projected mainly in indicative mode while proposal is mainly projected in imperative mode. For example:

3.16 a. The report that Rabobank stops its sponsorship hits me hard and raises a lot of questions. (COCA_WEB) (embedded locution: statement)
b. I'm just asking the question why was the word taken out? (COCA_SPOK) (embedded locution: question)
c. She believes Dilnot's call for a 35,000 cap on care costs may be too high and is not convinced by the proposal that individuals contribute up to 10,000 a year in residential care living costs. (COCA_ACAD) (embedded locution: offer)
d. Caribs at the beginning of every hurricane season with the request that they be informed if a storm was imminent. (COCA_MAG) (embedded locution: command)

3.17 a. We resist the notion that Lagos represents an African city en route to becoming modern. (COCA_BLOG) (finite embedded idea: statement)
b. I'm willing to give them the benefit of the doubt that they're not just yanking my chain. (COCA_WEB) (finite embedded idea: question)
c. I was given this book with the intention that I would review it within a month. (COCA_BLOG) (finite embedded idea: offer)
d. William and Harry have repeatedly expressed the wish that their mother be left to rest in peace. (COCA_MAG) (finite embedded idea: command)

Embedded locution and idea can also be non-finite. Non-finite embedded statement is realized by *of* + imperative and non-finite embedded question is realized by *whether* or WH- + perfective. Non-finite embedded offer is realized by *to* + perfective or *of* + imperfective. Non-finite embedded command is realized by *to* + perfective. For example:

3.18 a. I heard a rumor of using Microwave technology for subsurface coal gasification from coal. (COCA_BLOG) (non-finite embedded locution: statement)
b. When courts interpret precedents, they face the question whether to treat them as standards or rules. (COCA_ACAD) (non-finite embedded locution: question)
c. The proposal to legalize marijuana for adult recreational use was approved by voters (COCA_NEWS) (non-finite embedded locution: offer)
d. When I got the request to test out FORD's in Michigan I jumped on the opportunity. (COCA_WEB) (non-finite embedded locution: command)

3.19 a. But Aristotle's opinion of staying to watch the demonstration from the sidelines got put into words. (COCA_FIC) (non-finite embedded idea: statement)
b. Well, let's just say I have no doubt who to believe. (COCA_BLOG) (non-finite embedded idea: question)
c. It is our hope to make this second draft of history as definitive as possible. (COCA_MAG) (non-finite embedded idea: offer)
d. She waited for his command to exit. (COCA_FIC) (non-finite embedded idea: command)

All the embedded projected clauses of locution and idea are restrictive attributive clauses defining the head noun of the nominal group they are embedded into.

#### 3.2.3.2 Embedded Fact

Besides locution and idea, one more type of projection is identified as fact. Fact is not projected by any verbal or mental process and it comes as if it were readily packaged in projected form. The Head noun that embedded fact clause modifies is not the nominalization of any projecting process but that of "zero" (Halliday & Matthiessen 1999: 247). Embedded fact can be a modifier of the Head in a nominal group or stands on its own to be the Head in a nominal group. The former belongs to the attributive clause and the latter belongs to the nominal clause in traditional grammar. For example:

3.20 a. The growth of social media is based in the fact that it lets us be more human. (COCA_BLOG) (fact as modifier)
b. That people find themselves in rough situations is not debatable. (COCA_BLOG) (fact as head)

In 3.20a, *that it lets us be more human* serves as a modifier of the noun *fact* in the nominal group it is embedded. In 3.20b, *that people find themselves in rough situations* stands on its own as nominalization and serves as the head of the nominal group.

Fact nouns interact with modality in different ways and accordingly fall into four types: case, chance, proof and needs (Halliday & Matthiessen 2004). Cases are fact nouns of simple fact, bearing no interaction with modality. Chances are fact nouns accompanied by some degree of modalization. Proofs are nouns of indication equivalent to caused modality. Needs are nouns to which some degree of modulation is attached. Cases, chances and proofs go with propositions, while needs go with proposals. Cases and proofs are non-modalized, while chances and needs are modalized.

3.21 a. The fact that Rachel was not at the office only made Lynne more worried. (COCA_ FIC) (finite embedded case)
b. I would also like you to be open to the possibility that you are seeing what you expect to see. (COCA_BLOG) (finite embedded chance)
c. The missing source case-passenger is also a gap in the evidence that transmission occurred on the flight. (COCA_ACAD) (finite embedded proof)
d. It would rethink the obligation that troops return within 90 days. (COCA_ACAD) (finite embedded need)

3.22 a. In the case of driving with low vision, the question is whether a driver with low vision should be treated the same under the law as a driver who is fully sighted. (COCA_NEWS) (non-finite embedded case)
b. Despite the likelihood of rising rates, ARMs are doing brisk business. (COCA_MAG) (non-finite embedded chance)
c. It certainly carries the implication of using nuclear weapons. (COCA_SPOK) (non-finite embedded proof)
d. We are charged with the duty to judge the qualifications of the members of the House. (COCA_NEWS) (non-finite embedded need)

Among the four subclasses of fact nouns, only the embedded case can serve as head in the nominal group. Embedded case as head is "always agnate with an expanded nominal group with *fact* as head" (Halliday & Matthiessen 2004: 471). In this case, the fact clause is embedded though it stands as a nominalization on its own. Such embedded fact clauses are referred to as subject clauses and complement clauses in traditional grammar. They can be both finite and non-finite. For example:

3.23 a. That his ratings are slipping is beyond debate. (COCA_BLOG) (finite embedded case: subject)
b. I regret that I ever went on the expedition. (COCA_MAG) (finite embedded case: complement)

When embedded fact (case) stands on its own as head and serves as a complement (e.g., 3.23b), the simple clause containing an embedded fact appears in the same form as a clause complex of projection.

3.24 a. I think that's the strength of foster homes. (COCA_ACAD) (projected idea)
b. I regret that I took so long to come to this conclusion. (COCA_WEB) (embedded fact)

In the above examples, 3.24a, illustrate projected ideas and they are in the same form as 3.24b which illustrates the embedded fact. The projected idea is projected by the mental projecting process, and it is brought into existence in the course of the mental process. The embedded fact, however, exists prior to the occurrence of the mental process. The pre-existed fact enters a mental process rather than being projected by it. In 3.24e *I took so long to come to this conclusion* is not projected by *regret* but a phenomenon that enters the effective mental process of feeling regret. Hence, 3.24a is agnate with *In my opinion, that's the strength of foster homes* and 3.24e is agnate with *I took so long to come to this conclusion, which make me regret.*

Structural differences are put forward to distinguish hypotactic projected idea and embedded fact by Halliday and Matthiessen (2004). Firstly, projected idea (e.g., 3.24a) cannot be preceded by *the fact* while embedded fact, e.g., 3.24b, be expressed as *I regret the fact that I took so long to come to this conclusion.* Secondly, the projected idea cannot be replaced with a nominal group while the embedded fact can. For example, **I think the strength* is not acceptable but *I regret my decision* is acceptable. Thirdly, the projected idea can be substituted with *so,* while the embedded fact clause can be substituted by *it*: *I think so, I regret it.* What's more, embedded fact is the complement of the projecting verbal group and hereby can be changed from active voice into passive voice. Projected ideas are not the complement of the projecting verbal group and hereby passive voice is not acceptable (He 2019a). Subtypes of mental clauses vary in types of projections. A mental clause with an embedded fact clause is often emotive (e.g., *resent*, *worry*), perceptive (e.g., *hear*) and cognitive (e.g., *recognize, overlook*), while that with a projected idea is often cognitive (e.g., *think*) and desiderative (e.g., *hope*) (Halliday & Matthiessen 1999, 2004).

An embedded fact clause functioning as subject can be extraposed with a dummy pronoun *it* filling the slot of the subject. 3.23a is agnate with *It is beyond debate that his ratings are slipping.* Both finite and non-finite embedded fact clauses can be extraposed. For example:

3.25 a. Then it strikes me that the statute of limitations is long past. (COCA_FIC)
b. It scares me to see us losing that. (COCA_NEWS)

In the above examples, *it* is simply a subject placeholder. The fact clause is the subject of the clause, and it can occupy its position at the front. Facts can also be regarded as being "projected impersonally, either by relational process, by impersonal mental process or by impersonal verbal process" (Halliday & Matthiessen 2004: 472). Such "impersonal projection" is "not really a process at all" (Halliday & Matthiessen 2014: 549).

## 3.3 Cline in Projection

In this section, the notion of cline will be adopted to analyze the grammatical status of projecting clauses and projected clauses under different circumstances. The notion of cline will be introduced first and then three clines dealing with the grammatical status of projecting clause, projected clause and embedded projected clause will be presented, respectively.

### *3.3.1 The Notion of Cline*

In linguistic research, categorization is used to identify similarities and differences. However, there are always language units that do not have neat boundaries to fall into any language category. Such discreteness cannot be overlooked because they do exist and cannot be eradicated by various categorizations. SFL uses the term "cline" to refer to a continuum with two categories at the endpoints and members sharing various degrees of similarities to the two categories in between (Halliday & Matthiessen 1999).

A traditional approach to categorization is influenced by Aristotle's work. This approach is based on four assumptions: (1) categories are defined by necessary and sufficient features; law of contradiction (i.e., a thing cannot both belong and not belong to a category) and law of excluded middle (i.e., a thing must either belong to a category or not belong to it); (2) features are binary; (3) features have binaries; (4) all members of a category have equal status. With the traditional approach, the differences between categories are highlighted while the similarities are excluded and ignored (Yang 2003). Hereby uncertainty and indeterminacies are not accepted.

The cognitive approach to categorization is influenced by Wittgenstein's (1967: 32) idea of "the family resemblance," according to which the core of categorization is a prototype and the degree of membership depends on the degree of similarity. The cognitive approach accepts fuzziness and gradualness and regards categories as matters of gradience.

SFL orients toward rhetoric and ethnography and views language as a resource for making meaning. Compared with the cognitive approach that highlights human experience, SFL is concerned with how meaning is construed in naturally occurring speech. The approach of categorization SFL adopts is different from the above two. Halliday pointed out that "the distinction between closed system pattern and open set patterns in language is in fact a cline"; but they should be theoretically treated as "two distinct types of patterns requiring different categories". Consequenctly, general linguistic theory has to "provide both a theory of grammar and a theory of lexis, and also a means of relating the two" (Halliday 1961/2002: 41) and that "a cline resembles a hierarchy in that it involves relation along a single dimension; but instead of being made up of a number of discrete terms a cline is a continuum carrying potentially infinite gradation" (Halliday 1961/2002: 42).

The notion of cline can help explain a lot of language phenomena that formal linguistics fails to explain (He 2019a; Yang 2003). For example, traditional grammar identifies two types of interdependency relations between two clauses within a clause complex: coordination and subordination. The former refers to two clauses that share equal syntactic status and the latter refers to two clauses that have unequal syntactic status.

Typical coordination is symmetrical in that the order of the coordinate clauses can be reversed. However, asymmetrical coordination is also common nowadays, and the displacement of such coordinative clauses can make a difference in the meaning. For example:

3.26 a. Uncle Harrison Jones had graduated from the University of Georgia, and he was a great man. (COCA_ ACAD) (symmetrical coordination)
b. He offered the man $200, and the man accepted the offer. (COCA_NEWS) (asymmetrical coordination)
c. Remember me, and I will always be a part of you. (COCA_FIC) (asymmetrical coordination)

3.26a is symmetrical coordination and the two clauses can be transposed without changing the meaning. 3.26b and 3.26c are asymmetrical and the clauses cannot be displaced. 3.26b is syntactically coordinate but semantically asymmetrical. It should be noted that 3.26c is both asymmetrical in meaning and syntax because the initial clause is an imperative and the continuing one is a declarative. Such syntactic-meaning mismatches can exist in natural language coordination (Fabricius-Hansen & Ramm 2008). In this sense, the symmetrical and asymmetrical manifest different degrees of coordination.

Typical subordinate clauses include subject clause, object clause, adverbial clause, attributive clause and appositive clause. Subordination relation is hierarchical. The subordinate clauses are lower in syntactic status than the matrix clause. Subordinate clauses can be further classified into dependent clauses and embedded clauses. The dependent clause is attached to the matrix clause and the embedded clause assumes a constituent in the matrix clause. A subordinate clause is understood as being "embedded as a constituent of a matrix sentence" (Holler 2008: 188). The subject clause, object clause and adverbial clause are embedded to serve as subject, object and adverbial respectively in the matrix clause. Attributive clauses and appositive clauses are embedded to serve as modifiers within nominal groups. In this sense, both dependent and embedded clauses can be viewed as embedded clauses, and they manifest different degrees of embedding depth. For example:

3.27 a. When he wakes up, his mind is completely gone. (COCA_WEB) (adverbial clause)
b. Jackson, who died in 2009, repeatedly denied the allegations during his lifetime. (COCA_MAG) (attributive clause: nonrestrictive)
c. One man chooses to forgive the boy who killed his son. (COCA_NEWS) (attributive clause: restrictive)
d. It also carries with it the truth that you have failed in your obedience. (COCA_BLOG) (appositive clause)

e. That he lives shows the breadth of my magnanimity. (COCA_MOV) (subject clause)
f. I like that it has a clock and alarm. (COCA_WEB) (object clause)

An adverbial clause has the feature of asymmetrical coordination. Nonrestrictive attributive clauses are more likely to realize coordination than restrictive ones. Both adverbial clauses and nonrestrictive clauses function like adjuncts, and their matrix clauses can stand on their own without such syntactic adjuncts. In this sense, adverbial clauses and nonrestrictive attributive clauses are typical dependent clauses. Restrictive attributive clauses and appositive clauses are embedded as modifiers of nouns. They are not the indispensable part of the matrix clause and can be omitted. In this sense, they are typical embedded clauses. Subject clauses and object clauses are introduced by complementizer *that,* and they are indispensable for their matrix clauses. Hence, subject clauses and object clauses are neither typical dependent clauses nor typical embedded clauses.

The obscure distinction between coordination and subordination and that between dependent and embedded clauses can be explained by the notion of cline. In the Hallidayan sense, how two clauses within a clause complex or simplex relate to each other is determined by the degree of interdependency (i.e., parataxis, hypotaxis, embedding) and the logico-semantic relation (i.e., either expansion or projection). There is no clear boundary between three types of clauses combining: parataxis, hypotaxis and embedding. Types of interdependencies between clauses form a cline from the most typical parataxis to the most typical embedding, with paratactic projection, hypotactic expansion, hypotactic projection, embedded expansion and embedded projection in between (He 2019a). For example:

3.28 a. Unfortunately, the pastry was soggy and the apples had a mealy, mushy texture. (COCA_NEWS) (paratactic expansion)
b. He said: "I have good news for you. " (COCA_FIC) (paratactic projection)
c. She wants to be a computer engineer when she grows up. (COCA_MOV) (hypotactic expansion)
d. Similarly, Plato argued that groups are bound by an essential characteristic. (COCA_TV) (hypotactic projection)
e. I regret that I didn't spot this issue in my amicus. (COCA_WEB) (embedded projection as head: complement)
f. That he had some conflict with his golf club, also appears to be not true. (COCA_SPOK) (embedded projection as head: subject)
g. Don't believe the rumor that a flu shot can give you even a mild case of influenza. (COCA_WEB) (embedded projection as modifier)
h. One can't exploit the man who has nothing. (COCA_BLOG) (embedded expansion as modifier)

In 3.28, only paratactic expansion cannot be regarded as embedding. The other types of clause linking patterns can undergo double analysis in syntax and transitivity. Hereby, they can be viewed as both clause complexes and simple clauses with embedded elements. For example, the double analysis of 3.28b can be illustrated as follows:

| 3.28b | He | said: | "I | have | good news | for you." |
|---|---|---|---|---|---|---|
| Syntactic structure | Subject | Predicate | Subject | Predicate | Complement | Adjunct |
| | | | Complement | | | |
| Transitivity structure | Sayer | Process | Carrier | Process | Attribute | Circumstance |
| | | | Verbiage | | | |

Examples in 3.28 illustrate that the categories of parataxis, hypotaxis and embedding form a cline rather than being separated by a clear boundary. Members in between the categories demonstrate different degrees of clause combining. The degree of clause combining from 3.28a to 3.28f ranges from the weakest to the strongest, respectively. In the Hallidayan sense, a clause is composed of groups or phrases and a group or phrase is composed of words. Examples in 3.28 demonstrate different degrees of embedding depth. Paratactic clauses of projection, adjunct clause, complement clause and subject clause are embedded in clauses and realize participants. They belong to the group/phrase rank. Appositive clauses and modifier clauses are embedded in the nominal group, and hence they belong to the word rank. A more detailed cline of embedding depth is identified by He (2019a: 35): paratactic expansion < paratactic clauses of projection < adjunct clauses < complement clauses < subject clause < appositive clauses < modifier clauses.

Projection is manifested not only logically and experientially in the ideational domain but also interpersonally in the interpersonal domain (Halliday & Matthiessen 2004; Thompson 2005). Some projecting clauses can also serve as internal conjunctions to fulfill cohesive relations (Halliday & Hasan 1976). Hereby, PROJECTION RELATION is used to refer to how clauses are combined with each other in a clause complex or simplex involving a logico-semantic relation of projection. Clause complexes of projection involve different clause combining patterns, namely paratactic, hypotactic and embedding. Based on the views of cline in clause combining, the phenomenon of projection can be revisited and some controversial issues can be redefined.

### 3.3.2 *Cline of Projecting Clause*

One controversy about projection clause complexes is the grammatical and propositional status of the projected clause and the projecting clause. Whether the projecting clause or the projected clause should be regarded as maintaining a higher status remains controversial (e.g., Brinton 2008; Langacker 1987; Quirk et al. 1985; Thompson 2002; Verhagen 2005).

When a projecting clause construes the experience of a sayer's/sensor's verbal or mental behavior, it contains the main proposition being discussed. The projected clause construes the content projected by the projecting verb. The projected clause construes a second-order phenomenon and cannot exist without the projecting clause. The relationship between the projecting clause and projected clause is hence an interdependent relation. The projecting clause is the primary clause, and the projected clause is a secondary clause. The tense of the projected clause is determined by that of the projecting clause. Such clause complexes are referred to as ideational projection by Halliday and Matthiessen (2004) and experiential projection by Thompson (2005). The term used by Halliday and Matthiessen (2004) will be used in the current research. For example:

3.29 a. Mayor Garcetti says that the 2028 Olympics in Los Angeles will turn a $1-billion profit. (COCA_NEWS)
b. He said that his life is in danger. (COCA_SPOK)

The tag question added to 3.29a will be *does she* and that to 3.29b will be *did he.* This demonstrates that the information expressed by the projecting clause in ideational projection is viewed as the main proposition. The dual analysis of syntax and transitivity of example 3.29a are shown as follows:

| | Mayor Garcetti | said | that | the 2028 Olympics in Los Angeles | will | turn | a $1-billion profit |
|---|---|---|---|---|---|---|---|
| Syntactic structure | Subject | Predicate | complementizer | Subject | Predicate | | Complement |
| | Primary clause | | | Secondary clause | | | |
| Transitivity structure | Sayer | Process | Verbiage | | | | |
| | | | | Identified | Process | | Identifier |

| | Mayor Garcetti | (did) | said | that | the 2028 Olympics in Los Angeles | will | turn | a $1-billion profit |
|---|---|---|---|---|---|---|---|---|
| Mood structure | Subject | Finite | Predicator | | Subject | Finite | Predicator | Complement |
| | Mood | | Residue | | Mood | | Residue | |

In 3.29a, the projecting clause and the projected clause both belong to the clause rank and they form a hypotactic clause complex. The transitivity analysis indicates that the projected clause construes verbiage, and verbiage is brought into existence by the verbal process construed by the primary clause.

Some projecting clauses as ideational resources can be used "to do interpersonal service" (Halliday & Matthiessen 2004: 700). In such interpersonal projection, the projecting clauses usually contain the speaker or addresser as projector, e.g., *I think*, *do you think*, and they realize modality in the interpersonal domain. For example:

3.30 a. I would say that this advice has been ignored by linguistics, hasn't it? (Xin & Huang 2010: 66)
b. Luke lied often but I think it was more complicated than that. (COCA_FIC)

In 3.30a, the subject in the tag question consists of that in the projected clause, and this indicates that the projecting clause is semantically the main proposition. The projecting clause *I would say* serves as a modal adjunct to assess the modality of the proposition in the projected clause. Its function is similar to modal adverbs construing modality of probability, such as *probably*, *possibly* and *perhaps*. The dual analysis of syntax and transitivity of 3.30a is illustrated as follows:

| | I | would say | that | this advice | has been ignored | by linguistics, | hasn't it? |
|---|---|---|---|---|---|---|---|
| Syntactic structure | Subject | Predicate | Complementizer | Subject | Predicate | Adjunct | Tag question |
| Transitivity structure | Sayer | Process | | Phenomenon | Process | Sensor | |
| | Circumstance | | | | | | |

| | I | would say | that | this advice | has | been ignored | by linguistics, | hasn't | it? |
|---|---|---|---|---|---|---|---|---|---|
| Mood structure | Mood adjunct | | | Subject | Finite | Predicator | Adjunct | Finite | Subject |
| | Mood | | | | | Residue | | Mood tag | |

As shown in the above mood structure analysis of example 3.30a, the projecting clause as a whole can be viewed as a mood adjunct. The projected clause contains other mood elements, i.e., Subject, Finite and Residue. According to Halliday and Matthiessen (2004: 124), Adjunct in a clause "cannot be elevated to interpersonal status of modal responsibility". That is to say, an argument is constructed not around the Adjunct but most likely around the Subject. Seen in this way, the Subject lies in the projected clause and hereby the projected clause has a higher interpersonal status of modal responsibility than the projecting clause. This explains why the primary clause does not really express the main proposition in cases of interpersonal projection. Regarding the projecting clause as the mood element also indicates that the projecting clause in interpersonal projection bears constituent relations interpersonally with the projected clause.

In the clause complex of interpersonal projection, the interpersonal status of the projecting clause is lower than that in the clause complex of ideational projection. In ideational projection, the two clauses within the clause complex both express propositions and their mood structures are analyzed respectively. Both clauses contain Subject and Finite and maintain equal interpersonal status (see the mood structure of 3.29a). Therefore, interpersonal projection can be distinguished from ideational projection by the different interpersonal statuses of projecting clauses within the clause complex.

One way can help structurally distinguish ideational projection from interpersonal projection. In ideational projection, the secondary clause tends to be consistent with the primary clause in tense (e.g., *He said that he wanted to go back to America.*). In 3.30b, *I think* also construes modality and its tense is simple present tense, while the other clauses in the same clause complex are in past tense. *I think* seems to be a floating adjunct/parentheses that bears a weak connection with the rest part of the clause complex.

The projecting clause can serve as a discourse marker. In such cases, it is the projected clause rather than the projecting clause that expresses the main proposition. The projecting clause can be regarded as a textual Adjunct interpersonally. Such cases will be referred to as *textual projection* in the current research to distinguish them from ideational projection and interpersonal projection. Examples of textual projection are presented as follows:

3.31 a. I mean, it was like a home game here. (COCA_ NEWS)
b. And your work ethic, I mean, it's been unbelievable. (COCA_ SPOK)
c. That's not true, I mean. (COCA_MAG)
d. Well, I mean, I did but he could be the next Einstein, you know. (COCA_ MOV)

In 3.31a-d, the projected clauses express the propositions, and the projecting clause *I mean* fulfills the textual effect of discourse marker. They are usually separated from the projected clause by a comma and have positioning as flexible as parentheticals. Take 3.31a-c for example; *I mean* can appear in the initial position (see 3.31a), medial position (see 3.31b) or the ending position (see 3.31c). A projecting clause fulfilling textual effect can also appear with other discourse makers (i.e., *well, you know*) in the same utterance (see 3.31d). The following syntactic, transitivity and mood structure analysis of 3.31a shows in detail the grammatical status of *I mean.*

| 3.31a | I | mean, | it | was like | a home |
|---|---|---|---|---|---|
| Syntactic structure | Subject | Predicate | Subject | Predicate | Complement |
| | Conjunction | | | | |
| Transitivity structure | Sensor | Process | Identifier | Process | Identified |

| 3.31a | I | (do) | mean, | it | was | like | a home |
|---|---|---|---|---|---|---|---|
| Mood structure | Subject | Finite | Predicator | Subject | Finite | Predicator | Complement |
| | Conjunctive Adjunct | | | Mood | | Residue | |

According to the syntactic analysis of 3.31a, the projecting clause syntactically serves as a conjunction to indicate how the succeeding clause relates to other clauses in the context. A conjunction is not regarded as a constituent within the clause and hence does not belong to any rank in the clause (Yang 2003). Therefore, the projecting clause bears neither a clausal relationship (including interdependency and logico-semantic relationship) nor a constituency relationship with the projected clause. The projected clause stands alone as an independent clause, and the projecting clause serves as a conjunction outside the clause. In this sense, the projected clause is not projected by a projecting clause but a proposition standing on its own. The fact that there can be two projecting clauses (i.e., *I mean*, *you know*) but one projected clause in 3.31d can prove that the main proposition is not projected by either of the two projecting clauses. In this sense, *I mean* as a whole is better to be regarded as a conjunctive construction.

As shown in the mood structure analysis, *I mean* can be viewed as a conjunctive Adjunct. Conjunctive Adjunct is textual and does not express interpersonal meaning in the clause as an exchange of information. Compared to modal Adjunct that locates in Mood, conjunctive Adjunct neither locates in Mood nor in Residue and forms a constituent itself.

Both projecting clauses as conjunctive Adjunct in textual projection and those as modal Adjunct in interpersonal projection are not primarily fulfilling the ideational function of construing the verbal or mental process. Hereby, these two types of projections lead to clauses that appear to be projected in form but not in meaning. Such phenomenon is termed "pseudo-projected clauses" (Yang 2003: 120). Interpersonal projection and textual projection both involve pseudo-projected clauses. In this sense, the pseudo-projected clause is an independent clause standing on its own, with the projecting clause attached to it as a modal Adjunct or conjunctive Adjunct. The projecting clause as a modal Adjunct has a closer connection with the projected clause than that as a conjunction because the former is a constituent in the clause syntactically and part of the mood interpersonally while the latter functions outside the clause syntactically and not part of either the Mood or the Residue interpersonally.

To sum up, the status of projecting clauses can hereby form a cline from a grammatical perspective and helps to clarify the relation between the projecting clause and the projected clause. The cline is presented as follows (Fig. 3.1):

The syntactic status of the projecting clause forms a cline from ideational projection to interpersonal projection to textual projection, with the grammatical status ranging from higher to lower rank. The ideational projecting clause is a primary clause in a projection clause complex. The interpersonal projecting clause can be viewed as a modal adjunct serving as a constituent in an independent clause. The textual projecting clause can be viewed as a conjunctive adjunct functioning as a cohesive device outside the independent clause. The focus of the propositioncorrespondingly shifts from the projecting clause in ideational projection to the projected clause in interpersonal projection and textual projection.

People agree that alcohol is harmful for fetus. (Ideational projection)

I think alcohol is harmful for fetus. (Interpersonal projection)

You know, alcohol is harmful for fetus. (Textual projection)

**Fig. 3.1** Cline of projecting clause

### 3.3.3 Cline of Projected Clause

Another controversy in projection clause complex is the syntactic status of a projected clause (e.g., Langacker 1987; Quirk et al. 1985; Thompson 2002; Verhagen 2005). Whether a projected clause can be regarded as the object/complement of the projecting verb or not remains to be clarified. In SFL, clause nexus can be either clause complex containing a primary and a secondary clause, or clause simplex with an embedded clause. In clause complex of projection, the projected clause is the subordinate clause and bear interdependent relation with the projecting clause and hence cannot be viewed as the object of the corresponding projecting verb. In clause simplex of projection, the nominal group containing the embedded projected clause bears constituent relation with the corresponding verb and hence can be viewed as the direct object of verb. For example:

3.32 a. He thinks that it is impossible. (COCA_ACAD)
*b. That it is impossible is thought by him.
c. But we admit that we missed some good bars. (COCA_MAG)
d. That we missed some good bars is admitted.

3.32a is clause complex of hypotactic idea, and the projected clause cannot be viewed as direct object of the verb *think*. Therefore, 3.32b is not acceptable. 3.32c is clause simplex containing an embedded fact clause as head. Therefore, *admit* can be passivized and the embedded fact clause can serve as subject in 3.32d.

The clause complex of hypotactic projection (e.g., 3.32a) appears in the same form as the clause simplex with an embedded fact clause as head (e.g., 3.32c) and hereby the semantic analysis of the verbs are needed to clarify the grammatical status of the projected clauses. Verbs (e.g., *say, think*) that always project locutions or ideas can only appear in clause complexes. Verbs (e.g., *promise, believe*) that do not always project locutions or ideas may appear in either clause complexes or clause simplexes. Verbs (e.g., *regret, admit*) that are not able to project locutions or ideas only appear in clause simplexes. See Fig. 3.2.

As indicated by Fig. 3.2, though the above clause complexes and clause simplexes appear to be the same in form, the syntactic status of the dependent clauses ranges from the clause rank to the group rank. The verb *say* usually projects locutions and does not take nominal groups as direct objects except for its cognate nouns of speech such as *word* and *sentence*, and hence the projected clause cannot be regarded as the object of the projecting verb.

The verb *believe*, on the other hand, can project both ideas and facts. Accordingly, *I believe that John is a teacher* can be interpreted as *I think that John is a teacher,* and *believe* projects the succeeding idea. The same sentence can also be interpreted as *I believe the idea that John is a teacher,* and *believe* does not directly project the fact clause. *That John is a teacher* is not created by the process of believing but exists prior to the beginning of that process. In the former case, *believe* cannot introduce a nominal group object; whereas in the latter case, *believe* can take various nominal groups (e.g., *people, the story, science*) as its objects.

He said that John was a teacher. (Hypotacitc locution/ idea: clause)

I thought that Brandon Ross had a good day. (Hypotactic locution/ idea: clause)

I believe that John is a teacher. (Hypotactic locution/idea: clause)

I believe (the fact) that John is a teacher. (embedded fact: group)

I admit (the fact) that John is a teacher. (embedded fact: group)

**Fig. 3.2** Cline of projected clause

The last sentence in Fig. 3.2 demonstrates a clause with a verbal verb introducing a fact clause. Such verbs as *admit* and *regret* can take nouns as complements, and the fact clauses succeeding them can be regarded as complements.

Hereby, clause complexes of projection containing verbs with different semantic interpretations have to be analyzed from a semantic perspective to clarify the syntactic statuses of the continuing clauses.

### *3.3.4 Cline of Embedding Projection*

Embedding locutions and ideas are triggered by the nominalization of the projecting verbs, and embedded facts are the result of nominalization "from zero" (Halliday & Matthiessen 1999: 247). According to Halliday and Matthiessen (2014), under the conditions of nominalization, the semantic distinction between expansion and projection has reached a borderline.

The nominalization of the projecting verbal group in the clause complex would trigger certain syndromes. The nominal group realizing the projector can undergo downward rank-shift to realize the pre-modifier of the nominalization, and the projected clause also undergoes downward rank-shift to realize the post-modifier of the nominalization. For example:

3.33 a. They announced that they would be calling it quits this past July. The surprising news of course follows that.
b. The surprise news of course follows their announcement that they would be calling it quits this past July. (COCA_BLOG) (embedded locution with explicit projector)

3.34 a. Giovanni thought that the unexpected is part of polar trave and that touched me.
b. Giovanni touched me with his thought that the unexpected is part of polar travel. (COCA_WEB) (embedded idea with explicit projector)

In both 3.33b and 3.34b, the pre-modifier of the nominalization (i.e., *their* and *his*) is shifted from the projector (i.e., *they* and *Giovanni*) and the source of projection is clear. In this case the embedded projection is a packaged version of the original clause complex. The semantic relation between the projection noun and the embedded projected clause is close to the projection relation in their congruent forms. Hence the embedded clause is projected by the projection noun. What the embedded locution/idea construes is the second-order metaphenomenon.

Sometimes, the locution or idea noun has no pre-modifier indicating the projector, though the projection nouns indicate that the succeeding clauses are projected by someone. However, the absence of the projector responsible for the projecting behavior makes the projection noun and embedded projected clause appear to be standing on their own and are hence regarded as a pre-existing fact. For example:

3.35 The argument that next time will be different is unpersuasive. (COCA_NEWS)
3.36 The belief that nationalism is pre-modern is historically illiterate. (COCA_MAG)

In 3.35 and 3.36, the projection nouns *argument* and *belief* are nominalizations. However, the projector is unknown and Halliday and Matthiessen (2014) regard projected projections with unknown sources as facts. The semantic relationship between the locution/idea nouns and the embedded projected clause is projection. Such a phenomenon has reached the borderline between embedded locution/idea and embedded fact. On the one hand, the embedded clause is projected verbally or mentally by someone. On the other hand, the projector remains unknown.

Fact projection is the least prototypical form of the general category of projection. Fact nouns are not the nominalization of projecting verbs and no projectors are needed to project facts. Fact nouns are nouns that can define and be used to refer to the embedded clauses. Sometimes, fact nouns are attached to the language users' evaluation of the content in the embedded clauses. For example:

3.37 a. I'm going to teach you the lesson that it is not okay to be a freshman. (COCA_TV)
b. Do you have the certainty that she stole? (COCA_MOV)

In 3.37a and 3.37b, the fact nouns *lesson* and *certainty* define the corresponding content in the embedded clause. The fact clauses are not being projected by the fact nouns, but come as they are ready packaged in projected form (Halliday & Matthiessen 2014). A fact is impersonal projection. Embedded facts hereby demonstrate less degree of projection than embedded locution and idea. In 3.37b, *certainty* is attached to the language user's evaluation of the state of affairs. Modal fact nouns are attached to human evaluation while non-modalized ones are not. In this sense, facts modifying non-modalized fact nouns are more impersonal that those modifying modalized ones.

Compared with fact nouns with modality, fact nouns without modality are emptier in meaning and bear weaker connection with the embedded clauses. That is also the reason why case nouns like *fact* can be removed and the embedded fact clause stands on its own. Concerning the closeness of connection between fact nouns and corresponding embedded fact clauses, fact nouns with modality bear a closer relation with their embedded clauses than that without modality.

**his statement** that he's never paid less than a 13% tax rate (embedded locution/idea with explicit projector)

**the statement** that someone else said about audiences being stupid (embedded locution/idea without explicit projector)

**the need** that law shall conform itself to an end (embedded fact with modality)

**the fact** that there's a problem with the methodology (embedded fact without modality)

**that** she's not going to wait around (embedded fact as head)

**Fig. 3.3** Cline of embedding projection

Sometimes fact nouns of case can be removed and the embedded projected clauses appear to stand on their own. For example:

3.38 a. That his actions cause his lord's death is regrettable but also unavoidable. (COCA_ACAD)
b. Why you brought it up a second time is a puzzle. (COCA_MAG)

In 3.38a, *that his actions cause his lord's death* could modify a case noun *fact* or *case,* and in 3.38b, *why you brought it up a second time* could modify a case noun *question* defining the state of affairs. However, both the case nouns in these two examples are removed since they are quite empty in meaning. Complementizers *that* and *why* can also indicate the missing defining fact nouns. In these cases, the fact projection without fact nouns does not demonstrate projection in form or in meaning. It is the clausal nominalization that functions as a participant of the process. Projection, which originally refers to the logico-semantic relation between two language units, disappears because only one unit remains. Hereby, the fact projection standing on its own has the lowest degree of projection and is the most impersonal.

Based on the above discussion, the cline of projection degree within embedding projection is presented in Fig. 3.3.

To sum up, concerning embedding projection, the degree of projection can form a cline, in which embedded locutions or ideas with explicit projectors demonstrate the greatest degree of projection and embedded facts of case demonstrate the weakest degree of projection.

## 3.4 A Sketch of Grammatical Metaphor

In SFL, grammatical metaphor is "the expression of a meaning through a lexicogrammatical from which originally evolved to express a different kind of meaning" (Thompson 1996: 165). In the Hallidayan sense, grammatical metaphor includes ideational metaphor and interpersonal metaphor (Halliday 1985, 1994; Halliday & Matthiessen 2004). Some systemicists, such as Martin (1992, 1993), Thompson

(1996, 2014) Lassen (2003a, b) and He and Yang (2014), propose textual metaphor. The three types of grammatical metaphor in projection will be analysed in the following.

### 3.4.1 *Ideational Metaphor*

Ideational metaphor is a metaphor of transitivity (Halliday 1994). Ideational metaphor can be subcategorized into logical metaphor and experiential metaphor. Verbalization of conjunction groups is the resource for creating logical metaphor. Nominalization is the resource for creating experiential metaphor (Halliday 1985). See examples quoted from Halliday and Matthiessen (1999: 253):

3.39 a. They shredded the documents before they departed for the airport.
b. Their shredding of the documents preceded their departure for the airport.

The clause complex in 3.39a is the congruent realization and the simple clause in 3.39b is the metaphorical realization. The conjunction group *before* in 3.39a is verbalized as *preceded* in 3.39b and logical metaphor occurs. Verbal groups *shredded* and *departed* in 3.39a are nominalized as *shredding* and *departure* in 3.39b and experiential metaphor occurs. The verbalization and nominalization trigger the metaphorization of other lexicogrammatical items, i.e., adjectivization (*they - > their, their document - > of their document*) of nominal groups.

Besides verbal groups, many other grammatical classes are identified to have the potential to be nominalized. See the types of nominalizations quoted from the table illustrating 13 types of grammatical metaphors (Halliday & Matthiessen 1999: 247) (Table 3.1).

The grammatical metaphors of Type11 are fact nouns which can be considered as zero nominalization. That means the explicit transformation between the congruent form and the metaphorical form is absent. The fact noun *fact/case* can be regarded as a nominalization placeholder. Its existence is not always necessary. Once the speaker has evaluated the proposition or the proposal succeeding the fact noun, *fact/case* can be replaced with a more specific noun attached with modality or other evaluation. Hereby, fact nouns interacting with modality are also viewed as instances of zero nominalization attached with the speakers' evaluation. For example:

3.40 a. (The case) That I might become your Nobel colleague is finally settled.
b. (The possible case) That I might become your Nobel colleague is finally settled.
c. The chance that I might become your Nobel colleague is finally settled. (COCA_ACAD)

3.41 a. (The case) That all Americans must have insurance in 2014 still stands.
b. (The necessary/required case) That all Americans must have insurance in 2014 still stands.
c. The rule that all Americans must have insurance in 2014 still stands. (COCA_MAG)

**Table 3.1** Types of nominalization

| Types | Grammar shift | | Semantic element | | Example |
|---|---|---|---|---|---|
| | Grammar class | Grammatical functions | Congruent | Metaphorical | |
| 1 | Adjective = > noun | Epithet/Attribute = > Thing | Quality | Thing | Unstable = > instability |
| 2 | Verb = > noun | | Process | | |
| | | Event = > Thing | Event | | Transform = > transformation |
| | | Auxiliary = > Thing | Tense, modality | | Will = > prospect<br>can = > possibility |
| | | Catenative = > Thing | Phase, contingency | | Try to = > attempt |
| 3 | Preposition = > noun | | Circumstance | | |
| | Preposition | Minor Process = > thing | Minor process | | With = > accompaniment |
| | Prepositional phrase | Locution, Extent & c = > Classifier | Minor process + thing | | On the surface = > surface dust |
| 4 | Conjunction = > noun | Conjunctive = > Thing | Relator | | So = > cause, proof<br>If = > condition |
| 11 | + Noun | + Thing | [zero] | | [zero] = > the fact/ phenomenon of [zero] |

In 3.40a, *That I might become your Nobel colleague* is a zero nominalization. It can stand on its own or serve as a modifier of a nominalization placeholder *fact*. In 3.40b and 3.40c, the speaker's evaluation of this packaged proposition is that it is possible. The combination of *possible* and the nominalization placeholder would result in a fact noun with modality *chance*. In example 3.41, when the nominalization placeholder is attached with a judgment of being necessary, the fact noun of case turns into the fact noun of need *rule*.

### *3.4.2 Interpersonal Metaphor*

The language systems that can help adjust the negotiability and the arguability are Mood and Modality. Interpersonal metaphor consists of the metaphor of mood and the metaphor of modality (Halliday & Matthiessen 1999). Modality is realized in four semantic domains, i.e., subject, object, explicit and implicit. Implicit modalities are realized as modal verbs or modal adverbs within clauses, and explicit modalities are typically realized as subjective projecting clauses and objective projecting clauses in hypotactic clause complexes of projection. Implicit modalities are the congruent realization, and explicit modalities are the metaphorical realizations. For example:

3.41 a. I may be a head coach next year. (COCA_NEWS) (implicit subjective)
b. I think Colonel MacGregor agrees with me. (COCA_SPOK) (explicit subjective)
c. It is possible that Clayet Tomah was Clarissa Tomer. (COCA_ACAD) (explicit objective)

Apart from projecting clauses, there are other sources of interpersonal metaphor. When a nominal group (e.g., *the possibility*) realizes probability, interpersonal metaphor occurs (Martin 1992; Thompson 1996). See example quoted from Thompson (1996: 173):

3.42 But *the possibility* always existed of giving a second runway.

Proposition and proposal can also be modalized by being embedded (Matthiessen 1995). See example 3.43 quoted from Matthiessen (1995: 502):

3.43 That Henry has gone to London seems very likely.

Hereby, hypotactic projecting clauses and modalized fact nouns as well as embedded fact clauses are sources to construe interpersonal meaning metaphorically.

The mood system consists of two speech roles, i.e., giving and demanding, and two commodities exchanged, i.e., goods-&-services and information. Taking these two variables together can define four basic speech functions, i.e., statement, question, offer and command (Halliday 1994). The congruent realizations of the four speech functions are declarative, interrogative and imperative. When language is used with a non-congruent way to realize a speech function, interpersonal metaphor of mood occurs. For example:

3.44 a. Close the door!
b. Can you close the door?
c. I'm wondering whether you can close the door.
d. I want you to close the door.

In 3.44a, the speech function of command is realized congruently as an imperative, and the same speech function is realized metaphorically as an interrogative in 3.44b and as a declarative in 3.44c and 3.44d.

### *3.4.3 Textual Metaphor*

Textual metaphor is the realignment of structures (i.e., thematic, cohesive and information structures) that realize textual metafunction. Halliday and Hassan (1979)

**Table 3.2** Metaphorical realization of conjunctive relations

| Relation | Example |
|---|---|
| Meta-message relation | *Reason, example, point, factor, pointing out this* |
| Text reference | *This* |
| Negotiating texture | *Let me begin by …* |
| Internal conjunction | *A number of reasons, for examples, let me begin by, another example, as a final point, as a result of these factors* |

**Table 3.3** Types of internal conjunctions

| Types | Example |
|---|---|
| Addictive | *Well, okay, moreover* |
| Comparative | *I mean, in other words, in fact* |
| Temporal | *First, finally, at the same time* |
| Consequential | *Anyhow, admittedly, needless to say, accordingly, after all* |

distinguish two types of cohesive relations, i.e., external conjunction and internal conjunction. External conjunctions are experiential relations oriented to what is going on outside the text, and internal conjunctions encode the organization of text. Martin (1992) regards textual metaphor as language systems that can construe text as "material" social reality and identifies four types of textual metaphor from the internal and external text organization, i.e., meta-message relation, text reference, negotiating text and internal conjunction (Martin 1992). See examples quoted from Martin (1992: 416) (Table 3.2).

Within the subcategory of internal conjunction, Martin (1992) proposes four subcategories, i.e., additive, comparative, temporal and consequential, and the examples are presented as follows.

According to Table 3.3, projecting clauses such as *I mean* can serve as comparative internal conjunction.

## 3.5 Summary

This chapter has presented a brief introduction to the system of projection, the cline of projection relation and the theory of grammatical metaphor in SFL.

According to SFL, projection can be approached by the level of projection (i.e., locution, idea and fact) and the mode of projection (i.e., parataxis, hypotaxis and embedding) and speech functions of projection (i.e., proposition and proposal).

The notion of cline can help tackle some controversial issues about projection that traditional grammar fails to explain. The cline of projecting clauses clarifies the different grammatical statuses that projecting clauses can have. The projecting clause in an ideational projection has the highest grammatical status in modal responsibility, followed by that in interpersonal projection and finally in textual projection. This addresses the controversy about whether the projecting clause or the projected clause can be viewed as the proposition clause. The cline concerning clause nexuses of projection distinguishes the different grammatical statuses (i.e., clause rank, group rank) of projected clauses and identifies whether a projected clause can be viewed as an object of the projecting verbs. The cline of embedded projection demonstrates the varied degree of projection that different embedded projections can have and targets the constituent relation between projection nouns and projected clauses.

The theory of grammatical metaphor provides us a perspective to observe projection as a meaning potential to construe ideational, interpersonal and textual meanings metaphorically. Embedded projection involves nominalization of projecting verbal groups and nominalization of zero (Halliday & Matthiessen 1999). Hypotactic projecting clauses and modalized fact nouns can construe modality metaphorically, the former enhancing the negotiability of utterances while the latter lowering the arguability of the evaluation on certain propositions. The projecting clause in declarative can metaphorically realize the mood of command and question. Certain projecting clauses (e.g., *I mean*) can function as comparative internal conjunction to help construe text cohesion.

## References


Biber D, Johansson S, Leech G, Conrad S, Finegan E (1999) Longman grammar of spoken and written English. Longman, London

Brinton LJ (2008) The comment clause in English. Cambridge University Press, Cambridge

Eggins S (2004) Introduction to systemic functional linguistics. Continuum, New York/London

Fabricius-Hansen C, Ram W (2008) Editors' introduction: Subordination and coordination from different perspectives. In: Fabricius-Hansen C, Ramm W (eds) Subordination versus coordination in sentence and text: A cross-linguistic perspective. Benjamins, Amsterdam, pp 1–30

Halliday MAK (1985) An introduction to functional grammar. Arnold, London

Halliday MAK (1994) An introduction to functional grammar, 2nd edn. Arnold, London

Halliday MAK, Hasan R (1976) Cohesion in English. Longman, London

Halliday MAK, Matthiessen CMIM (1999) Construing experience through meaning: A language-based approach to cognition. Cassell, London/New York

Halliday MAK, Matthiessen CMIM (2004) An introduction to functional grammar, 3rd edn. Arnold, London

Halliday MAK, Matthiessen CMIM (2014) An introduction to functional grammar, 4th edn. Routledge, London/New York

Halliday MAK (1961/2002) Categories of the theory of grammar. In Webster J (Ed), Collected works of Halliday MAK, 1: On grammar (pp 35–94). Continuum, London

He Q (2019a) A corpus-based approach to clause combining in English from the systemic functional perspective. Springer, Singapore

He Q, Yang B (2014) A study of transfer directions in grammatical metaphor. Aust J Linguist 34(3):345–360

Holler A (2008) German dependent clauses from a constraint-based perspective. In: Fabricius-Hansen C, Ramm W (eds) Subordination versus coordination in sentence and text: A cross-linguistic perspective. Benjamins, Amsterdam, pp 187–216

Langacker RW (1987) Foundations of cognitive grammar, vol. 1: Theoretical prerequisites. Stanford University Press, Redwood

Lassen IM (2003a) Accessibility and acceptability in technical manuals: A survey of style and grammatical metaphor. John Benjamins, Amsterdam/Philadelphia

Lassen IM (2003b) Imperative readings of grammatical metaphor: A study of congruency in the imperative in A-M. Simon-Vandenbergen M Taverniers, Ravelli LJ (Eds), Gramm Metaphor: Views Syst Funct Linguist. John Benjamins, Amsterdam/Philadelphia, pp 279–308

Martin JR (1993) Life as a noun: Arresting the universe in science and humanities. In: Halliday MAK, Martin JR (eds) Writing science, literary and discourse power. Palmer Press, London, pp 241–293

Martin JR (1992) English text: System and structure. John Benjamins, Philadelphia/Amsterdam

Matthiessen CMIM (1995) Lexicogrammatical cartography. Int Lang Sci Publ, Tokyo

Quirk R, Sidney G, Geoffrey L, Svartvik J (1985) A comprehensive grammar of the English language. Longman, London

Thompson G (1996) Introducing functional grammar. Edward Arnold, London

Thompson SA (2002) "Object complements" and conversation towards a realistic account. Stud Lang 26(1):125–163

Thompson G (2005) But me some buts: A multidimensional view of conjunction. Text 25(6):763–791

Thompson G (2014) Introducing Functional Grammar (3rd edition). Routledge, London/New York

Verhagen A (2005) Constructions of intersubjectivity: Discourse, syntax, and cognition. Oxford University Press, Oxford

Wittgenstein L (1967) Philosophical investigation. Basil Blackwell, Oxford

Xin Z, Huang G (2010) Trigger mechanisms for the dynamic manifestation of projection across ideational and interpersonal metafunctions. Comput-Assist Foreign Lang Educ 8(1):44–50

Yang B (2003) A study of non-finite clause in English: A systemic functional approach. Foreign Lang Teach Res Press, Beijing

# Chapter 4
# Research Design

## 4.1 Research Questions

As discussed in Chap. 3, there are three types of projection, i.e., ideational projection, interpersonal projection and textual projection. The three types of projection all involve grammatical metaphor. Ideational projection is realized as a paratactic/hypotactic clause complex or nominal group with an embedded projected clause. Embedding projection is a metaphorical realization of the paratactic and hypotactic projection clause complex. Interpersonal projection is the metaphorical realization of interpersonal meaning. Textual projection is the metaphorical realization of cohesion.

Grammatical metaphor is a characteristic feature of written texts (Halliday 1989; Hyland 2009; Martin & Rose 2003). Among the written genres, grammatical metaphor tends to occur in scientific writing (Banks 2003, 2005; Biber 2006; Biber et al. 1999; Charles 2003; Colombi 2006; Devrim 2015; Galve 1998; Halliday 1998, 2004; Liardét 2016; Martin 1992, 1993; Yuliana 2011). Grammatical metaphor is also discipline sensitive. It occurs more in hard sciences than in soft sciences (Charles 2003; MacDonald 1994; Unsworth 1997). The present research is therefore to explore the synchronic distributions of different types of projections and the interplay between different types of projection in historical evolution. Specifically, the research intends to answer the following question:

**Question 1** What are the mode, genre and discipline distribution patterns of the different types of projection?

It is also found that the grammatical statuses of projecting clauses form a cline from a proposition clause to a modal adjunct in the proposition clause and finally to a conjunctive adjunct out of the proposition clause. Diachronically, the process of status shift along the cline is a process of grammaticalization.

This research is therefore to explore the diachronic evolution of projections. Specifically, the second question to be answered in the present research is:

**Question 2** What are the diachronic evolution trends of different types of projection?



M. Guo and Q. He, *A Corpus-Based Study of Projection in English from the Systemic Functional Perspective*, The M.A.K. Halliday Library Functional Linguistics Series,
https://doi.org/10.1007/978-981-97-5094-8_4

## 4.2 Research Methods

This research adopts a combined method of qualitative research and corpus-based quantitative research, which has become the mainstream linguistic research method nowadays. Qualitative research is the basis of quantitative research, and quantitative research will make qualitative research more accurate. The two methods are of great complementarity (Bunge 1995). SFL emphasizes the complementarity of quantitative research and qualitative research both in theory and practice.

SFL studies language-in-use, and its theoretical system is based on data collected from both spoken and written discourses. SFL studies bear close ties with corpus linguistics (Neale 2006). Corpus could benefit SFL studies in three ways: providing authentic texts, including spoken language data and facilitating quantitative ways of studying grammar.

In the present research, qualitative research was carried out first. Based on the literature review of traditional clausal linking patterns and complement clauses, this research classified different types of projection. Based on the theory of grammatical metaphor and the notion of cline, this research will identify transfers involving nominalization in embedding projection and propose the cline of combination between projection nominalizations and relative projected clauses.

Based on the above theoretical basis, quantitative research will be carried out to "test the objective theories by examining the relationship among variables" (Creswell 1994: 1). The study on the diachronic and genre distribution is basically quantitative. The creation of grammatical metaphor is theoretically a process of unidirectional transfer (He & Yang 2014). Therefore, the diachronic analysis can test the historical development and the formation of interpersonal and textual projections, and embedding projections as grammatical metaphor. The synchronic analysis of the mode, genre, and discipline distributions will help reveal the relationship between form, meaning and context. Search queries will be written to retrieve data from the COCA and the COHA. Then the data will be analyzed statistically using data analysis software such as SPSS 29.0.

## 4.3 Data Collection

SFL emphasizes that language is social semiotics and the meaning of language comes from its use. Based on this notion, except for directly cited example sentences, the examples in this study are collected from authentic language in use retrieved from the public online corpora COCA and COHA. The COCA will be used to conduct the synchronic study on the mode, genre and discipline distributions of projections. The COCA is large in size and genre-balanced. It contains more than one billion words (25 + million words each year during 1990–2019) from eight genres: spoken, fiction, popular magazines, newspapers, academic texts, and (with the update in March 2020) TV and movie subtitles, blogs and other web pages. The texts of the academic genre are balanced with various disciplines, e.g., Education, Technology, Medicine, Humanities and so on.

To facilitate the synchronic analysis, only the frequencies in Spoken, Fiction, Magazine, News and Academic will be retrieved in this study. Frequencies in Fiction, Magazine, News and Academics will be added up as frequencies in the mode of written texts to be compared with those in Spoken. Frequencies in Fiction, Magazine and News will be regarded as non-academic genres to compare with those in Academic. Among academic texts, texts of hard science are regarded as more technical than texts of social sciences (Copeck et al. 1997; He & Yang 2018). In the COCA, the disciplines of History, Education, Geography/Social Science, Law/Political Science, Humanities and Philosophy/Religion can be categorized as soft sciences, and the disciplines of Science/Technology and Medicine can be categorized as hard sciences.

The COHA will be used to facilitate the diachronic study of projection. The COHA is the largest structured corpus of historical English. It contains more than 475 million words from the 1820s to the 2010s, with the total number of words ranging from 6,981,389 in the 1820s to 35,452,806 in the 2010s. The COHA is also balanced by genre across the decades. For example, fiction + TV/movies (which are scripted, similar to fiction) accounts for 54–57% of the total in each decade (1820s–2010s), and the corpus is balanced across decades for sub-genres and domains as well (e.g., by Library of Congress classification for non-fiction; and by sub-genre for fiction—prose, poetry and drama). The corpus description of the COHA is presented in Table 4.1

The COHA can help investigate the diachronic distributions of different types of projection during the 200 years of language evolution.

## 4.4 Data Processing

The COHA and COCA are available online. Search queries will be written according to the CLAWS7 Tagset and the Query Syntax to automatically retrieve corresponding constructions in the corpora. Data retrieved from the COCA will be compared and analyzed to sum up the synchronic distribution of projection. SPSS 29.0 will also be used to conduct a chi-squared analysis to see whether the distributions of projection across modes, genres and disciplines show significant differences. Showing statistically significant differences is regarded as an indicator of mode, genre or discipline sensitivity. Data retrieved from the COHA will be divided into 20 phases, and the diachronic distributions of different projections will be tested using SPSS 29.0 software through correlation analysis and cluster analysis. Correlation analysis can help reveal how the historical development of one type of projection relates to that of another. Showing a significant positive correlation indicates that the two types of

**Table 4.1** Register, number of words and historical distribution in the COHA

| Decade | TV/movies | Fiction | Popular magazines | Newspaper | Non-fiction books | Total |
|---|---|---|---|---|---|---|
| 1820s | | 3,778,554 | 1,730,991 | | 1,471,844 | 6,981,389 |
| 1830s | | 7,492,464 | 3,158,784 | | 3,060,039 | 13,711,287 |
| 1840s | | 8,615,569 | 3,584,996 | | 3,606,482 | 15,807,047 |
| 1850s | | 9,175,764 | 4,243,240 | | 3,116,999 | 16,536,003 |
| 1860s | | 9,279,356 | 4,469,061 | 264,549 | 2,923,594 | 16,936,560 |
| 1870s | | 10,454,445 | 4,489,558 | 1,037,506 | 2,806,958 | 18,788,467 |
| 1880s | | 11,204,077 | 4,489,787 | 1,368,195 | 3,005,146 | 20,067,205 |
| 1890s | | 11,261,720 | 4,716,870 | 1,392,895 | 3,055,298 | 20,426,783 |
| 1900s | | 12,096,794 | 5,092,923 | 1,464,317 | 3,323,216 | 21,977,250 |
| 1910s | | 12,266,683 | 5,727,265 | 1,548,986 | 3,560,164 | 23,103,098 |
| 1920s | | 12,668,146 | 6,132,368 | 3,642,022 | 3,257,886 | 25,700,422 |
| 1930s | 2,994,552 | 11,959,731 | 6,048,788 | 3,651,557 | 3,053,251 | 27,707,879 |
| 1940s | 2,888,109 | 12,030,426 | 5,841,711 | 3,567,355 | 3,072,149 | 27,399,750 |
| 1950s | 4,003,700 | 12,014,411 | 5,961,487 | 3,570,759 | 3,110,917 | 28,661,274 |
| 1960s | 4,991,777 | 11,652,761 | 5,884,357 | 3,434,402 | 3,159,379 | 29,122,676 |
| 1970s | 4,982,750 | 11,652,921 | 5,767,353 | 3,402,783 | 3,023,418 | 28,829,225 |
| 1980s | 4,995,510 | 11,664,130 | 5,980,459 | 4,125,888 | 3,085,593 | 29,851,580 |
| 1990s | 5,039,323 | 13,337,688 | 7,552,995 | 4,069,742 | 3,149,570 | 33,149,318 |
| 2000s | 5,078,058 | 14,624,639 | 7,813,604 | 4,116,506 | 3,189,005 | 34,821,812 |
| 2010s | 5,061,478 | 15,150,555 | 7,552,354 | 4,546,307 | 3,142,112 | 35,452,806 |
| Total | 40,035,257 | 222,380,834 | 106,238,951 | 45,203,769 | 61,173,020 | 475,031,831 |

projection are of the same group of data, and showing a significant negative correlation indicates the historical development of the two types of projection is complementary. Cluster analysis can help categorize projections with similar historical development patterns.

## References

Banks D (2003) The evolution of grammatical metaphor in scientific writing. In: Simon-Vandenbergen AM, Taverniers M, Ravelli L (eds) Grammatical metaphor: Views from systemic functional linguistics. John Benjamins, Amsterdam/Philadelphia, pp 127–148

Banks D (2005) On the historical origins of nominalized process in scientific texts. Engl Specif Purp 24(3):347–357

Biber D, Johansson S, Leech G, Conrad S, Finegan E (1999) Longman grammar of spoken and written English. Longman, London

Biber D (2006) University language: A corpus-based study of spoken and written registers. John Benjamins, Philadelphia/Amsterdam

Bunge M (1995) Quality, quantity, pseudo quantity and measurement in social science. J Quant Linguist 2(1):1–10
Charles M (2003) 'This mystery … ': A corpus-based study of the use of nouns to construct stance in theses from two contrasting disciplines. J Engl Acad Purp 2(4):313–326
Colombi MC (2006) Grammatical metaphor: Academic language development in Latino students of Spanish. In: Byrnes H (ed) Advanced language learning: The contribution of Halliday and Vygotsky. Continuum, London, pp 147–163
Copeck T, Barker K, Delisle S (1997) What is technical language? Lang Sci 4:391–424
Creswell JW (1994) Research design: Qualitative and quantitative approaches. Sage, Thousand Oaks
Devrim DY (2015) Grammatical metaphor: What do we mean? What exactly are we researching? Funct Linguist 2(3):1–15
Galve IG (1998) The textual interplay of grammatical metaphor on the nominalizations occurring in written medical English. J Pragmat 30(3):363–385
Halliday MAK (1989) Spoken and written language. Oxford University Press, Oxford
Halliday MAK (1998) Things and relations: Regrammaticising experience as technical knowledge. In: Martin JR, Robert V (eds) Reading science: Critical and functional perspectives on discourses of science. Routledge, London, pp 185–235
Halliday MAK, Matthiessen CMIM (1999) Construing experience through meaning: A language-based approach to cognition. Cassell, London/New York
Halliday MAK, Matthiessen CMIM (2004) An introduction to functional grammar, 3rd edn. Arnold, London
Halliday MAK (2004) Language and knowledge: The unpacking of text. In: Webster J (ed) Collected works of M. A. K. Halliday, vol 5: The language of science. Continuum, London/New York, pp 24–48
He Q (2019) A corpus-based study of transfers in English nominal groups. Glottotheory 10(1–2):57–84
He Q (2021) A corpus-based study of interpersonal metaphors of modality in English. Stud Neophilol 93(1):50–71
He Q, Wen B (2017) A corpus-based study of textual metaphor in English. Aust J Linguist 37(3):265–285
He Q, Yang B (2014) A study of transfer directions in grammatical metaphor. Aust J Linguist 34(3):345–360
He Q, Yang B (2018) A corpus-based study of the correlation between text technicality and ideational metaphor in English. Lingua 203(2):51–65
He Q, Yang B, Wen B (2015) Textual metaphor from the perspective of relator. Aust J Linguist 35(4):334–350
Hyland K (2009) Academic discourse: English in a global context. Continuum, London
Köhler R (2012) Quantitative syntax analysis. De Gruyter Mouton, Berlin/New York
Liardét CL (2016) Nominalization and grammatical metaphor: Elaborating the theory. Engl Specif Purp 44:16–29
Liardét CL (2018) "As we all know": Examining Chinese EFL learners' use of interpersonal grammatical metaphor in academic writing. Engl Specif Purp 50:64–80
MacDonald SP (1994) Professional academic writing in the humanities and social sciences. Southern Illinois University Press, Carbondale
Martin JR (1992) English text: System and structure. John Benjamins, Philadelphia/Amsterdam
Martin JR (1993) Life as a noun: Arresting the universe in science and humanities. In: Halliday MAK, Martin JR (eds) Writing science, literary and discourse power. Palmer Press, London, pp 241–293
Martin JR, David R (2003) Working with discourse: Meaning beyond the clause. Continuum, London

Neale A (2006) Matching corpus data and system networks: Using corpora to modify and extend the system network for TRANSTIVITY in English. In: Thompson G, Hunston S (eds) System and corpus: Exploring connection. Equinox, London, pp 143–163

Schleppegrell MJ (2001) Linguistic features of the language of schooling. Linguist Educ 12(4):431–459

Unsworth L (1997) "Sound" explanation in school science: A functional linguistic perspective on effective apprenticing texts. Linguist Educ 9(2):199–226

Yang B (2019) Interpersonal metaphor revisited: Identification, categorization, and syndrome. Soc Semiot 29(2):186–203

Yuliana D (2011) An investigation of grammatical metaphor in students' writing and its effects on the texts' written characteristics (A Thesis of School of Post Graduate Studies). Indonesia University of Education

# Chapter 5
# Synchronic Study of Projection

In Chap. 3, the types of projection and the different syntactic structures realizing projection are reviewed within the framework of SFL. Three clines involving projection are put forward to understand how different types of projection relate to each other. In this chapter, quantitative research on the synchronic distribution of projection based on the COCA will be conducted. The comparative analysis will be conducted at the levels of mode, genre and discipline distributions.

## 5.1 Synchronic Distribution of Projections

In Sect. 3.4.1, we classified projection in English into ideational projection, interpersonal projection and textual projection.

Not all projecting clauses can serve as ideational, interpersonal and textual projections under different conditions. To facilitate comparison, the construction *I THNK* was chosen as the target to retrieve data for the three types of projection respectively because it is a typical interpersonal projection to realize explicit subjective modality (Halliday & Matthiessen 2004). *I THINK* can also appear to be attached like a parenthetical to a clause with a comma between it and the corresponding clause. In this case, it mainly fulfills the textual function as a discourse marker. Therefore, *I THINK* was taken as an example to observe how the ideational, interpersonal and textual *I THINK* distribute across modes, genres and disciplines.

Textual *I THINK* can appear in the initial, medial and final positions of a clause. Therefore, the following search queries were written to retrieve textual *I THINK* in different syntactic positions.

RE 5.1. I think,
RE 5.2. I think, "|'
RE 5.3, I think,

 
M. Guo and Q. He, *A Corpus-Based Study of Projection in English from the Systemic Functional Perspective*, The M.A.K. Halliday Library Functional Linguistics Series,
https://doi.org/10.1007/978-981-97-5094-8_5

RE 5.4, I think.

RE 5.1 can be described as any period followed by *I think* and a comma. It can be used to retrieve textual *I think* in clause-initial position. With this search query, *I think* in paratactic projecting clause complex is also retrieved. Therefore, search query RE 5.2 was written to retrieve *I think* in paratactic projecting clause complexes, and the number of tokens retrieved using RE 5.1 minus that retrieved using RE 5.2 will result in the frequency of textual *I THINK* in clause-initial position. See examples retrieved using RE 5.1 and RE 5.2:

5.1 a. I think, frankly, people also don't know where to begin. (COCA_NEWS)
b. I think, "I'm about to catch fire. This is terrible." (COCA_NEWS) (paratactic clause complex of projection)

RE 5.3 can be described as any comma followed by *I think* and a comma. Using RE 5.3 textual *I THINK* can be retrieved in clause-medial position. RE 5.4 can be described as any comma followed by *I think* and a period. RE 5.4 can be used to retrieve textual *I THINK* in clause-final position. For example:

5.2 a. The history of the township experiment shows, I think, that this is the wrong conclusion to draw. (COCA_ACAD)
b. It was the very last scene I shot, I think. (COCA_MAG)

Using REs 5.1, 5.2, 5.3, 5.4, 25,253 textual *I think* were retrieved in Spoken and Written texts in the COCA. The following search queries are written to retrieve interpersonal *I think*.

RE 5.5 [y*] I (don't/do not) think that_c*
RE 5.6 [y*] I (don't/do not) think [d*]|[at*]|[app*] [n*]|[pp*] [v*]
RE 5.7 [y*] I (don't/do not) think [n*]|[pp*] [v*]

RE 5.5 can be described as any punctuation followed by *I think* and a complementizer *that*. It can be used to retrieve interpersonal *I THINK* followed by *that* complementizer and a clause. *Don't* or *do not* are added in between *I* and *think* to retrieve the negative form of interpersonal *I THINK*. RE 5.6 can be described as any punctuation followed by *I think*, a determiner or article or possessive pronoun, a noun or personal pronoun and a verb. RE 5.7 can be described as any punctuation followed by *I think*, a noun or personal pronoun and a verb. RE 5.6 and RE 5.7 can help retrieve interpersonal *I THINK* and its negative form followed by clause without complementizer *that*. See examples retrieved using these three search queries:

5.3 a. I think that you will admit that there are no security standards from the FTC. (COCA_ACAD)
b. I don't think that anyone really cares whether something gets done or not. (COCA_FIC)
c. Also, I do not think that businesses should not be open on a day like Sunday. (COCA_NEWS)
d. I think this situation is connected primarily to the prime minister's personal legal woes. (COCA_FIC)

e. I don't think the department is gonna get a AAA-rating. (COCA_NEWS)
f. I do not think that hospitality comes easily to many. (COCA_ACAD)
g. I think he's going to be a star in this league. (COCA_NEWS)
h. I don't think he studied as much as he could have, but overall he did fine. (COCA_ACAD)
i. I do not think we can give up the word so easily. (COCA_MAG)

Using RE 5.6 and RE 5.7, 143,815 interpersonal *I THINK* were retrieved from spoken and written texts in the COCA. Interpersonal *I THINK* functions as modal adjunct and it can be viewed as a construction with internal fixation in form and allows less variation in tense, aspect and modality. Thus, *I THINK* construction in past tense or modified by an adverb can in turn signal its being ideational. Hereby the past tense of the verb *think* can be searched as ideational *I THINK*. Apart from that, *THINK* modified by adverbs can also be searched. Being modified by adverbs shows that the meaning of the verb *THINK* matters and *I THINK* is not a lexicalized and fixed construction that cannot be added with other elements in the internal construction. The following search queries were written to retrieve ideational *I THINK*.

RE 5.8 I thought that_c*
RE 5.9 I didn't/did not think that_c*
RE 5.10 I thought [d*]|[at*]|[app*] [n*]|[pp*] [v*]
RE 5.11 I didn't/did not think [d*]|[at*]|[app*] [n*]|[pp*] [v*]
RE 5.12 I thought [n*]|[pp*] [v*]
RE 5.13 I didn't/did not think [n*]|[pp*] [v*]
RE 5.14 I [rr*] THINK that_c*
RE 5.15 I [rr*] THINK [d*]|[at*]|[app*] [n*]|[pp*] [v*]
RE 5.16 I [rr*] THINK [n*]|[pp*] [v*]

RE 5.8 can be described as any *I thought* followed by conjunction *that*. This search query can be used to retrieve ideational *I THINK* with complementizer *that* followed by a projected clause. RE 5.9 is used to retrieve the corresponding negative form for ideational *I think*. For example:

5.4 a. I thought that the advice I was giving my clients was special. (COCA_ACAD)
b. I didn't think that overalls would be back. (COCA_SPOK)
c. I did not think that turning around and going back was a good idea. (COCA_NEWS)

RE 5.10 can be described as *I thought* followed by a determiner, article or possessive pronoun and a noun or personal pronoun and a verb. RE 5.11 can be used to search the corresponding negative form of the projecting clause *I think*. RE 5.12 can be described as *I thought* followed by a noun or personal pronoun and a verb. RE 5.13 can be used to search the negative form of *I THINK* in past tense followed by a noun or a pronoun and a verb. These four search queries can be used to retrieve ideational projecting clauses in past tense followed by a projected clause without complementizer *that*. For example:

5.5 a. I thought the Knight had missed Walter. (COCA_FIC)
b. I didn't think the expectations were crazy. (COCA_NEWS)
c. I did not think the passage was difficult, simply because of the type of questions asked. (COCA_ACAD)
d. I thought I could fix it but got trapped by my ego and refusal to fail. (COCA_ACAD)
e. I didn't think you could get a real workout from a DVD. (COCA_MAG)
f. I did not think we would see that by this time a month ago. (COCA_SPOK)

RE 5.14 can be described as a pronoun *I* followed by an adverb, any form of the verb *think* and a conjunction *that*. RE 5.15 can be described as pronoun *I* followed by an adverb, any form of the verb *think*, a determiner or article or possessive pronoun, a noun or personal pronoun and a verb. RE 5.16 can be described as any pronoun *I* followed by an adverb, any form of the verb *think*, a noun or a personal pronoun and a verb. These three search queries can be used to retrieve ideational *I THINK* construction in which the verb *think* is modified by adverbs.

5.6 a. I frankly thought that I didn't deserve it. (COCA_FIC)
b. I always thought each generation ought to be a little better than the other. (COCA_NEWS)
c. Did I really think I could go into a lab full of specialists and get anything from this for my classroom? (COCA_ACAD)

Using the eight search queries from RE 5.8 to RE 5.16, a total of 48,949 ideational *I THINK* were retrieved from spoken and written texts in the COCA.

The raw frequencies of textual, interpersonal and ideational *I THINK* in different sub-corpora are shown in Table 5.1.

Textual projection serves the same as conjunctions or discourse markers of saying. It is syntactically flexible and can be categorized as "pragmatic connectives" that are "mainly used in oral texts" (Cuenca & Crible 2019). Hence it can be hypothesized that textual *I THINK* is more likely to appear in spoken texts regarding mode distribution, in non-academic texts regarding genre distribution and in soft science texts regarding discipline distribution. Interpersonal projection helps enact interpersonal relationship. It tends to occur more in non-technical fiction texts (He 2021). Hereby it can be hypothesized that interpersonal *I THINK* is also more prevalent in spoken texts regarding mode distribution, in non-academic texts regarding genre distribution

**Table 5.1** Frequencies of textual, interpersonal and ideational *I THINK* in the COCA

| | Spoken | Written | | | | | | Total |
|---|---|---|---|---|---|---|---|---|
| | | Fiction | Magazine | Newspaper | Academic | | | |
| | | | | | Soft sci | Hard sci | Misc | |
| Textual | 19,151 | 3187 | 1127 | 991 | 615 | 40 | 142 | 25,253 |
| Interpersonal | 95,303 | 17,933 | 10,497 | 17,251 | 2289 | 240 | 302 | 143,815 |
| Ideational | 18,279 | 17,886 | 5414 | 6285 | 797 | 110 | 178 | 48,949 |

and in soft science texts regarding discipline distribution. In the same vein, we can hypothesize that ideational *I THINK* is of similar distribution trend to interpersonal *I THINK*.

### *5.1.1 Mode Distribution of Projections*

The raw frequencies of textual, interpersonal and ideation *I THINK* are converted into normalized frequencies per million words in spoken and written texts in the COCA (see Table 5.2).

To facilitate comparison, the total normalized frequencies of textual *I THINK* (164.43) and ideational *I THINK* (208.08) were further converted to that of interpersonal *I THINK* (855.61). Their mode distributions are shown in Fig. 5.1.

As shown in Fig. 5.1, the mode distribution patterns of the three types of projection are in consistency with the hypothesis. All the three types of *I THINK* constructions tend to occur more in spoken texts. The textual *I THINK* is the most prevalent in spoken texts and the ideational *I THINK* is the most prevalent in written texts. The mode distributions of the textual, interpersonal and ideational *I THINK* manifest a significant difference ($\chi^2 = 182.636$, $df = 2$, $p = 0.000 < 0.01$). Textual *I THINK*, similar to other discourse markers of saying like *I mean*, *you know*, are categorized as pragmatic connectives. They are appositional syntactically and function to bracket units of talks such as indicating turn-taking and topic-changing in dialogue (Cuenca & Crible 2019). Written texts are more technical and the conjunctions mainly indicate

**Table 5.2** Normalized frequencies of textual, interpersonal and ideation *I THINK*

| | Spoken | Written | Total |
|---|---|---|---|
| Textual | 151.8715 | 12.55814 | 164.4297 |
| Interpersonal | 755.7732 | 99.83947 | 855.6127 |
| Ideational | 144.9564 | 63.11998 | 208.0764 |

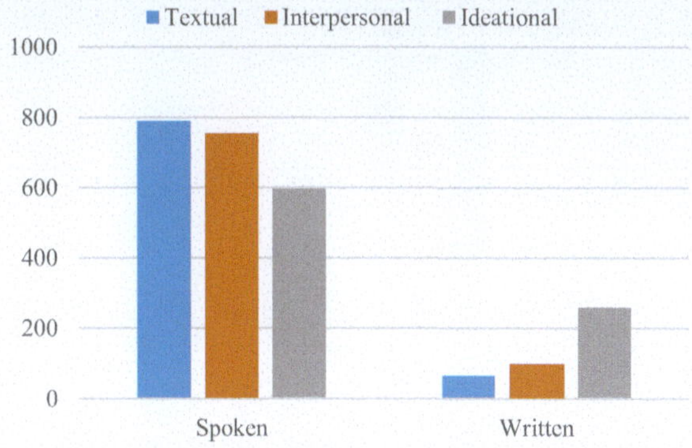


**Fig. 5.1** Mode distributions of textual, interpersonal and ideational *I THINK*

grammatical relations between language units (e.g., subordination and coordination) and the logico-argumentative meaning (e.g., exemplification, definition, addition). Textual projection is colloquial and dialogic and hereby the most prevalent in spoken texts.

### 5.1.2 Genre Distribution of Projections

Based on the mode distributions of textual, interpersonal and ideational *I THINK*, it can be hypothesized that textual projection is the most prevalent in the least technical genre and ideational projection is the most prevalent in the most technical genre. The normalized frequencies of textual, interpersonal and ideational *I THINK* in Fiction, Magazine, Newspaper and Academic genres in the COCA are shown in Table 5.3.

To facilitate comparison, the total normalized frequencies of textual *I THINK* (50.67) and ideational *I THINK* (254.83) were converted to that of interpersonal *I THINK* (400.21). Their genre distributions are shown in Fig. 5.2.

As shown in Fig. 5.2, all the three types of *I THINK* constructions tend to occur the most in non-academic fiction texts. This is in consistency with their mode distribution. The genre distributions of textual, interpersonal and ideational *I THINK* manifest significant difference ($\chi^2 = 83.194$, $df = 6$, $p = 0.000 < 0.01$). Textual *I THINK* is the most prevalent in academic genre, followed by interpersonal *I*

**Table 5.3** Normalized frequencies of textual, interpersonal and ideational *I THINK* across genres

| | Fiction | Magazine | Newspaper | Academic | Total |
|---|---|---|---|---|---|
| Textual | 26.9399831 | 8.937351 | 8.142975 | 6.652755 | 50.67306 |
| Interpersonal | 151.58918 | 83.24346 | 141.7502 | 23.63105 | 400.2139 |
| Ideational | 151.191885 | 42.93418 | 51.64339 | 9.056761 | 254.8262 |

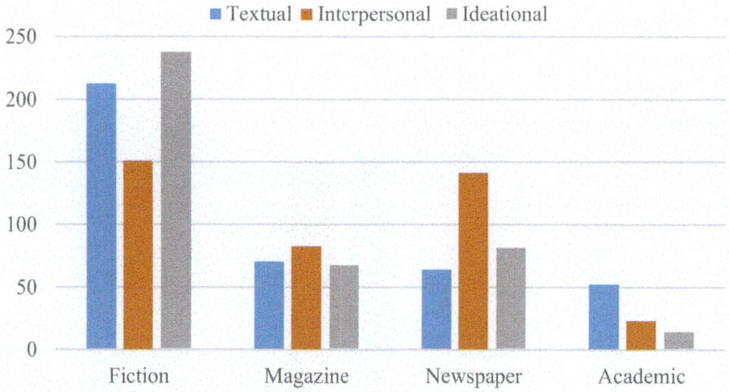


**Fig. 5.2** Genre distributions of textual, interpersonal and ideational *I THINK*

*THINK* and finally ideational *I THINK*. The distribution pattern is the opposite of their mode distribution pattern. In fiction texts, ideational *I THINK* is the most prevalent, followed by textual *I THINK* and finally interpersonal *I THINK*. This is not consistent with their mode distribution pattern. The reason might be that the use of the first-person singular pronoun *I* is considered an informal feature of academic texts (Chang & Swales 1999).

### *5.1.3 Discipline Distribution of Projections*

The normalized frequencies of textual, interpersonal and ideational *I THINK* in soft science and hard science texts in the COCA were worked out in Table 5.4.

To facilitate comparison, the total normalized frequencies of textual *I THINK* (8.6) and ideational *I THINK* (13.21) were converted into that of interpersonal *I THINK* (35.25). Their discipline distributions are shown in Fig. 5.3.

As shown in Fig. 5.3, all the three types *of I THINK* tend to occur more in soft science texts. Their discipline distributions do not show a significant difference ($\chi^2 = 1.296$, $df = 2$, $p = 0.523 > 0.01$). In soft science texts, textual *I THINK* is the most prevalent while in hard science texts, ideational *I THINK* is the most prevalent. This is in consistency with their mode distributions. However, it can also been seen that the distribution of the three types of *I THINK* in hard science texts with regard to discipline distribution is opposite of that in academic texts with regard to genre

**Table 5.4** Normalized frequencies of textual, interpersonal and ideational *I THINK* across disciplines

| | Soft science | Hard science | Total |
|---|---|---|---|
| Textual | 7.19298246 | 1.413428 | 8.60641 |
| Interpersonal | 26.7719298 | 8.480565 | 35.2525 |
| Ideational | 9.32163743 | 3.886926 | 13.20856 |

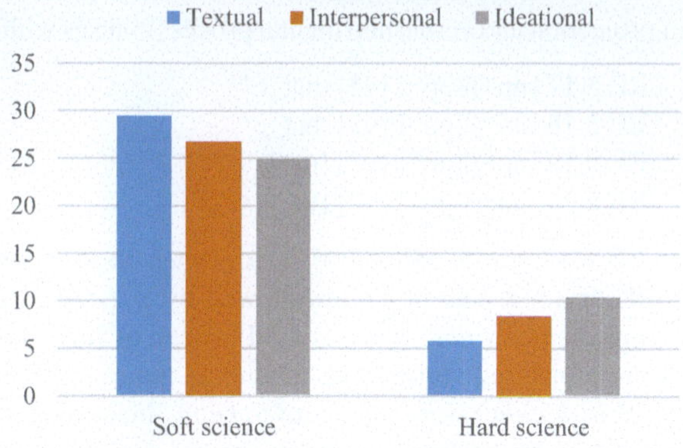


**Fig. 5.3** Discipline distributions of textual, interpersonal and ideational *I THINK*

distribution. The reason might be that although all the three types of *I THINK* do not tend to occur in hard science texts textual projection is characteristic of oral language.

## 5.2 Synchronic Distribution of Projected Clauses

According to the discussion in Sect. 3.4.2, the syntactic status of projected clause can be interpreted by the semantic analysis of the verbs preceding the projected clauses. Projected clauses succeeding verbal and mental projecting verbs function at the clause rank and a projecting clause and a projected clause form a hypotactic clause complex. Embedded fact clauses function at the group rank and the embedded fact clause is a constituent of the matrix clause. Projecting clause complexes are of higher grammatical intricacy while clauses with embedded fact are of higher lexical density. The technicality of language is determined by lexical density instead of grammatical intricacy. Therefore, it can be hypothesized that hypotactic clause complexes of projection are more prevalent in spoken texts regarding mode distribution, more prevalent in fiction texts regarding genre distribution and more prevalent in soft science texts regarding discipline distribution while clauses with embedded fact are oppositely distributed.

Typical projecting verbal and mental verbs are selected from the list provided by Halliday and Matthiessen (2014: 514, 517, 523, 536). Verbal verbs include projecting verbs with locution such as *tell*, *remark*, *announce*, *suggest*, *offer*, *threaten*, *promise*, *agree*, *ask*, *order* and *decide* and non-projecting declarative verbs with fact such as *admit*. Mental verbs include projecting verbs with idea such as *think*, *wish*, *hope*, *want* and *intend* and non-projecting verbs with fact such as *accept*, *overlook*, *recognize*, *regret* and *worry*. Verbs that can be interpreted either as projecting verbs with idea or as non-projecting verbs with fact are removed from the list to avoid overlapping in the calculation. For example, *believe* is excluded because it can be a projecting cognitive mental verb projecting idea or a non-projecting cognitive mental verb perceiving fact.

The following search queries were written to retrieve hypotactic clause complexes of projection and verbal and mental process clauses with embedded fact in the COCA.

RE 5.17 [np*]|[pp*] [v*] that_c*
RE 5.18 [nn*]|[pp*] [v*] that_c*
RE 5.19 [np*]|[pp*] [v*] [to*]
RE 5.20 [nn*]|[pp*] [v*] [to*]|[v?g*]

RE 5.17 can be described as a proper noun neutral for number (e.g., Andes, IBM) or a personal pronoun followed by a specific verbal or mental verb and the complementizer *that*. [np*] is used instead of [nn*] because with [nn*] the subject of the projecting verb can be inanimate nouns such as *book* in *this book tells that the British didn't want the world to know*. Inanimate nouns cannot realize sensor or sayer. Hereby, such constructions are not projecting verbal processes but relational

**Table 5.5** Frequencies of projected clauses in the COCA

| | | Spoken | Written | | | | | | Total |
|---|---|---|---|---|---|---|---|---|---|
| | | | Fiction | Magazine | Newspaper | Academic | | | |
| | | | | | | Hard sci | Soft sci | Misc | |
| Hypotactic | Locution | 22,808 | 8410 | 13,761 | 17,409 | 8926 | 1590 | 690 | 73,594 |
| | Idea | 53,463 | 12,609 | 8415 | 7274 | 5076 | 1067 | 891 | 88,795 |
| Embedding | Fact | 2324 | 1252 | 2449 | 2332 | 1952 | 327 | 141 | 10,777 |
| Total | | 78,595 | 22,271 | 24,625 | 27,015 | 15,954 | 2984 | 1722 | 173,166 |

processes. Search query RE 5.17 can be used to search hypotactic clause complexes with finite projected clausees. For example:

5.7 a. But he said that this only counts if I'm injured due to someone else's actions. (COCA_FIC)
b. As a result of the inventories, Mr. Zinther determined that the Multimedia Club and School Yearbook Club held the greatest potential. (COCA_ACAD)

Search query RE 5.18 can be described as a noun or personal pronoun followed by a specific verbal or mental verb and the complementizer *that* [nn*] is used instead of [np*] here because mental or verbal verbs with fact do not appear with inanimate nouns. RE 5.18 is used to retrieve clauses of mental or verbal processes with embedded fact. For example:

5.8 a. I regret that I didn't do something or I didn't say something. (COCA_NEWS)
b. She admitted that the block class had its struggles in the beginning. (COCA_ACAD)

RE 5.19 can be described as a proper noun or personal pronoun followed by a specific projecting verb and an infinitive marker *to*. This search query can be used to retrieve hypotactic clause complexes of projection with non-finite projected clauses. For example:

5.9 a. I promise to see if the damage can be undone. (COCA_FIC)
b. In this work, we propose to learn a long-term filter Formula omitted to address this problem. (COCA_ACAD)

Using the above four search queries, 73,594 hypotactic clause complexes of locution, 88,795 hypotactic clause complexes of idea and 10,777 clauses with embedded facts were retrieved from the COCA. Their raw frequencies are shown in Table 5.5.

### *5.2.1 Mode Distribution of Projected Clauses*

The frequencies of hypotactic clause complex of locution and idea were added up as the frequency of hypotactic clause complexes of projection. The normalized

**Table 5.6** Normalized frequencies of hypotactic projections and embedded facts across modes

| | Spoken | Written | Total |
|---|---|---|---|
| Hypotactic projection | 604.8454 | 176.0259 | 780.8713 |
| Embedded fact | 18.42982 | 17.39658 | 35.8264 |

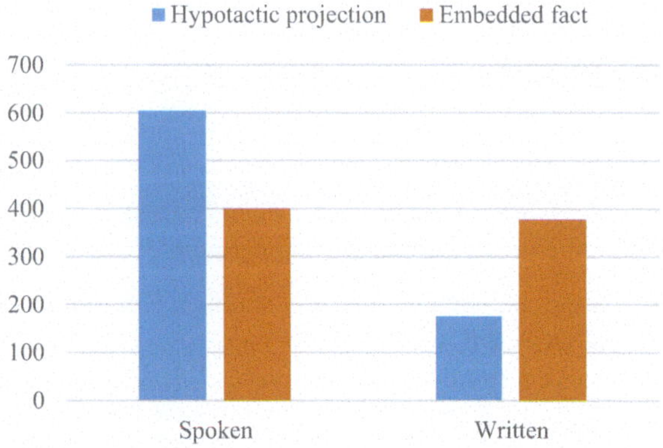


**Fig. 5.4** Mode distributions of hypotactic projections and embedded facts

frequency of hypotactic clause complexes of projection and that of clause simplexes with embedded fact in spoken and written texts are shown in Table 5.6.

To facilitate comparison, the total normalized frequency of the clause simplexes with embedded fact (35.83) was converted to that of the hypotactic clause complexes of projection (780.87). Their mode distributions are shown in Fig. 5.4.

The mode distribution of hypotactic clause complexes of projection shows a significant difference from that of clause simplexes with embedded fact ($\chi^2 = 115.173$, $df = 1$, $p = 0.000 < 0.01$). Hypotactic clause complexes of projection manifest considerable preference in spoken texts instead of written texts. Clause simplexes with embedded fact are nearly evenly distributed in spoken texts and written texts. In spoken texts, hypotactic clause complexes of projection are more prevalent. In written texts, clause simplexes with embedded fact are more prevalent. This is consistent with the hypothesis that clause simplexes with embedded fact are more prevalent in written texts. The reason is that clause simplexes with embedded fact have lower grammatical intricacy but higher lexical density, which is consistent with the feature of written texts. The syntactic status of embedded fact is at the group rank and hence increases the lexical density in the nominal group in which it is embedded.

### 5.2.2 *Genre Distribution of Projected Clauses*

Based on the mode distributions of hypotactic clause complexes of projection and clause simplexes with embedded fact, it can be hypothesized that clause simplexes with embedded fact are more prevalent in academic texts than in other genres. The normalized frequencies of hypotactic clause complexes of projection and clause simplexes with embedded fact in Fiction, Magazine, Newspaper and academic texts were worked out to compare their genre distributions (see Table 5.7).

To facilitate comparison, the total normalized frequency of clause simplexes with embedded fact (69.37) was converted to that of hypotactic clause complexes of projection (708.61). The genre distributions are shown in Fig. 5.5.

The genre distributions of hypotactic clause complexes of projection and clause simplexes with embedded fact show a significant difference ($\chi^2 = 26.694$, $df = 3$, $p = 0.000 < 0.01$). As shown in Fig. 5.5, the two types of data are oppositely distributed in fiction texts and in academic texts. Hypotactic clause complexes of projection tend to occur more in fiction texts while clause simplexes with embedded fact tend to occur more in academic texts. This is consistent with the hypothesis that clause simplexes with embedded fact are more likely to occur in academic texts. The reason is that academic language is more technical and the technicality of language relies on lexical density instead of syntactic complexity.

**Table 5.7** Normalized frequencies of hypotactic projections and embedded facts across genres

| | Fiction | Magazine | Newspaper | Academic | Total |
|---|---|---|---|---|---|
| Hypotactic projection | 177.6754 | 175.8604 | 202.8184 | 152.2538 | 708.60799 |
| Embedded fact | 10.58326 | 19.42109 | 19.16187 | 20.20033 | 69.366565 |

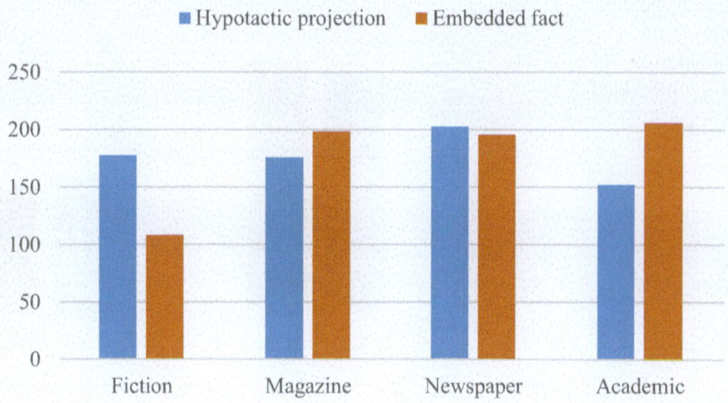


**Fig. 5.5** Genre distributions of hypotactic clause complexes of projection and clause simplexes with embedded fact

### *5.2.3 Discipline Distribution of Projected Clauses*

Based on the mode and genre distributions of hypotactic clause complexes of projection and clause simplexes with embedded fact, it can be hypothesized that hypotactic clause complexes of projection are more likely to occur in soft science texts while clause simplexes with embedded fact are more likely to occur in hard science texts. The normalized frequencies of the two groups of data are shown in Table 5.8.

To facilitate comparison, the total normalized frequency of simple clauses with embedded fact (34.39) was converted to that of hypotactic clause complexes of projection (257.65). Their discipline distributions are illustrated in Fig. 5.6.

Figure 5.6 shows that the discipline distribution of hypotactic clause complexes of projection and that of clause simplexes with embedded fact do not show a significant difference ($\chi^2 = 0.417$, $df = 1$, $p = 0.518 > 0.05$). Both of them tend to occur more in soft science texts than in hard science texts. This is not in agreement with our hypothesis.

**Table 5.8** Normalized frequencies of hypotactic projections and embedded facts across disciplines

| | Soft science | Hard science | Total |
|---|---|---|---|
| Hypotactic projection | 163.7661 | 93.88693 | 257.653 |
| Embedded fact | 22.83041 | 11.55477 | 34.38518 |

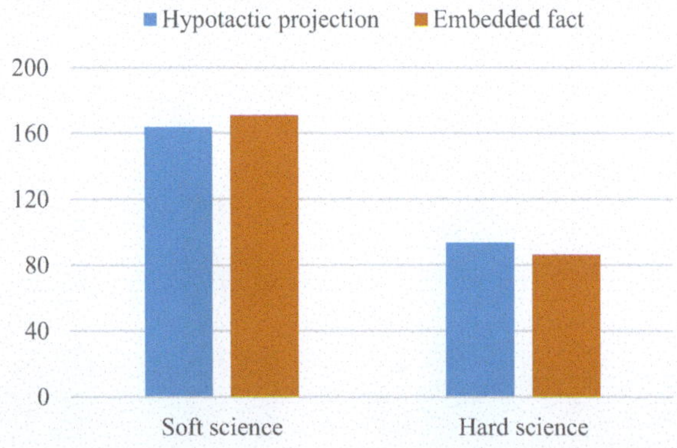


**Fig. 5.6** Discipline distributions of hypotactic clause complexes of projection and clause simplexes with embedded fact

## 5.3 Synchronic Distribution of Embedding Projections

Embedded projection involves the rank-shift of a projected clause from clause rank to group rank or word rank. The investigation of embedded projection can be conducted from the perspectives of the level of projection, the degree of projection and the finiteness of projected clauses.

Nominal groups with embedded projection demonstrate different degrees of projection. Embedded projections with possessive pronouns can indicate the projector and hence maintain a higher degree of projection. The degree of projection decreases with embedded locution/idea without indicator of projector, embedded fact with modality, embedded fact without modality and finally embedded fact without head noun. Hereby the following search queries were written to retrieve the corresponding constructions.

RE 5.20 [app*] [nn*] that|[rrq*] –[v*]
RE 5.21 [app*] [nn*] of [v?g*]
RE 5.22 [app*] [nn*] to [v*]
RE 5.23 [app*] [nn*] for|of [pp*]|[ppx*]|[nn*]|[np*]|[pn*] to [v*]

RE 5.20 can be described as any possessive pronoun followed by a noun, the complementizer *that* or a *wh*-word not preceding a verb. This search query can be used to retrieve embedded projection with explicit projector indicated by the pre-modifier. Examples of results retrieved using RE5.20 are shown in 5.10. RE 5.21 can be described as any possessive pronoun followed by a noun and an *of* phrase. RE 5.21 can be used to retrieve non-finite embedded projections of proposition with explicit projector. RE 5.22 can be described as any possessive pronoun followed by a noun and a *to* infinitive. RE 5.23 can be described as any possessive pronoun followed by a noun, a preposition *for* or *of*, a pronoun or reflexive personal pronoun or noun or proper noun or indefinite pronoun and a *to* infinitive. RE. 5.22 and RE 5.23 can be used to retrieve non-finite embedded projections of proposal with explicit projector. Examples retrieved using RE 5.21, RE 5.22 and RE 5.23 are shown in 5.11.

5.10 a. His statement that he is valued as a 13 instead of a one, is associated with his statements that he wanted to be valued more in other parts of his life. (COCA_NEWS)
b. I'm not sure how to address your suggestion that I haven't provided any kind of explanation. (COCA_BLOG)

5.11 a. Your suggestion of having the child follow along in the book as he listens to the tape may be very good. (COCA_WEB)
b. Is he standing by his threat to close the border? (COCA_SPOK)
c. That was when I launched into my plea for him to allow us to have a cocktail party in this house. (COCA_FIC)

The results retrieved using RE 5.22 and RE 5.23 are different in that the former are proposal of offer (e.g., 5.11b) which construes inclination that the projector will do and the latter are proposal of command (e.g., 5.11c) that requires a second person to meet an expectation from the projector.

Locution and idea nouns are the nominalization of corresponding verbal and mental verbal groups. The absence of projector after nominalization enables the projected content to appear as packaged locution or idea that is projected by someone unknown. The following search queries were written to retrieve embedded locutions and ideas without projectors.

RE 5.24 the [nn*] that|[rrq*] [d*]|[at*]|[app*] [n*]|[pp*] [v*]
RE 5.25 the [nn*] that|[rrq*] [n*]|[pp*] [v*]
RE 5.26 the [nn*] of [v?g*]
RE 5.27 the [nn*] to [v*]
RE 5.28 the [nn*] for|of [pp*]|[ppx*]|[nn*]|[np*]|[pn*] to [v*]

RE 5.24 can be described as a noun following a definite article *the* and preceding the complementizer *that* or a *wh*-word, a determiner or article or possessive pronoun, a noun or pronoun, and a verb. RE 5.25 can be described as a noun followed by the complementizer *that* or a *wh*-word, a noun or pronoun, and a verb. RE 5.26 can be described as a definite article *the* followed by a noun and an *of* phrase. RE 5.27 can be described as a definite article *the* followed by a noun and a *to* infinitive. RE 5.28 can be described as a noun following a definite article *the* and preceding a preposition *for* or *of*, a pronoun or reflexive personal pronoun or noun or proper noun or indefinite pronoun, and a *to* infinitive. RE 5.24 and RE 5.25 can be used to retrieve finite embedded projections serving as the appositives of projection nouns or fact nouns. RE 5.26, RE 5.27 and RE 5.28 can be used to retrieve non-finite embedded projections serving as the appositives of projection nouns or fact nouns. For example:

5.12 a. A child who is dwelling on the thought that the world would be better without him needs immediate help too. (COCA_MAG)
b. Instead of answering the inquiry how he came there, Jesus blamed their asking. (COCA_WEB)
c. Spence was asked about the possibility of facing Terence Crawford, but he's eyeing the Filipino veteran. (COCA_MAG)
d. Then the police chief gives the order to move the trucks slowly, even though the protesters are lying underneath. (COCA_SPOK)
e. But we, like you, recognize the need for them to experience as many different aspects of life as possible, to arm them spiritually and emotionally for the years ahead. (COCA_SPOK)

The above examples illustrate some finite embedded projections without projector. Different groups of typical projection nouns (see Appendix E) can be used to further distinguish locution, idea, modalized and non-modalized facts and so on.

The last type of embedded projection does not follow any head noun and stands on its own as nominalization. The absent head nouns can only be fact nouns of case since they are vague in meaning. Therefore, all the embedded projections without head nouns are embedded facts. Embedded fact nouns as head can serve as the subject or the complement in the clause it is embedded in. The following search queries were designed to retrieve subject embedded fact nouns.

RE 5.29.|! that [d*]|[at*]|[app*] [nn*]|[pp*] [v*]
RE 5.30.|! that [pp*] [v*]
RE 5.31 [y*] it [vb*] [j*] that
RE 5.32 it [vb*] [j*] to [v*]

RE 5.29 can be described as a period or an exclamation mark followed by the complementizer *that*, a determiner or article or possessive pronoun, a noun or pronoun, and a verb. RE 5.30 can be described as a period or an exclamation mark followed by the complementizer *that*, a pronoun, and a verb. RE 5.29 and RE 5.30 can be used to retrieve fact projections serving as the subject in the clause it is embedded in. RE 5.31 can be described as a punctuation followed by a pronoun *it*, a BE verb, an adjective, and the complementizer *that*. RE 5.31 can be used to retrieve fact projections serving as extraposed subjects. RE 5.32 can be described as a pronoun *it* followed by a BE verb, an adjective, and a *to* infinitive. It can be used to retrieve non-finite fact clauses standing on their own and serving as extraposed subjects. In such constructions, *it* is a subject placeholder and the embedded fact clause is the real subject. For example:

5.13 a. That my daughter could have been greatly affected by this just overwhelms me! (COCA_BLOG)
b. That he had some conflict with his golf club, also appears to be not true. (COCA_SPOK)
c. It is incomprehensible that a human being had the freedom to rise from the dead. (COCA_MAG)
d. Still, it's fun to see the old gang again. (COCA_MAG)

However, the number of constructions retrieved using RE 5.29 and RE 5.30 is limited and some of the constructions are not embedded facts. For example:

5.14 a. That a Mormon will run the world. (COCA_BLOG)
b. That we should ask. (COCA_FIC)

Hereby, the data retrieved using RE 5.31 and RE 5.32 will be used to represent embedded facts as subject.

To retrieve embedded facts as complement, typical verbal (e.g., *admit*) or mental verbs (e.g., *regret*) that can take fact as complement were employed to write the following search queries:

RE 5.33
REJOICE|WORRY|RECOGNIZE|REGRET|ADMIT|ACCEPT|OVERLOOK
|RESENT that [d*]|[at*]|[app*] [n*]|[pp*] [v*]
RE 5.34
REJOICE|WORRY|RECOGNIZE|REGRET|ADMIT|ACCEPT|OVERLOOK
|RESENT that [nn*]|[pp*] [v*]

RE 5.33 can be described as any of the verbal or mental verbs followed by the complementizer *that*, a determiner or article or possessive pronoun, a noun or pronoun, and a verb. RE 5.34 can be described as any of the verbal or mental verbs followed by the complementizer *that*, a noun or pronoun, and a verb. These two search queries can be used to retrieve fact projections that stand on their own and serve as the complements in the clauses they are embedded in. For example:

5.15 a. And he admits that the experience left him shaken. (COCA_ACAD)
b. And okay, I resent that he's going to marry someone else. (COCA_FIC)

The other typical environment that fact projections without a head noun will appear is a relational (e.g., *it may be that*) process, an impersonal mental (e.g., *it is believed that*) or verbal process (e.g., *it is said that*) in which the fact projection is "projected impersonally" (Halliday & Matthiessen 2014: 539). Hereby, the following search queries were written to retrieve fact clauses as heads.

RE 5.35 [y*] the [nn*] [vb*] that_c*
RE 5.36 [y*] it [vb*] [v?n*] that
RE 5.37 [y*] it [vm*] [vb*] [v?n*] that
RE 5.38 [y*] it happens|occurs|appears|seems that

RE 5.35 can be described as any punctuation followed by the definite article *the*, a noun, a BE verb, and the complementizer *that*. RE 5.36 can be described as any punctuation followed by the pronoun *it*, a BE verb, a past participle of a lexical verb, and the complementizer *that*. RE 5.37 can be described as any punctuation followed by the pronoun *it*, a modal auxiliary, a BE verb, a past participle of lexical verb, and a complementizer *that*. RE 5.38 can be described as any punctuation followed by the pronoun *it*, any one of the verbs (i.e., *happens, occurs, appears, seems*) and the complementizer *that*. These search queries can be used to retrieve embedded projections that stand on their own and serve as a constituent in a clause which means to bring the fact into existence. For example:

5.16 a. The issue is that there is no perfect way to control for complex population structure and environmental heterogeneity. (COCA_ACAD)
b. In the end, it was agreed that the tribe elders should decide what to do. (COCA_FIC)
c. Though, it can be assumed that's his horse at the end. (COCA_NEWS)
d. It seems that he had spent quite some time on the issue back in 1983. (COCA_BLOG)

Using the above search queries, 310,717 embedded projections were retrieved from the COCA. The detailed frequencies are shown in Table 5.9.

As shown in Table 5.9, the speech functions of embedded locution and idea are divided into proposition and proposal and further categorized by giving and demanding. Sometimes, the speech function of proposal is not further categorized because some locution or idea nouns are hard to be distinguished as nominalization of verbs that construe offering or demanding. For example, *desire* and *hope* are idea nouns indicating goods-&-services exchange but it is impossible to judge whether

**Table 5.9** Frequencies of embedded projections retrieved from the COCA

| | | | Finite | Non-finite | Total | |
|---|---|---|---|---|---|---|
| Locution/idea with explicit projector | Proposition | Statement | 9240 | 717 | 9957 | 24,228 |
| | | Question | 17 | 0 | 17 | |
| | Proposal | Order | 1764 | 11,848 | 13,612 | |
| | | Command | | 642 | 642 | |
| Locution/idea without explicit projector | Proposition | Statement | 33,487 | 17,729 | 51,216 | 68,042 |
| | | Question | 57 | 6 | 63 | |
| | Proposal | Order | 4715 | 12,048 | 16,763 | |
| | | Command | | | | |
| Fact with modality | Proposition | Chance | 5571 | 7290 | 12,861 | 32,353 |
| | Proposal | Need | 1051 | 18,441 | 19,492 | |
| Fact without modality | Proposition | Case | 67,089 | 4799 | 71,888 | 73,101 |
| | | Proof | 1159 | 54 | 1213 | |
| Fact as head | Proposition | Case | 77,155 | 107,796 | 184,951 | 184,951 |
| Total | | | 201,305 | 181,370 | 310,717 | 310,717 |

their appositive would convey an offer or command merely by the projection noun. Hence some projections of proposal will not be further classified.

The embedded projections retrieved are merely some typical ones and do not cover all the occurrences of the corresponding types of projection. The proportions of their frequencies are not the overall proportions of different types of embedded projections but they can serve the purpose of exploring the mode, genre and discipline distributions of embedding projections. The raw frequencies of embedded projections in different genres in the COCA are presented in Table 5.10.

Using the above search queries, a total of 70,461 embedded projections in different disciplines were retrieved from the COCA. The frequencies are shown in Table 5.11.

According to Table 5.11, a total of 57,887 embedded projections in soft science texts and 12,574 embedded projections in hard science texts were retrieved from the COCA.

### 5.3.1 *Synchronic Distribution of Embedded Locutions, Ideas and Facts*

Projections of locution and projections of idea show different distribution trends across genres (Halliday & Matthiessen 2014; He 2019b). For example, reporting ideas dominate in fiction texts while reporting locutions dominate in news and academic texts (Biber et al. 1999).

According to Biber et al. (1999), the head nouns in nominal groups with embedded clauses, either finite or non-finite, are generally found to be more prevalent in the academic genre, followed by the news genre (Biber et al. 1999).

**Table 5.10** Frequencies of embedded projections across genres in the COCA

| | | | Spoken | Fiction | Magazine | Newspaper | Academic | Total |
|---|---|---|---|---|---|---|---|---|
| Locution/ idea with projector | Locution | Finite | 365 | 187 | 320 | 442 | 532 | 1846 |
| | | Non-finite | 1001 | 502 | 837 | 753 | 1264 | 4357 |
| | Idea | Finite | 295 | 292 | 262 | 386 | 191 | 1426 |
| | | Non-finite | 1115 | 1001 | 1528 | 1757 | 1588 | 6989 |
| Locution/ idea without projector | Locution | Finite | 898 | 355 | 699 | 595 | 933 | 3480 |
| | | Non-finite | 47 | 18 | 53 | 63 | 87 | 268 |
| | Idea | Finite | 5365 | 2599 | 3946 | 2942 | 5382 | 20,234 |
| | | Non-finite | 3258 | 3151 | 4099 | 3862 | 4381 | 18,751 |
| Fact with modality | Chance | Finite | 619 | 444 | 745 | 550 | 1399 | 3757 |
| | | Non-finite | 626 | 432 | 960 | 844 | 2292 | 5154 |
| | Need | Finite | 95 | 35 | 109 | 137 | 296 | 672 |
| | | Non-finite | 1249 | 969 | 2186 | 1858 | 5723 | 11,985 |
| Fact without modality | Case | Finite | 14,450 | 4977 | 6320 | 5079 | 6776 | 37,602 |
| | | Non-finite | 439 | 568 | 436 | 339 | 625 | 2407 |
| | Proof | Finite | 373 | 60 | 101 | 55 | 126 | 715 |
| | | Non-finite | 11 | 2 | 2 | 3 | 15 | 33 |
| Fact as head | Case | Finite | 7787 | 4001 | 7915 | 4851 | 20,211 | 44,765 |
| | | Non-finite | 15,971 | 7450 | 13,035 | 10,157 | 13,992 | 60,605 |
| Total | | | 35,179 | 17,988 | 53,964 | 27,043 | 43,553 | 34,673 |

#### 5.3.1.1 Mode Distribution of Embedded Locutions, Ideas and Facts

The total normalized frequencies of embedded locution, idea and fact are added up to compare their mode distributions. Their normalized frequencies in spoken and written texts are shown in the following Table 5.12.

It can be seen from Table 5.12, among the embedded projections retrieved, the normalized frequencies of embedded ideas and facts are higher than that of embedded locutions. To facilitate comparison, the total normalized frequency of embedded locutions (34.05) and embedded ideas (156.47) were converted to that of embedded facts (589.52). Their mode distributions are demonstrated in Fig. 5.7.

Figure 5.7 shows that embedded projections on the whole tend to appear in spoken texts. The distributions of the three levels of projections are not significantly different in spoken and written texts ($\chi^2 = 3.203$, $df = 2$, $p = 0.202 > 0.05$). Comparatively, embedded facts are the most prevalent in spoken texts while embedded ideas are the most prevalent in written texts.

This is different from Biber et al.'s (1999) finding that head nouns taking noun complement clauses do not tend to occur in the conversational genre. Two reasons may account for this difference. Firstly, the typical head nouns Biber et al. (1999) used are mostly locution and idea nouns that have corresponding verbs, including only

**Table 5.11** Frequencies of embedded projections across disciplines in the COCA

| | | | Soft science | Hard science | Total |
|---|---|---|---|---|---|
| Locution/idea with projector | Locution | Finite | 477 | 24 | 501 |
| | | Non-finite | 157 | 20 | 177 |
| | Idea | Finite | 1061 | 116 | 1177 |
| | | Non-finite | 1414 | 100 | 1514 |
| Locution/idea without projector | Locution | Finite | 694 | 74 | 768 |
| | | Non-finite | 142 | 17 | 159 |
| | Idea | Finite | 4470 | 522 | 4992 |
| | | Non-finite | 3519 | 561 | 4080 |
| Fact with modality | Chance | Finite | 1036 | 290 | 1326 |
| | | Non-finite | 1629 | 569 | 2198 |
| | Need | Finite | 261 | 26 | 287 |
| | | Non-finite | 4454 | 1065 | 5519 |
| Fact without modality | Case | Finite | 5577 | 806 | 6383 |
| | | Non-finite | 487 | 94 | 581 |
| | Proof | Finite | 86 | 26 | 112 |
| | | Non-finite | 8 | 4 | 12 |
| Fact as head | Case | Finite | 20,117 | 4709 | 24,826 |
| | | Non-finite | 12,298 | 3551 | 15,849 |
| Total | | | 57,887 | 12,574 | 70,461 |

**Table 5.12** Normalized frequencies of embedded locutions, ideas and facts across modes

| | Spoken | Written | Total |
|---|---|---|---|
| Locution | 18.32672 | 15.7234 | 34.05012 |
| Idea | 79.56384 | 76.90265 | 156.4665 |
| Fact | 330.0555 | 259.4669 | 589.52248 |

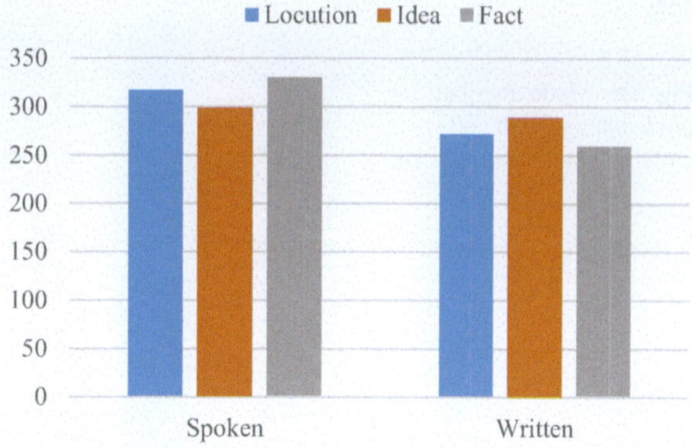


**Fig. 5.7** Mode distributions of embedded locutions, ideas and facts

three fact nouns, i.e. *fact, possibility* and *ground*. Nouns that have corresponding verbs are the nominalizations of the verbs and hence tend to appear more in academic texts. Secondly, Biber et al. (1999) do not include embedded facts standing on their own in noun complement clauses. Embedded facts standing on their own usually enter a mental, verbal or relational process to function as a participant. Typical mental verbs taking embedded fact clauses standing on their own are emotive such as *regret*, *rejoice* and *recent*. Biber et al. (1999) refer to such embedded fact clauses as post-predicate *that*-clauses, and found that post-predicate *that*-clauses tend to occur more in conversational texts. It is those embedded fact clauses that contribute to the higher frequency in the spoken texts.

We then take idea nouns as examples to compare the distributions of locution nouns with corresponding verbs (e.g., *belief*, *thought*, *feeling*, *notion*, *prediction*, *assumption*) and those without corresponding verbs (e.g., *idea*, *view*, *opinion*) to see whether the latter ones occur more in spoken texts. The normalized frequencies of embedded ideas with and without corresponding mental verbs are shown in Table 5.13.

To facilitate comparison, the total normalized frequency of locution nouns without corresponding verbs (23.03) was converted to that of those with corresponding verbs (43.93). Their mode distributions are shown in Fig. 5.8.

As shown in Fig. 5.8, idea nouns with corresponding verbs tend to occur more in written texts while those without corresponding verbs tend to occur more in spoken texts. This is consistent with the analysis and supports the first reason discussed above.

The normalized frequency of fact projections standing on their own is also observed specifically. Such constructions are excluded from Biber et al.'s (1999)

**Table 5.13** Normalized frequencies of idea nouns with and without corresponding verbs across modes

| Idea nouns | Spoken | Written | Total |
|---|---|---|---|
| With corresponding verbs | 10.28549 | 12.74542 | 23.03 |
| Without corresponding verbs | 28.62014 | 15.31385 | 43.93 |

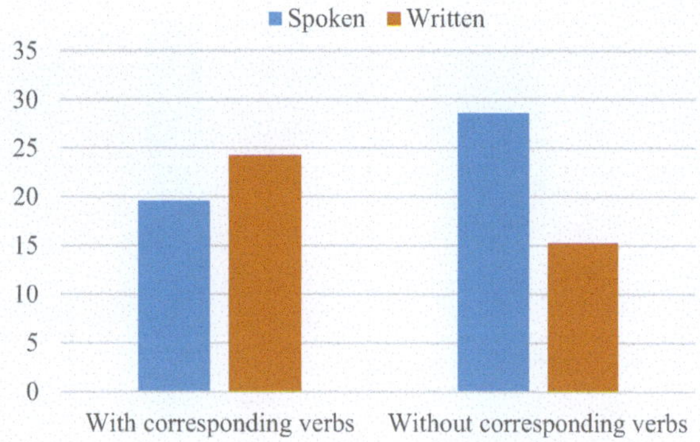


**Fig. 5.8** Mode distributions of idea nouns with and without corresponding verbs

**Table 5.14** Raw and normalized frequencies of facts as head across modes in the COCA

| | Spoken | Written |
|---|---|---|
| Raw frequency | 23,758 | 81,612 |
| Normalized frequency | 188.406027 | 167.9604857 |

calculation of constructions of head nouns with noun complement clauses. The normalized frequencies of all the fact clauses standing on their own (i.e., fact as head) are shown in Table 5.14.

As shown in Table 5.14, although the raw frequency of fact as head is higher in written texts, the normalized frequency is higher in spoken texts because the total number of words in spoken texts (126.1 million words) is far lower than that in written texts (485.9 million words). Therefore, fact clauses standing on their own without a head noun tend to occur far more in spoken texts than in written texts. This contributes to the higher frequency of embedded fact projections in spoken texts and confirms the hypothesis put forward on the second reason discussed above. Hereby, fact projections, either being modifier or head, tend to occur more in spoken texts.

#### 5.3.1.2 Genre Distribution of Embedded Locutions, Ideas and Facts

Based on the mode distributions of embedded locutions, ideas and facts, it is hypothesized that embedded facts are the most prevalent in fiction texts and embedded ideas are the most prevalent in academic texts. The total normalized frequencies of embedded locutions, ideas and facts across different genres are calculated (see Table 5.15).

Among the embedded projections retrieved, embedded facts have the highest normalized frequency. Since the retrieved data consist of typical constructions of embedded projection, their general distribution trends in different genres will be worked out and their proportion in specific genres will not be taken into consideration. To facilitate comparison, the total normalized frequencies of embedded locutions (62.85) and embedded ideas (307.39) were converted to that of embedded facts (1038.007). The genre distributions of embedded locutions, ideas and facts are presented in Fig. 5.9.

According to Fig. 5.9, embedded projections of locution, idea and fact all tend to appear more in academic texts than in fiction texts. This is opposite to the present

**Table 5.15** Normalized frequencies of embedded locutions, ideas and facts across genres

| | Fiction | Magazine | Newspaper | Academic | Total |
|---|---|---|---|---|---|
| Locution | 8.977177 | 15.13878 | 15.22597 | 23.50584 | 62.84776 |
| Idea | 59.53508 | 77.99366 | 73.51684 | 96.34391 | 307.3895 |
| Fact | 160.0845 | 252.2522 | 196.1627 | 429.5075 | 1038.007 |

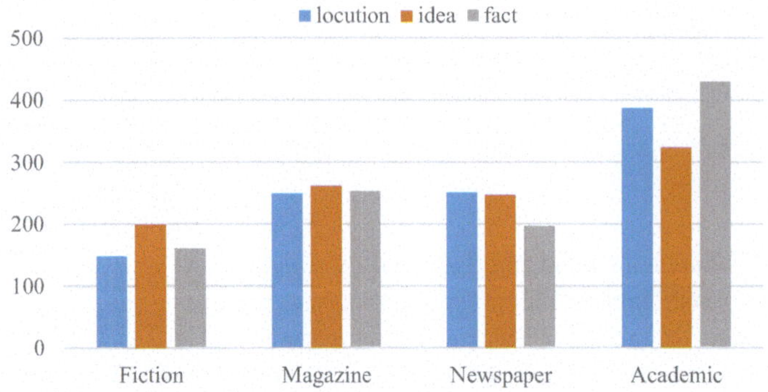


**Fig. 5.9** Genre distributions of embedded locutions, ideas and facts

hypothesis. Fiction texts are regarded as the least technical one among the four written genres.

The genre distributions of embedded locutions, ideas and facts show a significant difference ($\chi^2 = 32.404$, $df = 6$, $p = 0.000 < 0.01$). In fiction texts, the most prevalent embedded projections are embedded ideas. In academic texts, the most prevalent are embedded facts. This is opposite to their mode distributions in which embedded facts are the most prevalent in spoken texts and embedded ideas are the most prevalent in written texts.

#### 5.3.1.3 Discipline Distributions of Embedded Locutions, Ideas and Facts

Embedded projections of locution, idea and fact are not mode sensitive but they are genre sensitive. Embedded facts are more likely to appear in academic texts while embedded ideas are more likely to appear in fiction texts. Hereby it can be hypothesized that embedded facts are more likely to appear in hard science texts while embedded ideas are more likely to appear in soft science texts. The normalized frequencies of embedded locutions, ideas and facts are shown in Table 5.16.

To facilitate comparison, the total normalized frequency of embedded locution (21.96) and embedded idea (168.29) were converted to that of embedded fact (931.1). Their discipline distributions are shown in Fig. 5.10.

As shown in Fig. 5.10, all the three types of embedded projection tend to occur more in soft science texts. The discipline distributions of the three types of

**Table 5.16** Normalized frequencies of embedded locutions, ideas and facts across disciplines

| | Soft science | Hard science | Total |
|---|---|---|---|
| Locution | 17.19298 | 4.770318 | 21.9633 |
| Idea | 122.386 | 45.90106 | 168.287 |
| Fact | 537.462 | 393.6396 | 931.1016 |

Fig. 5.10 Discipline distributions of embedded locutions, ideas and facts

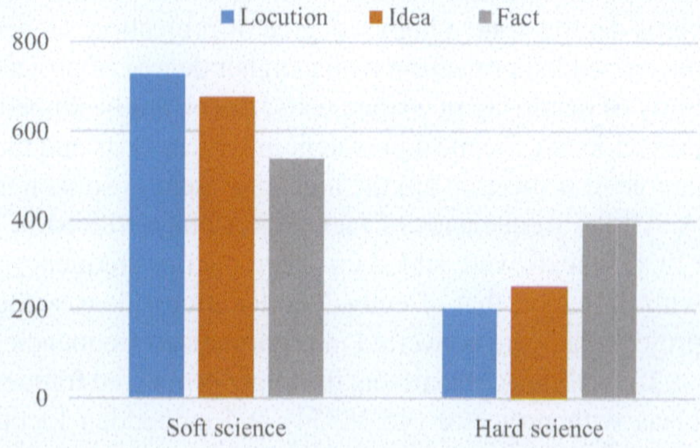


projection show a significant difference ($\chi^2 = 100.61, df = 2, p = 0.000 < 0.01$). In hard science texts, embedded facts are the most prevalent, which is in consistency with the genre distribution feature that facts are the most prevalent in academic texts. In soft science texts, embedded locutions are the most prevalent, which is not in consistency with the genre distribution that embedded ideas are the most prevalent in fiction texts.

## 5.3.2 *Synchronic Distribution of Embedded Projections*

### 5.3.2.1 Mode Distribution of Embedded Projections

Embedded projections result from nominalization. The nominalization of projecting verbs would lead to the adjectivization of the nominal group that realizes the projector and the downward rank-shift of the projected clause. Some embedded locutions and ideas are pre-modified by possessive pronouns. The pre-modifier realized by possessive pronouns can be regarded as the adjectivization of the nominal group realizing projector in the clause complex of projection. Hence embedded locutions and ideas with explicit projectors maintain the closest degree of projection with their congruent projection clause complexes.

Embedded locutions and ideas without explicit projectors are weaker in degree of projection because projectors are implicit and the unknown source makes the projected idea or locution appear on its own. Embedded facts are the nominalization of zero. Having no projector means no projecting processes are involved in creating a fact. Hence embedded facts maintain the weakest degree of projection. The greater degree of projection means the stronger interdependency relation between the projection/fact noun and the projected clause.

In Sect. 5.3.1.1 (Mode distributions of embedded locutions, ideas and facts), it is found that locution nouns with corresponding projecting verbs tend to occur more in written texts than those without corresponding verbs. Nouns with corresponding verbs demonstrate a higher degree of projection. Hence it can be hypothesized that the embedded projection with a higher degree of projection will have a higher possibility of occurring in written texts. Accordingly, embedded projections with explicit projectors are the most prevalent in written texts and fact projections with the lowest degree of projection are the most prevalent in spoken texts.

All the frequencies of fact projections retrieved in written (77,382) and spoken (29,415) texts were added up. Then the raw frequency of embedded locutions/ideas with projector, that of embedded locutions/ideas without projector and that of fact projections were converted into normalized frequencies (see Table 5.17).

To facilitate comparison, the total normalized frequencies of embedded locutions/ideas with projector (46.38554) and embedded locutions/ideas without projector (144.1311) were converted to that of fact projections (589.5225). Their mode distribution patterns are shown in Fig. 5.11.

As shown in Fig. 5.11, embedded projections with projector show opposite mode distribution patterns to those without projector ($\chi^2 = 8.798$, $df = 2$, $p = 0.012 < 0.05$). Embedded locutions/ideas with projector are more likely to occur in written texts while embedded locutions/ideas without projector and fact projections are more likely to occur in spoken texts. Embedded facts are the most prevalent in spoken texts while embedded locutions/ideas with projector are the most prevalent in written texts. Their mode distribution patterns are consistent with the present hypothesis. One reason may be that the nominal groups realizing embedded locutions/ideas with projector have more pre-modifiers. The higher complexity of a nominal group will lead to higher lexical density. Written language features higher lexical

**Table 5.17** Normalized frequencies of different types of nominalization acorss modes

| | Spoken | Written | Total |
|---|---|---|---|
| Locution/idea with explicit projector | 22.01427 | 24.37126981 | 46.38554 |
| Locution/idea without explicit projector | 75.87629 | 68.25478494 | 144.1311 |
| Fact projection | 330.0555 | 259.4669685 | 589.5225 |

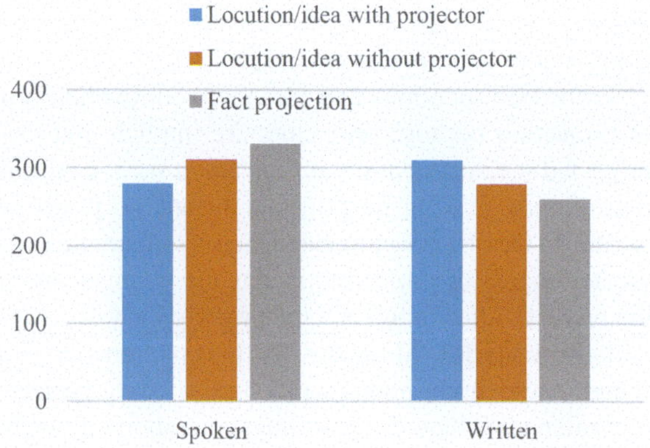


**Fig. 5.11** Mode distributions of embedded projections in cline of projection degree

density and spoken language features higher grammatical intricacy (Halliday 1989). Hereby embedded projections with pre-modifier indicating explicit projector are more prevalent in written texts.

As for fact projection, modalized fact nouns, i.e., chance and need nouns, bear a stronger relation with embedded facts because they define and evaluate epistemically the probability and obligation of the proposition in the embedded fact. The stance attached to chance and need nouns is regarded somehow as "nominalized from adjectives," e.g., *feasibility* in *the feasibility of using standing waves to measure the cloud density* is derived from *feasible* in *it is feasible to use standing waves to measure the cloud density* (Dong et al. 2020: 6). Compared with non-modalized fact nouns that just define the projected clause, modalized fact nouns bear stronger relations with the fact clauses. It can hence be hypothesized that modalized fact projections are more prevalent in written texts and non-modalized fact projections are more prevalent in spoken texts.

Fact projections as post-modifiers of modalized and non-modalized fact nouns were retrieved and their raw frequencies were converted into normalized frequencies. Their normalized frequencies are shown in Table 5.18.

To facilitate comparison, the total normalized frequency of the modalized fact projections (59.5908) was converted to that of non-modalized fact projections (173.57). Their mode distribution pattern is shown in Fig. 5.12.

According to Fig. 5.12, modalized and non-modalized facts show significantly different mode distribution features ($\chi^2 = 43.712, df = 1, p = 0.000 < 0.01$). Modalized facts tend to occur more in written texts while non-modalized facts tend to occur more in spoken texts. This is consistent with the distribution pattern of embedded

**Table 5.18** Normalized frequencies of facts modifying modalized and non-modalized fact nouns across modes

| | Spoken | Written | Total |
|---|---|---|---|
| Modalized | 20.53132435 | 39.05947726 | 59.5908016 |
| Non-modalized | 121.1181602 | 52.44700556 | 173.5651657 |

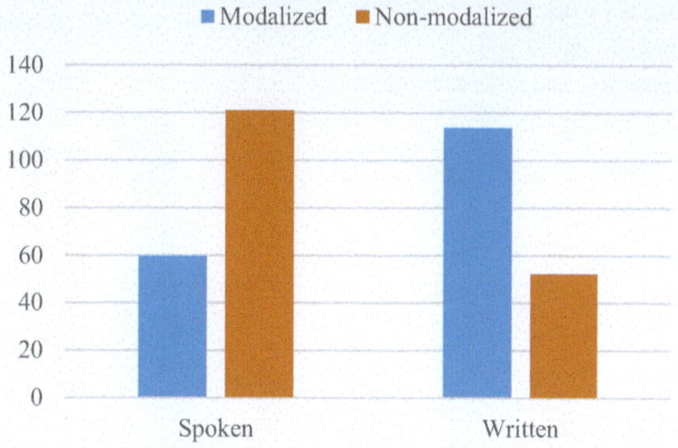


**Fig. 5.12** Mode distributions of facts modifying modalized and non-modalized nouns

locutions and ideas. Generally speaking, a closer relation between the head noun and the embedded clause as appositive contributes to the tendency to occur in written texts.

A fact clause can follow a head noun to serve as its appositive or stand on its own to serve as the head. Fact as appositive bears an interdependency relationship with its head noun. In the case of fact as head, the absence of the head noun indicates that the interdependency relation no longer exists. Hereby, it can be hypothesized that facts as appositive dominate in written texts and facts as head dominate in spoken texts. The normalized frequencies of facts serving as appositive of both modalized and non-modalized fact nouns are added up to work out the normalized frequency of all the fact projections serving as appositive. The normalized frequencies of facts as appositive and facts as head are shown in Table 5.19.

To facilitate comparison, the total normalized frequency of facts as head (159.37) was converted to that of facts as appositive (356.37). Their mode distributions are shown in Fig. 5.13.

As shown in Fig. 5.13, the mode distributions of facts as appositive and facts as head show a significant difference ($\chi^2 = 4.621$, $df = 1$, $p = 0.032 < 0.05$). Both of them tend to occur more in spoken texts. In spoken texts, facts as appositive are more prevalent. As for written texts, facts as head are more prevalent. Their mode distributions pattern is not in agreement with the present hypothesis.

Fact nouns that can be removed to allow the fact clause to stand on its own are usually fact nouns of case. Facts as appositives modify both modalized and non-modalized fact nouns. Modalized facts tend to appear in written texts. This may affect the mode distribution of facts as the appositives of head nouns and make it hard to identify what factor contributes to the mode sensitivity. Hence the comparative mode

**Table 5.19** Normalized frequencies of facts as appositive and facts as head across modes

| | Spoken | Written | Total |
|---|---|---|---|
| Fact as appositive | 141.6495 | 91.50648 | 233.156 |
| Fact as head | 188.406027 | 167.9604857 | 356.3665127 |

**Fig. 5.13** Mode distributions of facts as appositive and facts as head

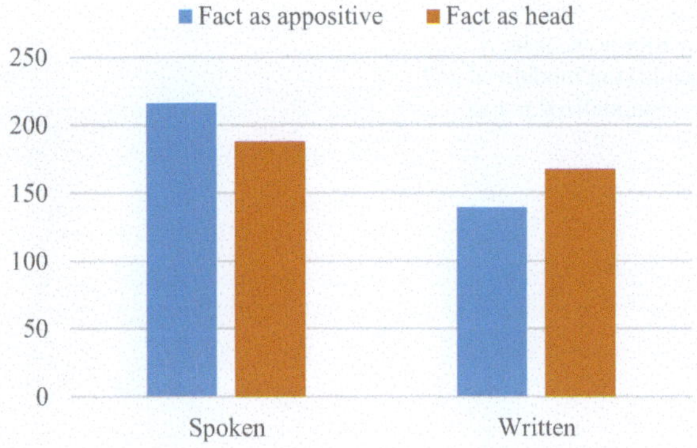

distribution analysis between the facts of case as appositive and the facts as head is necessary.

Fact nouns of case do not interact with modality and are vague in meaning. The case noun can be removed so that the embedded fact clause stands on its own as head. Comparing the mode distributions of facts of case as appositive and as head can reveal whether nouns modified by embedded clauses or embedded clauses as head are more technical. The normalized frequencies of embedded facts of case as appositive and those as head are shown in Table 5.20.

To facilitate comparison, the total frequency of cases as appositive (169.77) was converted to that of cases as head (356.37) to compare their distributions (see Fig. 5.14).

Figure 5.14 shows that both types of fact of case tend to appear in spoken texts. Their mode distributions show a significant difference ($\chi^2 = 20.822$, $df = 1$, $p = 0.000 < 0.01$). Embedded facts of case as appositive dominate in spoken texts while embedded facts of case as head dominate in written texts.

To sum up, seen from the perspective of nominalization, the closeness of interdependency relation between the projection/fact noun and the embedded projected clause can contribute to the mode sensitivity. Head nouns that bear a closer relation with embedded projected clauses also manifest a higher degree of projection. The above analysis indicates that embedded projections involving closer constituency relations and a higher degree of projection tend to appear more in written texts.

**Table 5.20** Normalized frequencies of embedded cases as appositive and as head across modes

| | Spoken | Written | Total |
|---|---|---|---|
| Case as appositive | 118.073 | 51.69788 | 169.7708 |
| Case as head | 188.406027 | 167.9604857 | 356.3665127 |

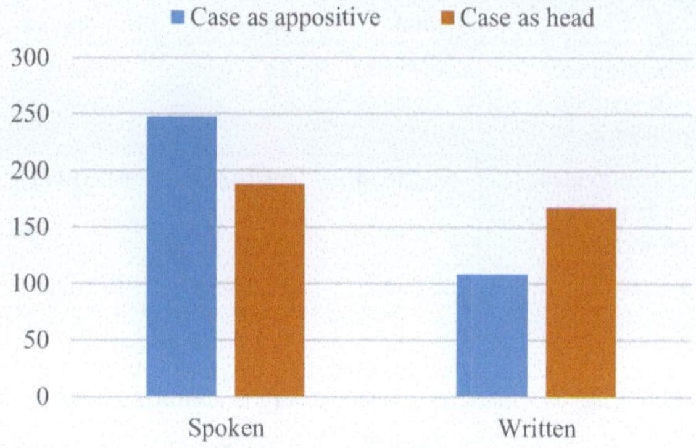


**Fig. 5.14** Mode distributions of embedded cases as appositive and as head

#### 5.3.2.2 Genre Distribution of Embedded Projections

Embedded projection involves different types of nominalization and leads to various degrees of projection. The genre distribution of the nominalizations of verbs and that of the nominalizations of zero will be observed first. The analysis of their mode distributions shows that embedded projections with a stronger degree of projection tend to dominate in written texts. Accordingly, it can be hypothesized that embedded locutions/ideas with explicit projector are the most technical while embedded projections of fact as a whole are the least technical. The normalized frequencies of all the embedded facts as appositive and as head are added up to work out the total normalized frequency of fact projections to compare with that of embedded locutions/ideas with and without explicit projector (see Table 5.21).

The normalized frequencies of embedded locutions/ideas with and without projector were added up to work out the total normalized frequency of embedded projections involving the nominalization of projecting verbs. This will facilitate the comparison of embedded projections resulting from the nominalization of verbs and that of zero. See their normalized frequencies across genres in Table 5.22.

To facilitate comparison, the total normalized frequency of the nominalizations of projecting verbs (370.24) was converted to that of the nominalizations of zero (1038.01) (see Fig. 5.15).

Embedded projections involving the nominalization of verbs and that of zero tend to occur more in academic texts. This is because embedded projection as a whole helps package up information in a nominal group and enhance the lexical density of the text. This can contribute to the conciseness of academic texts. The genre distributions of the nominalizations of verbs and those of zero in fiction and academic texts show a significant difference ($\chi^2 = 11.040, df = 1, p = 0.001 < 0.01$).

**Table 5.21** Normalized frequencies of embedded cases as appositive and as head across genres

| | Fiction | Magazine | Newspaper | Academic | Total |
|---|---|---|---|---|---|
| Locution/idea with explicit projector | 16.75402 | 23.37034 | 27.4281 | 29.8414 | 97.39386 |
| Locution/idea without explicit projector | 51.75824 | 69.76209 | 61.31471 | 90.00835 | 272.8434 |
| Fact | 160.08453 | 252.25218 | 196.162695 | 429.50751 | 1038.0069 |

**Table 5.22** Normalized frequencies of the nominalizations of verbs and of zero across genres

| | Fiction | Magazine | Newspaper | Academic | Total |
|---|---|---|---|---|---|
| Nominalization of verbs | 68.51226 | 93.13243 | 88.74281 | 119.8497 | 370.2373 |
| Nominalization of zero | 160.08453 | 252.25218 | 196.162695 | 429.5075 | 1038.0069 |

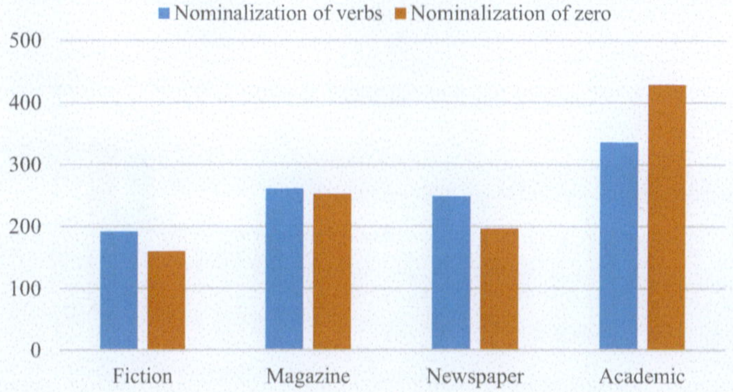


**Fig. 5.15** Genre distributions of nominalizations of verbs and of zero

Nominalizations of zero are more technical and hereby more prevalent in academic texts while nominalizations of verbs are less technical and more prevalent in fiction texts.

According to the genre distributions of embedded projections resulting from the nominalization of verbs and zero, projection nouns bearing a closer relationship with embedded clauses and having a higher degree of projection are less technical because a lower degree of projection can contribute to a higher degree of abstractness. Therefore, it can be hypothesized that embedded locutions/ideas without explicit projector are more technical than embedded projections with explicit projector. The genre distributions of embedded locutions/ideas with and without explicit projector will be compared to check whether this hypothesis is true or not. See Table 5.21 for their normalized frequencies across genres.

To facilitate comparison, the total normalized frequency of embedded locutions/ideas with explicit projector (97.39) and that of embedded locutions/ideas without projector (272.84) were converted to that of facts (1038.01). The genre distributions are shown in Fig. 5.16.

According to Fig. 5.16, the three types of embedded projection all tend to appear more in academic texts, with fact projection being the most genre sensitive. They demonstrate a significant difference in fiction and academic genre distributions ($\chi^2 = 14.353$, $df = 2$, $p = 0.001 < 0.01$). Nominalizations of zero are the most prevalent in academic texts, followed by embedded locutions/ideas without explicit projector and embedded locutions/ideas with explicit projector. Nominalizations of verbs with explicit projector are less prevalent than those without explicit projector. This is consistent with the hypothesis that a weaker degree of projection and a lower degree of closeness between the head noun and the embedded clause will lead to a higher degree of text technicality. However, the genre distributions of embedded locutions/ideas with and without explicit projector in fiction and academic texts do not show a significant difference ($\chi^2 = 0.032$, $df = 1$, $p = 0.859 > 0.05$). This indicates that the degree of projection does not result in genre sensitivity within the construction involving the nominalization of projecting verbs.

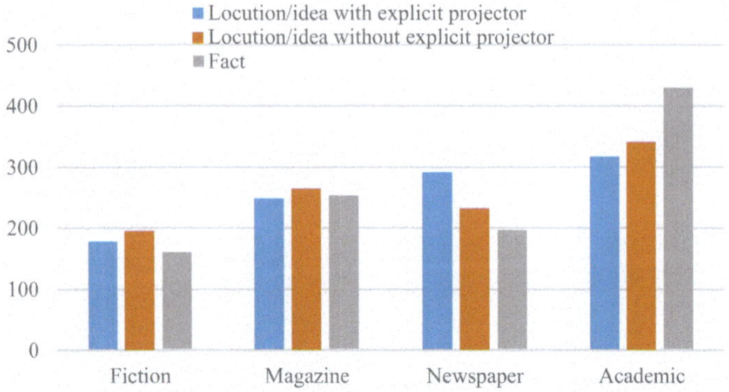


**Fig. 5.16** Genre distributions of types of nominalization

Fact projections can serve as an appositive to modify a fact noun or stand on their own to serve as the head. Fact clauses modifying head nouns manifest a higher degree of projection and closeness in interdependency relationship than fact clauses standing on their own. Based on the above findings in genre distribution, it can be hypothesized that fact clauses modifying head nouns are less prevalent than fact clauses standing on their own in academic texts. To compare their genre distributions, the total normalized frequency of embedded facts serving as appositive to modify modalized and non-modalized fact nouns were added up and compared with that of those serving as head (see Table 5.23).

To facilitate comparison, the total normalized frequency of facts as appositive (366.25) was converted to that of facts as head (671.75). Their genre distributions are shown in Fig. 5.17.

According to Fig. 5.17, both facts as appositive and facts as head generally tend to appear more in academic texts than in fiction texts. This is opposite to their mode distribution trend that facts tend to appear in spoken texts. Facts serving as head are more prevalent in academic texts and facts serving as appositive are more prevalent in fiction texts. This distribution feature is in consistency with their mode distribution trend that facts serving as head are more prevalent in written texts. Fact nouns are vague in meaning and the absence of fact nouns can contribute to the conciseness of language. Their distributions do not show a significant difference ($\chi^2 = 3.243$, $df = 3$, $p = 0.356 > 0.05$).

**Table 5.23** Normalized frequencies of facts as appositive across genres

| | Fiction | Magazine | Newspaper | Academic | Total |
|---|---|---|---|---|---|
| Fact as appositive | 63.28825 | 86.1142 | 72.84306 | 144.0067 | 366.2522 |
| Fact as head | 96.79628 | 166.13799 | 123.3196 | 285.5008 | 671.7547 |

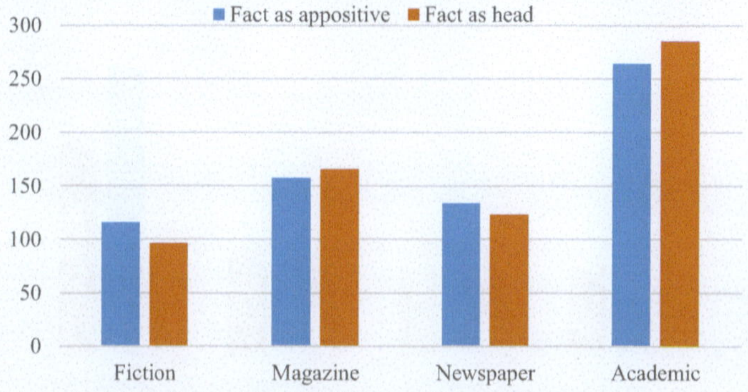


**Fig. 5.17** Genre distributions of fact as appositive and fact as head

Facts as appositive can modify either modalized or non-modalized fact nouns. Fact projections result from the nominalization of zero. Accordingly, facts as appositive can be categorized as modalized and non-modalized nominalizations of zero. The mode distribution analysis shows that the modality of fact nouns does contribute to the mode sensitivity of facts as appositive. Based on the previous finding that facts modifying modalized fact nouns are more prevalent in academic texts than those modifying non-modalized fact nouns, it can be hypothesized that facts modifying modalized fact nouns will be more prevalent than those modifying non-modalized fact nouns in academic texts. See in Table 5.24 their normalized frequencies.

The total normalized frequency of modalized fact nouns (156.51) was converted to that of non-modalized fact nouns (881.50). Their genre distributions are shown in Fig. 5.18.

The distribution pattern of modalized and non-modalized nominalizations of zero is consistent with the present hypothesis. Modalized ones are more prevalent in academic texts and non-modalized ones are more prevalent in fiction texts. Their distributions in different genres show a significant difference ($\chi^2 = 31.751$, $df = 3$, $p = 0.000 < 0.01$).

Facts of case can serve as appositives to modify case nouns or as heads standing on their own. Case nouns involving no modality are vague in meaning and the relation between the case nouns and the corresponding facts as appositive is weak. The mode distribution analysis shows that facts of case as head are more prevalent in written

**Table 5.24** Normalized frequencies of facts modifying modalized and non-modalized fact nouns across genres

| | Fiction | Magazine | Newspaper | Academic | Total |
|---|---|---|---|---|---|
| Modalized fact nouns | 15.8918 | 31.72086 | 27.84717 | 81.05175 | 156.5116 |
| Non-modalized fact nouns | 144.1927 | 220.5313 | 168.3155 | 348.4558 | 881.4953 |

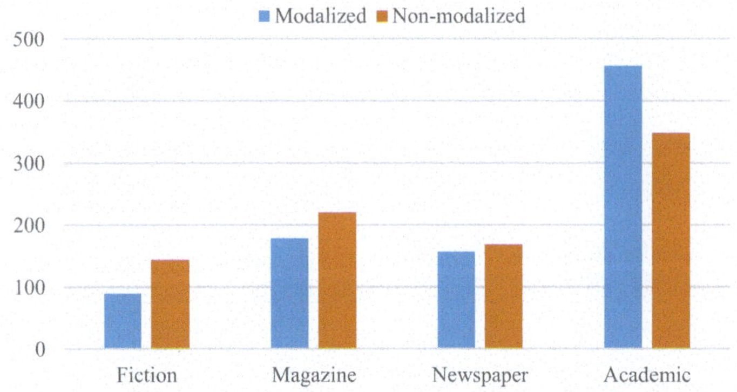


**Fig. 5.18** Genre distributions of facts modifying modalized and non-modalized fact nouns

texts. Hereby it can be hypothesized that facts of case as head are more prevalent in academic texts. The normalized frequencies of cases as appositives and as heads in the four genres are presented in Table 5.25.

The total normalized frequency of cases as appositive (206.75) was converted to that of cases as head (671.75). The genre distribution patterns of cases as appositive and as head are shown in Fig. 5.19.

The genre distributions of cases as appositive and that as head are consistent with the present hypothesis. Both cases as appositive and cases as head tend to occur more

**Table 5.25** Normalized frequencies of facts of case across genres

| | Fiction | Magazine | Newspaper | Academic | Total |
|---|---|---|---|---|---|
| Case as appositive | 46.87236 | 53.57653 | 44.51931 | 61.77796 | 206.7462 |
| Case as head | 96.79628 | 166.138 | 123.3196 | 285.5008 | 671.7547 |

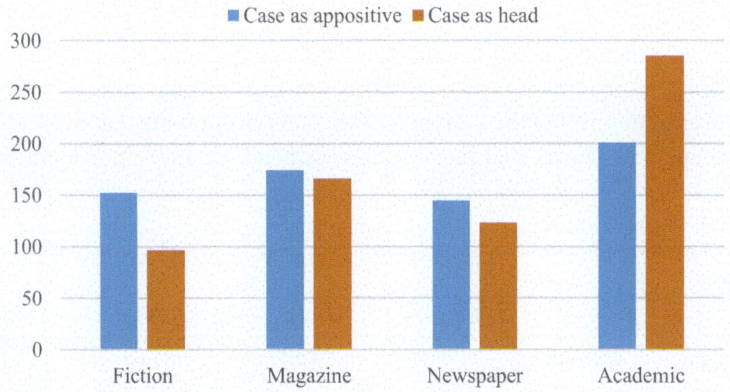


**Fig. 5.19** Genre distributions of cases as appositive and as head

in academic texts. Cases as head dominate in academic texts while cases as appositive dominate in fiction texts. Their genre distributions show a significant difference ($\chi^2 = 28.979$, $df = 3$, $p = 0.000 < 0.01$).

#### 5.3.2.3 Discipline Distribution of Embedded Projections

The degree of projection varies among different types of embedded projections. The stronger the relationship between projection/fact nouns and embedded projected clauses, the higher the degree of projection in the corresponding embedded projections. In this section, we will observe whether the degree of projection and that of closeness in constituent relationship determine the discipline sensitivity.

The above genre analysis shows that nominalizations of zero occur more in academic texts and nominalizations of verbs occur more in fiction texts. Thus, it can be hypothesized that nominalizations of zero are more technical and will occur more in hard science texts. The normalized frequencies of nominalizations of projecting verbs and zero are shown in Table 5.26.

The total normalized frequency of nominalizations of verbs (370.85) was converted to that of nominalizations of zero (637.9) for further comparison. The discipline distributions of the two types of embedded projections are shown in Fig. 5.20.

**Table 5.26** Normalized frequencies of nominalization of verbs and nominalization of zero across disciplines

| | Fiction | Magazine | Newspaper | Academic | Total |
|---|---|---|---|---|---|
| Nominalization of verbs | 68.51226 | 93.13243 | 88.74281 | 119.8497 | 370.2373 |
| Nominalization of zero | 97.92899 | 143.2752 | 108.1841 | 288.5142 | 637.9024 |

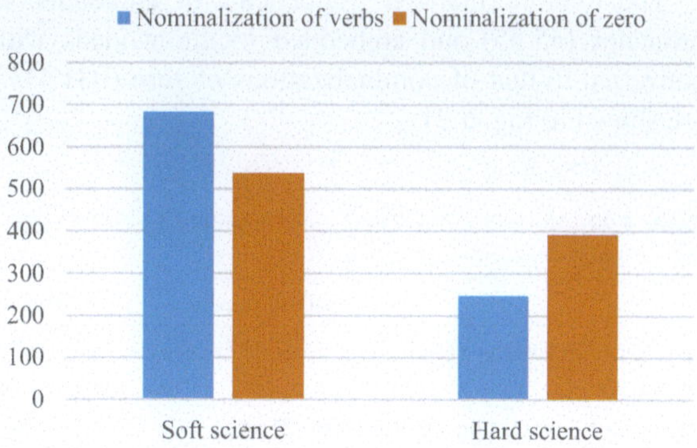


**Fig. 5.20** Discipline distributions of nominalizations of verbs and nominalizations of zero

Figure 5.20 shows that both the nominalizations of projecting verbs and of zero tend to occur more in soft science texts. Their discipline distributions show a significant difference ($\chi^2 = 50.675$, $df = 1$, $p = 0.000 < 0.01$). Nominalizations of projecting verbs are more prevalent in soft science texts while nominalizations of zero are more prevalent in hard science texts. This is consistent with the hypothesis that nominalizations of zero are more technical. Soft science texts involve more integration of ideas and statements while hard science texts involve more descriptions of experimental evidences (Charles 2007). The nominalization of verbal verbs and mental verbs enables writers to discuss and evaluate the locution and idea as entity. The nominalization of zero enables writers to define and evaluate epistemically the corresponding proposition. See the following examples:

5.17 a. The results are relevant to the suggestion that different juries be employed in the two phases. (COCA_ACAD)
b. The chance that you'll get defensive and snarky is pretty high. (COCA_BLOG)

The nominalization of the verb *suggest* into the noun *suggestion* construes an entity that can be further discussed and referred to. Hence, another entity *the results* can be brought into discussion and its relation with the proposition suggested is able to be pointed out in one sentence. In this sense, the nominalization of projecting verbs is a device to integrate different voices. In 5.17b, *chance* is the nominalization of zero and defines the succeeding proposition as not being factual but being possible.

Fact nouns resulting from the nominalization of zero manifest a lower degree of projection and weaker relation between the head noun and the embedded projected clause. Nominalizations of projecting verbs with explicit projector manifest a stronger degree of projection than those without explicit projector. It can hence be hypothesized that nominalizations of verbs with explicit projector are less technical than those without explicit projector, and nominalizations of verbs without explicit projector are less technical than nominalizations of zero. The following table presents the normalized frequencies of these three types of embedded projection (see Table 5.27).

The total normalized frequencies of embedded locutions/ideas with explicit projector (45.55) and embedded locutions/ideas without projector (144.7) were converted to that of nominalizations of zero (931.1). Their discipline distributions are shown in Fig. 5.21.

**Table 5.27** Normalized frequencies of nominalization of verbs with/without projector and nominalization of zero across disciplines

| | Soft science | Hard science | Total |
|---|---|---|---|
| Locution/idea with explicit projector | 36.36257 | 9.187279 | 45.54985 |
| Locution/idea without explicit projector | 103.2164 | 41.4841 | 144.7005 |
| Nominalization of zero | 537.462 | 393.6396 | 931.1016 |

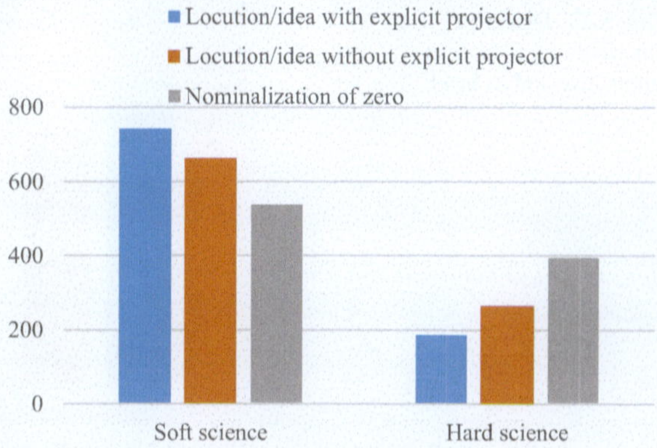


**Fig. 5.21** Discipline distributions of nominalization of verbs with/without projector and nominalization of zero

Figure 5.21 shows that the discipline distributions of the three types of embedded projection are consistent with their genre distributions. Their discipline distributions are significantly different ($\chi^2 = 109.669$, $df = 2$, $p = 0.000 < 0.01$). In soft science texts, nominalizations of verbs with projector are the most prevalent, while in hard science texts, nominalizations of zero are the most prevalent. Therefore, the degree of projection determines the text technicality of embedded projections.

Embedded projections of fact can be categorized as embedded facts as appositive and as head. They are not mode sensitive but are genre sensitive. Embedded facts modifying fact nouns are found to be less prevalent in written texts with regard to mode distribution and in academic texts with regard to genre distribution than embedded facts as head. Hereby it can be hypothesized that embedded facts as head are more prevalent in hard science texts and embedded facts as appositive are more prevalent in soft science texts. Their normalized frequencies are shown in Table 5.28.

To facilitate comparison, the total normalized frequency of facts as appositive (260.11) was converted to that of facts as head (671). Their distribution patterns in soft and hard science texts are shown in Fig. 5.22.

As shown in Fig. 5.22, both facts as appositive and facts as head tend to occur more in soft science texts than in hard science texts. In hard science texts, facts as head are more prevalent, which is consistent with the hypothesis that facts as head are more technical. However, their discipline distributions do not show a significant difference ($\chi^2 = 2.584$, $df = 1$, $p = 0.108 > 0.05$). Therefore, whether serving as appositive or as head does not determine the discipline sensitivity of embedded fact projections.

**Table 5.28** Normalized frequencies of facts as appositive and as head across disciplines

| | Soft science | Hard science | Total |
|---|---|---|---|
| Fact as appositive | 158.3392 | 101.7668 | 260.106 |
| Fact as head | 379.1228 | 291.8728 | 670.9956 |

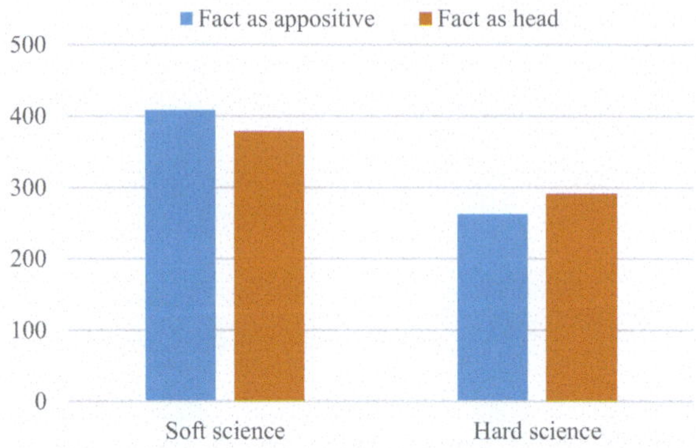


**Fig. 5.22** Discipline distributions of facts as appositive and as head

As for facts as appositive, the fact nouns they modify can be modalized or non-modalized. Modalized fact nouns bear a closer relationship with fact clauses than non-modalized fact nouns. Previous mode and genre analyses show that modalized fact nouns modified by embedded fact clauses are more likely to appear in written texts than in spoken texts and in academic texts than in fiction texts. Hence it can be hypothesized that modalized fact nouns modified by fact clauses are more technical and prevalent in hard science texts than non-modalized ones. See their normalized frequencies in Table 5.29.

The total normalized frequency of facts as appositive of non-modalized fact nouns (104.89) was converted to that of facts as appositive of modalized fact nouns (155.2204). Their discipline distributions are shown in Fig. 5.23.

**Table 5.29** Normalized frequencies of facts modifying modalized and non-modalized fact nouns across disciplines

| | Soft science | Hard science | Total |
|---|---|---|---|
| Modalized fact nouns | 86.31579 | 68.90459 | 155.2204 |
| Non-modalized fact nouns | 72.02339 | 32.86219 | 104.8856 |

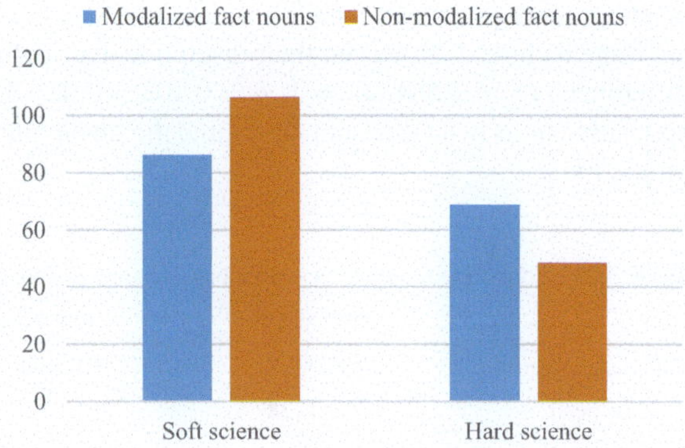


**Fig. 5.23** Discipline distributions of facts modifying modalized and non-modalized fact nouns

According to Fig. 5.23, both facts as appositive of modalized and non-modalized fact nouns tend to appear more in soft science texts. Their discipline distributions show a significant difference ($\chi^2 = 5.672$, $df = 1$, $p = 0.017 < 0.05$). Their discipline distributions are consistent with the present hypothesis. Facts as appositive modifying modalized fact nouns are more technical and prevalent in hard science texts than in soft science texts. The reasons for this are the same as those explaining their mode and genre distributions.

Facts as appositive include both facts as the appositives of modalized and non-modalized fact nouns. Modality may affect the discipline sensitivity of corresponding constructions. Next, only facts of case will be observed to see whether being appositive or head will determine the discipline sensitivity. See Table 5.30 for the normalized frequencies of cases as appositive and as head.

The total normalized frequency of cases as appositive (102.7261) was converted to that of cases as head (670.9956). Their discipline distributions are shown in Fig. 5.24.

According to Fig. 5.24, both cases as appositive and cases as head tend to occur more in soft science texts. Their discipline distributions show a significant difference ($\chi^2 = 22.492$, $df = 1$, $p = 0.000 < 0.01$). Facts of cases as head are more technical and they dominate in hard science texts. Their discipline distribution is in consistency with their mode and genre distributions. The reason is that cases as head contribute more to the conciseness and effectiveness of scientific language.

**Table 5.30** Normalized frequencies of cases as appositive and as head across disciplines

| | Soft science | Hard science | Total |
|---|---|---|---|
| Case as appositive | 70.92398 | 31.80212 | 102.7261 |
| Case as head | 379.1228 | 291.8728 | 670.9956 |

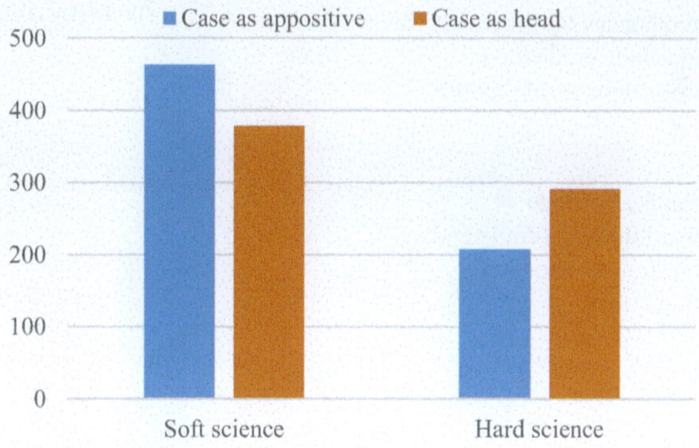


**Fig. 5.24** Discipline distributions of cases as appositive and as head

## 5.3.3 *Synchronic Distributions of Finite and Non-finite Embedded Projections*

### 5.3.3.1 Mode Distributions of Finite and Non-finite Embedded Projections

In embedded projections, the projected clauses result from the downward rank-shift from the clause rank to the word rank. Being embedded allows the projected clause to be further compressed in form and results in the change in finiteness. All embedded projected clauses can be either finite or non-finite. Non-finite clauses are more compressed in form. It can be hypothesized that non-finite embedded projections tend to appear more in written texts.

All the frequencies of finite and non-finite embedded projections were added up to see their general mode distributions. Their normalized frequencies in spoken and written texts are shown in Table 5.31.

The total normalized frequency of non-finite embedded projections (366.78) was converted to that of finite embedded projections (413.25). The mode distributions of finite and non-finite embedded projections are shown in Fig. 5.25.

Figure 5.25 shows that finite embedded projections tend to occur in spoken texts and non-finite embedded projections exhibit almost similar likelihood to appear in spoken and written texts. The general mode distributions of finite and non-finite embedded projections manifest a significant difference ($\chi^2 = 3.831$, $df = 1$, $p = 0.05$). This is consistent with the present hypothesis.

Locution and idea nouns are the nominalizations of verbal and mental verbs and facts are the nominalizations of zero. Next, we will examine whether finiteness

**Table 5.31** Normalized frequencies of finite and non-finite embedded projections across modes

| | Spoken | Written | Total |
|---|---|---|---|
| Finite | 239.8652 | 173.3896 | 413.2548 |
| Non-finite | 188.0809 | 178.7034 | 366.7843 |

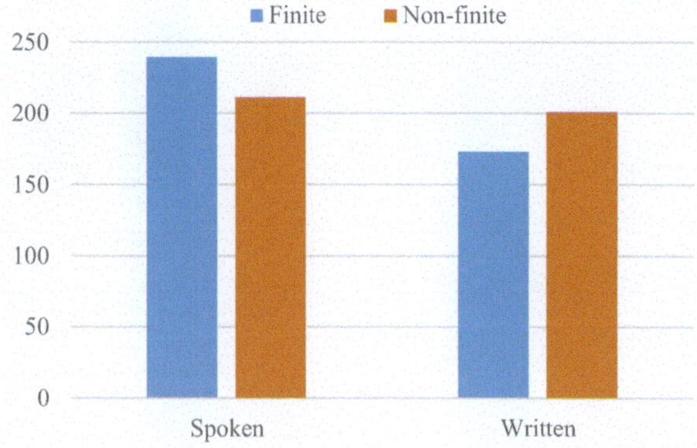


**Fig. 5.25** Mode distributions of finite and non-finite embedded projections

affects these two types of nominalizations in their mode distributions. The normalized frequencies of finite and non-finite embedded locutions/ideas and that of facts are worked out and presented in Table 5.32.

To facilitate comparison, the total normalized frequencies of finite embedded locutions/ideas (93.14), non-finite embedded locutions/ideas (94.33) and non-finite embedded facts (272.46) were converted to that of the total normalized frequency of finite embedded facts (317.06). The mode distributions of finite and non-finite embedded locutions/ideas and facts are shown in Fig. 5.26.

Nominalizations of verbs are modified by embedded locutions/ideas and nominalizations of zero are modified by embedded facts. As shown in Fig. 5.26, both nominalizations of verbs and nominalizations of zero show similar preferences of finiteness in the embedded clauses across modes. In spoken texts, finite embedded clauses in both nominalizations of verbs and zero are more prevalent than finite ones. In written texts, non-finite embedded clauses in both nominalizations of verbs and zero are more prevalent than finite ones. The mode distributions of finite and non-finite embedded locutions/ideas are significantly different ($\chi^2 = 11.414$, $df = 1$, $p = 0.001 < 0.01$) while those of embedded facts are not significantly different ($\chi^2 = 1.637$, $df = 1$, $p = 0.201 > 0.05$). That is to say, finiteness plays a larger role in determining the mode sensitivity of embedded locutions/ideas. Finiteness, on the other hand, does not determine the mode sensitivity of embedded facts. In written

**Table 5.32** Normalized frequencies of finite and non-finite nominalizations of verbs and of zero across modes

| | | Spoken | Written | Total |
|---|---|---|---|---|
| Nominalization of verbs | Finite | 54.90087 | 38.24244 | 93.14331 |
| | Non-finite | 42.98969 | 51.33567 | 94.32536 |
| Nominalization of zero | Finite | 184.9643 | 132.0992 | 317.0635 |
| | Non-finite | 145.0912 | 127.3678 | 272.459 |

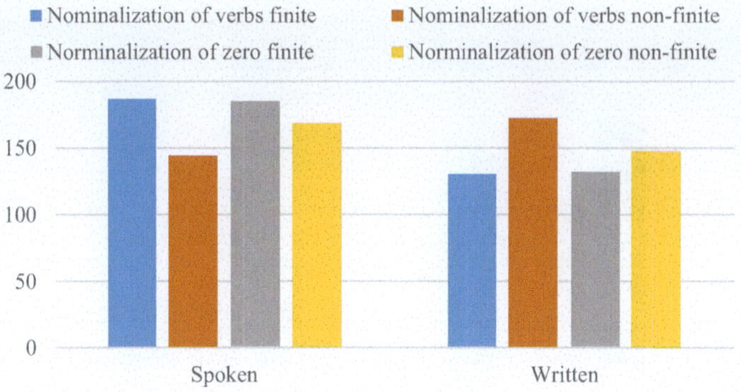


**Fig. 5.26** Mode distributions of finite and non-finite embedded locutions/ideas and facts

texts, nominalizations of projecting verbs followed by non-finite embedded locutions/ideas are the most prevalent. In spoken texts, nominalizations of zero followed by finite embedded facts are the most prevalent.

Finiteness plays a larger role in determining the mode sensitivity of embedded locutions/ideas than it does for embedded facts. Embedded locutions/ideas result from nominalizations of verbs that exhibit a higher degree of projection. Hereby it can be hypothesized that finiteness has a greater impact on the mode distributions of embedded locutions/ideas with explicit projector than those without explicit projector. See their normalized frequencies across modes in Table 5.33.

The total normalized frequency of finite embedded locutions/ideas with explicit projector (7.56), non-finite embedded locutions/ideas with explicit projector (35.78) and non-finite embedded locutions/ideas without explicit projector (58.55) were converted to that of finite embedded locutions/ideas without explicit projector (85.58). Their mode distributions are shown in Fig. 5.27.

According to Fig. 5.27, embedded locutions/ideas with and without explicit projector show the same preference for finiteness across modes. In spoken texts, finite embedded locutions/ideas dominate non-finite ones. In written texts, non-finite embedded locutions/ideas are more prevalent than finite ones. The mode distributions of finite and non-finite embedded locutions/ideas with explicit projector are significantly different ($\chi^2 = 43.712$, $df = 1$, $p = 0.000 < 0.01$) while those of embedded

**Table 5.33** Normalized frequencies of finite and non-finite embedded locutions/ideas with and without explicit projector across modes

| | | Spoken | Written | Total |
|---|---|---|---|---|
| Embedded locution/idea with explicit projector | Finite | 5.233941 | 2.327639 | 7.561581 |
| | Non-finite | 16.78033 | 18.99568 | 35.77601 |
| Embedded locution/idea without explicit projector | Finite | 49.66693 | 35.9148 | 85.58173 |
| | Non-finite | 26.20936 | 32.33999 | 58.54935 |

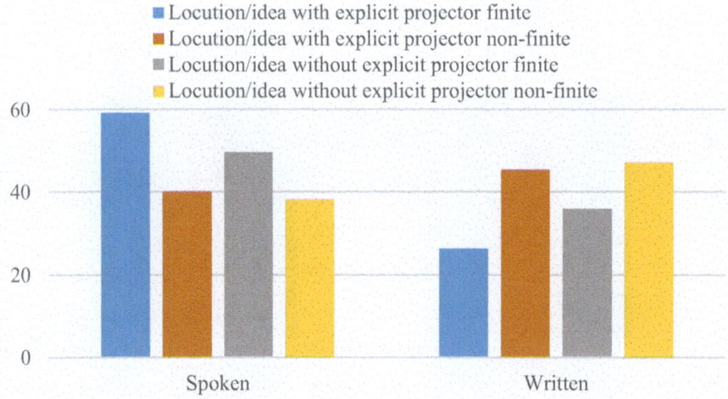


**Fig. 5.27** Mode distributions of finite and non-finite embedded locutions/ideas

locutions/ideas without projector are not significantly different ($\chi^2 = 3.088$, $df = 1$, $p = 0.079 > 0.05$). This indicates that finiteness has a considerably larger impact on the mode sensitivity of embedded locutions/ideas with explicit projector, but not on those without explicit projector. Finiteness of embedded clauses tends to contribute to the mode sensitivity of embedded projections with a higher projection degree.

For embedded projections resulting from the nominalization of zero, embedded facts as appositive bear a relationship with the head nouns. Fact clauses modifying modalized fact nouns demonstrate a higher degree of projection than those modifying non-modalized fact nouns. It can hereby be hypothesized that finiteness has a greater impact on the mode sensitivity of facts modifying modalized fact nouns more than on thoes modifying non-modalized fact nouns. The normalized frequencies of facts modifying modalized and non-modalized fact nouns are shown in Table 5.34.

Seen from the normalized frequencies per million words in Table 5.34, fact clauses modifying modalized fact nouns show a preference for non-finiteness, while fact clauses modifying non-modalized fact nouns show a preference for finiteness. The normalized frequency of non–finite fact clauses modifying non-modalized fact nouns is especially low. The reason lies in the semantic focus of the corresponding embedded projections. Modalized fact nouns not only define the succeeding information but also construe the epistemic evaluation. Attaching modality to the fact noun makes the modality an entity to be discussed and referred to. Hence modality is foregrounded and becomes the semantic focus of the whole construction. The finiteness of the embedded clause matters less because the embedded clause does not shoulder much responsibility for indicating the modality. Compared to finite clauses, non-finite clauses do not contain a subject or a finite operator that expresses tense and modality (Halliday & Matthiessen 2004). Hereby for fact clauses modifying modalized fact nouns, non-finiteness is preferred because modality is expressed in modalized fact nouns. Non-modalized fact nouns, on the other hand, are vague in meaning and the semantic focus lies on the embedded clauses. The finite element is complete in finite clauses and it shoulders the responsibility to express the modality for the proposition in the embedded fact clauses.

To facilitate comparison, the total normalized frequencies of finite (13.3) and non-finite (46.28) fact clauses modifying modalized fact nouns and non-finite fact clauses modifying non-modalized fact nouns (7.66) were converted to that of fact clauses modifying non-modalized fact nouns (165.90). Since the modality of the

**Table 5.34** Normalized frequencies of finite and non-finite facts modifying modalized and non-modalized fact nouns across modes

| | | Spoken | Written | Total |
|---|---|---|---|---|
| Fact modifying modalized fact nouns | Finite | 5.662173 | 7.645606 | 13.30778 |
| | Non-finite | 14.86915 | 31.41387 | 46.28302 |
| Fact modifying non-modalized fact nouns | Finite | 117.5496 | 48.35151 | 165.9011 |
| | Non-finite | 3.568596 | 4.095493 | 7.664089 |

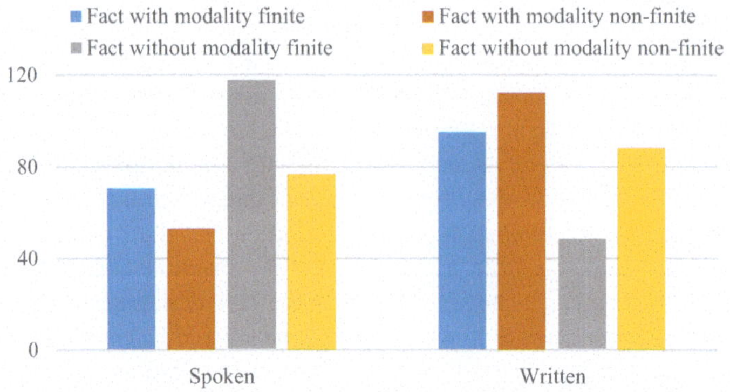


**Fig. 5.28** Mode distributions of finite and non-finite facts modifying modalized and non-modalized fact nouns

fact nouns determines the mode and genre sensitivity of embedded fact projections, it can be hypothesized that non-finite facts modifying modalized fact nouns are the most technical. Additionally, finiteness is expected to have a greater impact on the mode sensitivity of facts modifying modalized fact nouns than those modifying non-modalized fact nouns. Their mode distributions are shown in Fig. 5.28.

According to Fig. 5.28, both fact clauses modifying modalized and non-modalized fact nouns prefer finiteness in spoken texts and non-finiteness in written texts. Finite fact clauses modifying non-modalized fact nouns are the most prevalent in spoken texts and non-finite fact clauses modifying modalized fact nouns are the most prevalent in written texts. This is consistent with the present hypothesis. The mode distributions of finite and non-finite fact clauses modifying modalized fact nouns manifest a significant difference ($\chi^2 = 4.171$, $df = 1$, $p = 0.041 < 0.05$), and the mode distributions of finite and non-finite fact clauses modifying non-modalized fact nouns manifest a significant difference ($\chi^2 = 20.891$, $df = 1$, $p = 0.000 < 0.01$). The results of the chi-squared test indicate that finiteness has a greater influence on the mode distributions of facts modifying non-modalized fact nouns than on those modifying modalized fact nouns. This is not in consistency with the present hypothesis. For nominalizations of zero, finiteness determines the mode sensitivity more in embedded projections that manifest a lower degree of projection. The reason lies in the construal of the modality of the proposition. For appositive fact clauses modifying modal facts, the responsibility for the modality of the proposition lies in the modal fact nouns and hence the finiteness of embedded clauses does not matter a lot to affect negotiability. For appositive fact clauses modifying non-modal facts, the responsibility for the modality of the proposition lies in the embedded clause and hereby the finiteness of embedded clauses plays a larger role in shaping the negotiability of the discussed proposition.

Fact clauses modifying non-modalized case nouns can have the case nouns absent and stand on their own. The absence of case nouns may increase the likelihood of the embedded facts being finite so that the modality of the proposition in fact clauses can be completely expressed. Based on the previous finding that finiteness plays a larger role in determining mode sensitivity of embedded clauses shouldering the responsibility for realizing modality, it can be hypothesized that finite and non-finite cases as head will demonstrate a more significant difference in mode distribution than cases as appositive. It is also hypothesized that both cases, whether as appositive or as head, prefer non-finiteness in written texts. Their normalized frequencies in spoken and written texts are shown in Table 5.35.

To facilitate comparison, the total normalized frequencies of finite cases as appositive (162.24), non-finite cases as appositive (7.53) and finite cases as head (137.85) were converted to that of finite cases as head (218.51). Their mode distributions are shown in Fig. 5.29.

According to Fig. 5.29, both finite and non-finite cases, weather as appositive or as head, show differences in mode distribution. For embedded cases as appositive, finite ones are more prevalent in spoken texts while non-finite ones are more prevalent in written texts. The mode distributions of cases as appositive manifest a significant difference ($\chi^2 = 27.036$, $df = 1$, $p = 0.000 < 0.01$). For cases as head, finite ones dominate in written texts while non-finite ones dominate in spoken texts. The mode distributions of cases as head also manifest a significant difference ($\chi^2 = 7.686$, $df = 1$, $p = 0.006 < 0.01$).

**Table 5.35** Normalized frequencies of finite and non-finite cases as appositive and as head across modes

| | | Spoken | Written | Total |
|---|---|---|---|---|
| Case as appositive | Finite | 114.5916 | 47.64766 | 162.2393 |
| | Non-finite | 3.481364 | 4.050216 | 7.53158 |
| Case as head | Finite | 61.75258 | 76.10208 | 137.8547 |
| | Non-finite | 126.6534 | 91.85841 | 218.5119 |

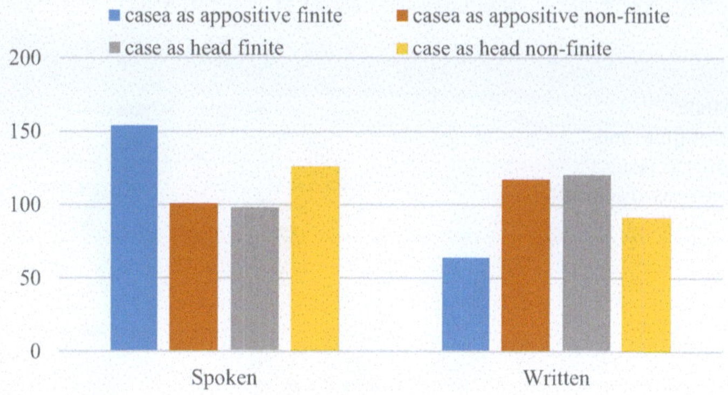


**Fig. 5.29** Mode distributions of finite and non-finite cases as appositive and as head

Why do finite cases as head dominate in written texts? The finite embedded cases as head retrieved include those serving as pre-predicate, extraposed subject, and complement while the non-finite embedded cases as head all serve as extraposed subject (see examples 5.13c, 5.13d). To exclude the variety of serving different syntactic roles, finite and non-finite embedded facts as head that serve solely as extraposed subject will be compared to see whether non-finite cases as head are more prevalent in spoken texts while finite ones are more prevalent in written texts. Their normalized frequencies are shown in Table 5.36.

To facilitate comparison, the total normalized frequency of finite cases as head serving as extraposed subject (41.61) was converted to that of non-finite ones (218.51). Their mode distributions are presented in Fig. 5.30.

As can be seen in Fig. 5.30, finite and non-finite cases as head serving as extraposed subject are oppositely distributed across modes. The non-finite ones are more prevalent in spoken texts and the finite ones are more prevalent in written texts. Their mode distributions show a significant difference ($\chi^2 = 17.362$, $df = 1$, $p = 0.000 < 0.01$). Finiteness does determine the mode sensitivity of cases as head serving as extraposed subject. For example:

5.18 a. It is important that students do not become sidetracked with alternate problems. (COCA_ACAD)
b. It is important to keep fledglings safe and to allow the parents to continue feeding them. (COCA_WEB)

5.18a contains a finite case as head serving as extraposed subject and 5.18b contains a non-finite case as head serving as extraposed subject. When the adjective in the relational process clause construes modal assessment such as usuality,

**Table 5.36** Normalized frequencies of finite and non-finite cases as head serving as extraposed subject across modes

| | Spoken | Written | Total |
|---|---|---|---|
| Finite | 15.82078 | 25.78514 | 41.60592 |
| Non-finite | 126.6534 | 91.85841 | 218.5118 |

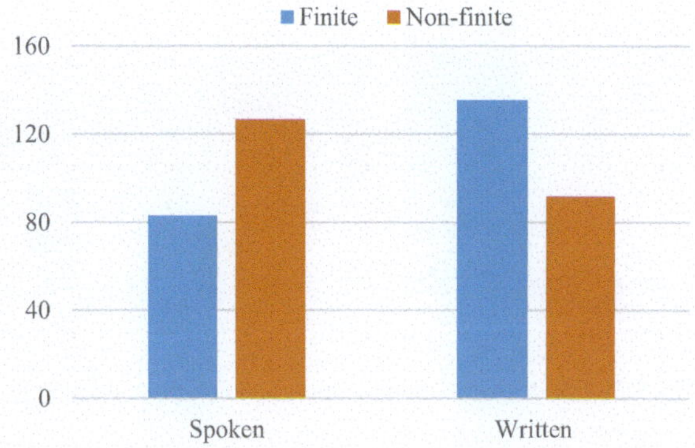


**Fig. 5.30** Mode distributions of finite and non-finite cases as head serving as extraposed subject

validity and obligation, the clause in which the fact of case is embedded no longer contains the main proposition but functions as a modal expression to assess the proposition contained in the embedded case. For example:

5.19 a. It is likely that teachers within a school share common experiences. (COCA_ACAD)
b. It is rare that a single contrivance has such a profound social effect. (COCA_ACAD)
c. It is imperative that the police force continue to develop professionally. (COCA_ACAD)
d. It is possible to conceptualise Bitcoin as either a currency or an asset. (COCA_ACAD)
e. It is rare to find an example as large as the tiara in Plate VI. (COCA_MAG)
f. It is necessary to foster a true culture of debate in the church. (COCA_MAG)

In examples in 5.19a–f, *it is ADJ* construes explicit objective modality and the main propositions lie in the embedded clauses. The embedded cases, whether finite or non-finite, can be viewed as clauses containing the propositions. In examples of 5.18a–b the adjectives in the clause of relational process express attitudinal evaluation rather than modal assessment. Hence the matrix clauses in examples 5.18a–b do not turn into a modal construction and express the main proposition. Explicit objective modality is interpersonal metaphor found to be more technical in genre distributions (He 2021). The mode distribution difference of the finite and non-finite embedded facts as head is affected by modal expressions. It may be the types of evaluation construed by the adjective that determine the mode distribution. Those construing modal assessment are more likely to appear in written texts while those construing attitudinal assessment are more likely to appear in spoken texts.

The most common adjectives that go with the finite and non-finite extraposed cases as head in the COCA were retrieved to see whether the two types of projections prefer different types of adjectives. The top ten adjectives that collocate with finite and non-finite extraposed cases as head are shown in Table 5.37.

According to Table 5.37, five of the top ten adjectives co-occurring with finite extrapose cases of modal assessment. Their total frequency reaches 3491, accounting for 64.48% of the total frequency of the top ten adjectives co-occurring with finite extrapose cases. Of the top ten non-finite extraposed cases as head co-occurring with adjectives, three realize modal assessment and their total frequency is 1323, accounting for 17.84% of the total frequency of the top ten adjectives co-occurring with non-finite extraposed cases. Therefore, the preference for collocating adjectives realizing modal assessment may contribute to the prevalence of finite extraposed cases as head in written texts. Spoken texts allow more personal opinions and the preference of attitudinal adjectives enables non-finite extraposed cases as head to dominate in spoken texts.

**Table 5.37** Top ten adjectives collocating with finite and non-finite extraposed cases as head

| | Finite | Frequency | Non-finite | Frequency |
|---|---|---|---|---|
| 1 | Possible | 1303 | Important | 2356 |
| 2 | True | 1151 | Hard | 1145 |
| 3 | Clear | 751 | Difficult | 922 |
| 4 | Likely | 573 | Easy | 756 |
| 5 | Important | 512 | Possible | 593 |
| 6 | Obvious | 270 | Impossible | 521 |
| 7 | Unlikely | 244 | Interesting | 462 |
| 8 | Imperative | 220 | Good | 242 |
| 9 | Interesting | 219 | Better | 212 |
| 10 | Noteworthy | 171 | Necessary | 209 |
| Total frequency of modal adjectives | 3491 | | 1323 | |
| Total | 5414 | | 7418 | |

#### 5.3.3.2 Genre Distribution of Finite and Non-finite Embedded Projection

The mode distribution analysis shows that non-finite embedded clauses are more technical than finite embedded clauses and tend to appear in written texts. Hereby it can be hypothesized that finite embedded projections are more likely to appear in fiction texts while non-finite embedded projections are more likely to appear in academic texts. To start with, the overall genre distributions of finite and no-finite embedded projections in the COCA will be compared. The normalized frequencies of all the finite and non-finite embedded projected clauses are added up. See their normalized frequencies in Table 5.38.

To facilitate comparison, the total normalized frequency of finite embedded projections (694.1519) was converted to that of non-finite embedded projections (714.09). Their genre distributions are presented in Fig. 5.31.

As shown in Fig. 5.31, both finite and non-finite embedded projections tend to occur more in academic texts than in fiction texts, which is opposite to their mode distributions. In fiction texts, finite and non-finite embedded projections share similar proportions. In academic texts, finite embedded projections dominate non-finite ones. The genre distributions of finite and non-finite embedded projections are significantly different ($\chi^2 = 10.926$, $df = 3$, $p = 0.012 < 0.05$). Hereby finiteness determines the overall genre distributions of embedded projections. That finite embedded projection

**Table 5.38** Normalized frequencies of finite and non-finite embedded projections across genres

| | Fiction | Magazine | Newspaper | Academic | Total |
|---|---|---|---|---|---|
| Finite | 109.4675 | 161.9112 | 123.5579 | 299.2154 | 694.1519 |
| Non-finite | 119.1293 | 183.4734 | 161.3476 | 250.1419 | 714.0922 |

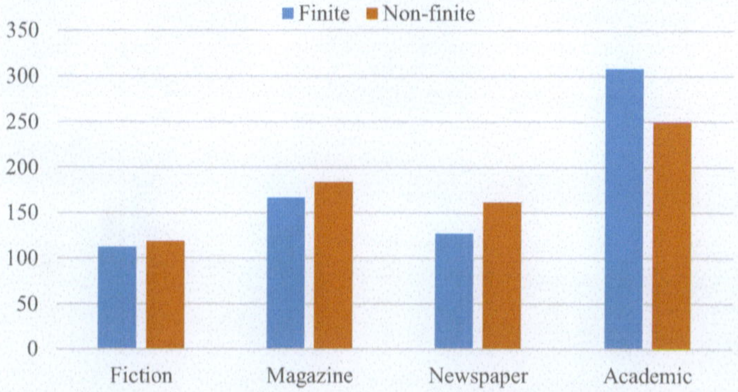


**Fig. 5.31** Genre distributions of finite and non-finite embedded projections

dominates in academic texts is not in consistency with the present hypothesis. A further analysis on the different types of nominalizations involving projection is needed to explore what contributes to the higher text technicality of finite embedded projections.

The non-finite embedded locutions/ideas and facts are more technical and tend to occur in written texts with regard to mode distribution. Hereby, it can be hypothesized that the non-finite embedded locutions/ideas and facts tend to occur in academic texts with regard to genre distribution. The normalized frequencies of finite and non-finite embedded locutions/ideas and that of finite and non-finite facts are added up (see Table 5.39).

To facilitate comparison, the total normalized frequencies of finite embedded locutions/ideas (165.09), non-finite embedded locutions/ideas (205.15) and non-finite embedded facts (508.94) were converted to that of finite embedded facts (529.07). Their genre distributions are presented in Fig. 5.32.

The genre distributions of finite and non-finite embedded locutions/ideas in fiction and academic texts are not significantly different ($\chi^2 = 4.774$, $df = 3$, $p = 0.189 > 0.05$), and those of finite and non-finite embedded facts are not significantly different either ($\chi^2 = 8.517$, $df = 3$, $p = 0.036 < 0.05$). This indicates that finite and non-finite embedding locutions/ideas do not show genre sensitivity but finite and non-finite facts do. In academic texts, finite embedded facts dominate non-finite ones and this is opposite to the hypothesis that non-finite facts are more technical.

**Table 5.39** Normalized frequencies of finite and non-finite embedded locutions/ideas and facts

| | | Fiction | Magazine | Newspaper | Academic | Total |
|---|---|---|---|---|---|---|
| Nominalization of verbs | Finite | 29.01944 | 41.45123 | 35.86689 | 58.74791 | 165.0855 |
| | Non-finite | 39.49281 | 51.68121 | 52.87592 | 61.10184 | 205.1518 |
| Nominalization of zero | Finite | 80.44801 | 120.46 | 87.69104 | 240.4674 | 529.0665 |
| | Non-finite | 79.63652 | 131.7922 | 108.4717 | 189.0401 | 508.9405 |

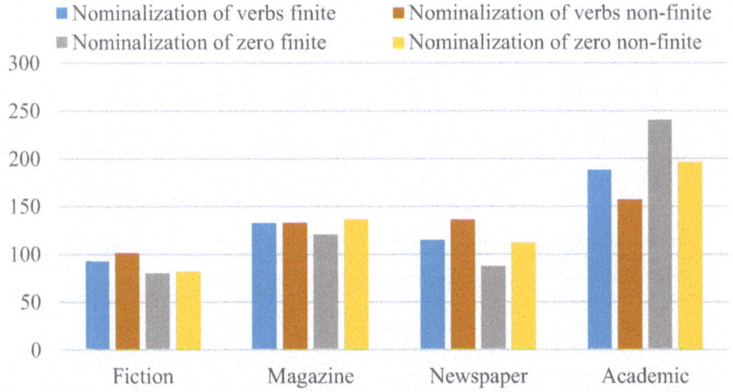


**Fig. 5.32** Genre distributions of finite and non-finite embedded locutions/ideas and facts

Next, a more detailed examination will be conducted on the genre distributions of embedded locutions/ideas and facts, respectively. Embedded locutions /ideas with explicit projector can have a higher degree of projection than those without explicit projector. The mode distribution analysis shows that non-finite embedded locutions / ideas without projector are more prevalent in written texts than in spoken texts. Hence it can be hypothesized that non-finite embedded locutions/ideas without explicit projector are more prevalent in written texts than those with explicit projector. Their normalized frequencies across genres are shown in Table 5.40.

To facilitate comparison, their total normalized frequencies were converted to that of finite embedded locutions/ideas without explicit projector (142.58). Their genre distributions are shown in Fig. 5.33.

According to Fig. 5.33, non-finite embedded locutions/ideas with explicit projector are more prevalent than their finite equivalents in academic texts. For embedded locutions/ideas without explicit projector, finite ones are more prevalent than non-finite ones in academic texts. This is not in consistency with their mode distribution pattern. However, neither the embedded locutions/ideas with explicit projector ($\chi^2 = 0.441$, $df = 1$, $p = 0.507 > 0.05$) nor the one without explicit projector ($\chi^2 = 1.661$, $df = 1$, $p = 0.197 > 0.05$) show a statistically significant difference in their distributions in fiction and academic texts. Hereby, finiteness does

**Table 5.40** Normalized frequencies of embedded projections with and without projector across genres

| | | Fiction | Magazine | Newspaper | Academic | Total |
|---|---|---|---|---|---|---|
| With projector | Finite | 4.049028 | 4.615385 | 6.803615 | 6.035058 | 21.50309 |
| | Non-finite | 12.70499 | 18.75496 | 20.62449 | 23.80634 | 75.89077 |
| Without projector | Finite | 24.97041 | 36.83584 | 29.06327 | 52.71285 | 143.5824 |
| | Non-finite | 26.78783 | 32.92625 | 32.25144 | 37.29549 | 129.261 |

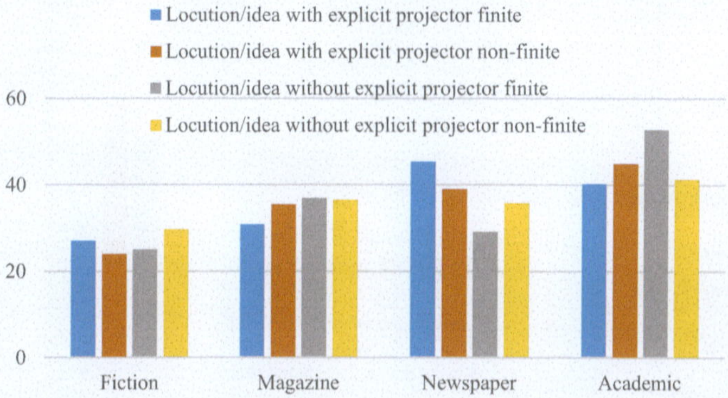


**Fig. 5.33** Genre distributions of embedded locutions/ideas with and without explicit projector

not determine the genre distributions of embedded locutions/ideas with and without explicit projector.

Embedded facts modifying modalized and non-modalized fact nouns are found to prefer finiteness in spoken texts and non-finiteness in written texts. Finiteness has a greater impact on the mode distributions of embedded facts modifying modalized fact nouns than on those modifying non-modalized fact nouns. Therefore, it can be hypothesized that non-finite embedded facts modifying modalized fact nouns are the most prevalent in academic texts while finite embedded facts modifying non-modalized fact nouns are the most prevalent in spoken texts. See the normalized frequencies of finite and non-finite embedded facts modifying modalized and non-modalized fact nouns in Table 5.41.

Among the occurrences retrieved, facts modifying modalized fact nouns have more non-finite fact clauses than finite ones while facts modifying modalized fact nouns have more finite fact clauses than non-finite ones. Their total normalized frequencies were converted to that of finite fact clauses modifying non-modalized fact nouns (193.30). Their genre distributions are shown in Fig. 5.34.

According to Fig. 5.34, both facts modifying modalized and non-modalized fact nouns are more prevalent in academic texts than fiction texts. Both of them prefer non-finiteness in academic texts. This is in consistency with the present hypothesis. Facts modifying modalized fact nouns are more sensitive in genre distribution.

**Table 5.41** Normalized frequencies of finite and non-finite embedded facts modifying modalized and non-modalized fact nouns across genres

| | | Fiction | Magazine | Newspaper | Academic | Total |
|---|---|---|---|---|---|---|
| Fact with modality | Finite | 4.049028 | 6.772403 | 5.645029 | 14.14858 | 30.61504 |
| | Non-finite | 11.84277 | 24.94845 | 22.20214 | 66.90317 | 125.8965 |
| Fact without modality | Finite | 42.57819 | 50.9199 | 42.1857 | 57.61269 | 193.2965 |
| | Non-finite | 4.818259 | 3.473434 | 2.810189 | 5.342237 | 16.44412 |

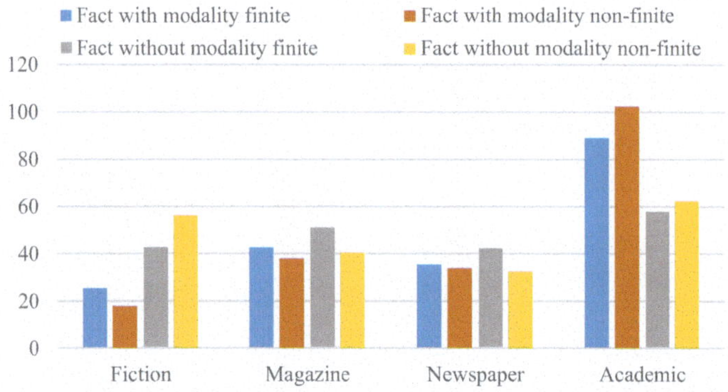


**Fig. 5.34** Genre distributions of finite and non-finite facts modifying modalized and non-modalized fact nouns

However, neither the finite and non-finite facts modifying modalized fact nouns ($\chi^2 = 2.324$, $df = 1$, $p = 0.127 > 0.05$) nor the finite and non-finite facts modifying non-modalized fact nouns ($\chi^2 = 0.537$, $df = 1$, $p = 0.464 > 0.05$) show a significant difference in distributions in fiction and academic texts. Therefore, finiteness does not significantly determine the genre distributions of the facts modifying modalized and non-modalized fact nouns.

Genre distribution can also be affected by modality. To specify the impact of finiteness on genre distribution, only finite and non-finite facts of case will be compared because case nouns do not involve modality and can be omitted to allow the embedded facts to serve as head. Whether finiteness contributes to the genre distributions of embedded facts of cases as appositive and as head can be clarified without the influence from other factors. Based on the mode distribution that finite cases as head and non-finite cases as appositive are more prevalent in written texts, it can be hypothesized that finite cases as head occur more in academic texts than non-finite ones and non-finite cases as appositive occur smore in academic texts than finite ones. See their normalized frequencies in Table 5.42.

To facilitate comparison, their total normalized frequencies were converted to that of non-finite cases as head (366.60). Their genre distributions are shown in Fig. 5.35.

As shown in Fig. 5.35, non-finite cases as appositive dominate finite ones and finite cases as head dominate non-finite ones in academic texts. This is consistent

**Table 5.42** Normalized frequencies of finite and non-finite cases as appositive and as head across genres

| | | Fiction | Magazine | Newspaper | Academic | Total |
|---|---|---|---|---|---|---|
| Case as appositive | Finite | 42.07101 | 50.11895 | 41.73377 | 56.56093 | 190.4847 |
| | Non-finite | 4.801352 | 3.457573 | 2.785538 | 5.217028 | 16.26149 |
| Case as head | Finite | 33.82079 | 62.76764 | 39.86031 | 168.7062 | 305.1549 |
| | Non-finite | 62.97549 | 103.3703 | 83.45933 | 116.7947 | 366.5998 |

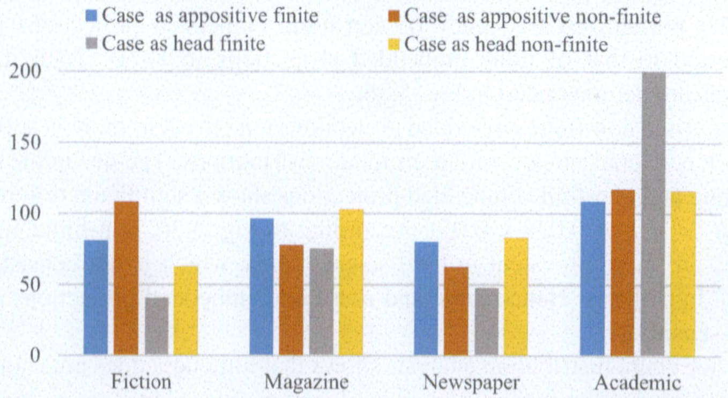


**Fig. 5.35** Genre distributions of finite and non-finite cases as appositive and as head

with the present hypothesis. The genre distributions of cases as appositive in fiction and academic texts are not significantly different ($\chi^2 = 1.107$, $df = 1$, $p = 0.293 > 0.05$). This indicates that finite and non-finite cases as appositive do not show genre sensitivity. The genre distributions of cases as head in fiction and academic texts are significantly different ($\chi^2 = 18.528$, $df = 1$, $p = 0.000 < 0.01$). Therefore, finite and non-finite cases as head demonstrate more significant genre sensitivity. As mentioned above, such genre sensitivity has more to do with the modal assessment construed by the adjectives in relational process clauses in which the facts of cases are embedded.

To sum up, finite and non-finite embedded projections do not show a significant difference in genre distribution, except for embedded cases as head.

#### 5.3.3.3 Discipline Distribution of Finite and Non-finite Embedded Projection

The genre distribution analysis of finite and non-finite embedded projections shows that they both tend to occur in academic texts, with finite ones dominating non-finite ones in academic texts. Based on the previous study, it can be hypothesized that finite embedded projections are more technical and more prevalent in hard science texts than non-finite embedded projections.

The normalized frequencies of all the finite and non-finite embedded projections were added up. See their normalized frequencies in Table 5.43.

**Table 5.43** Normalized frequencies of finite and non-finite embedded projections across disciplines

| | Soft science | Hard science | Total |
|---|---|---|---|
| Finite | 395.076 | 232.9682 | 628.0442 |
| Non-finite | 281.9649 | 211.3428 | 493.3077 |

The total normalized frequency of non-finite embedded projections (493.31) was converted to that of finite embedded projections (628.04). Their discipline distributions are demonstrated in Fig. 5.36.

Both finite and non-finite embedded projections tend to occur more in soft science texts, which is in consistency with their mode distributions. The discipline distributions of finite and non-finite embedded projections show a significant difference ($\chi^2 = 4.301$, $df = 1$, $p = 0.038 < 0.05$). According to Fig. 5.36, non-finite embedded projections are more prevalent in hard science texts, which is not consistent with the present hypothesis. Hence finite and non-finite embedded projections manifest discipline sensitivity.

The above genre distribution analysis shows that finiteness does not significantly affect the genre distributions of embedded locutions/ideas but it does significantly affect that of embedded facts. Non-finite embedded locutions/ideas and embedded facts are more prevalent in academic texts. Hence it can be hypothesized that non-finite embedded locutions/ideas and facts all dominate finite ones in hard science texts. The normalized frequencies of finite and non-finite embedded projections involving nominalizations of verbs and zero are shown in Table 5.44.

The total normalized frequencies of finite clauses modifying nominalizations of verbs (104.4) and non-finite ones (85.86) and non-finite clauses modifying nominalizations of zero (407.45) were converted to that of finite clauses modifying nominalizations of zero (523.65). Their discipline distributions are shown in Fig. 5.37.

**Fig. 5.36** Discipline distributions of finite and non-finite embedded projections

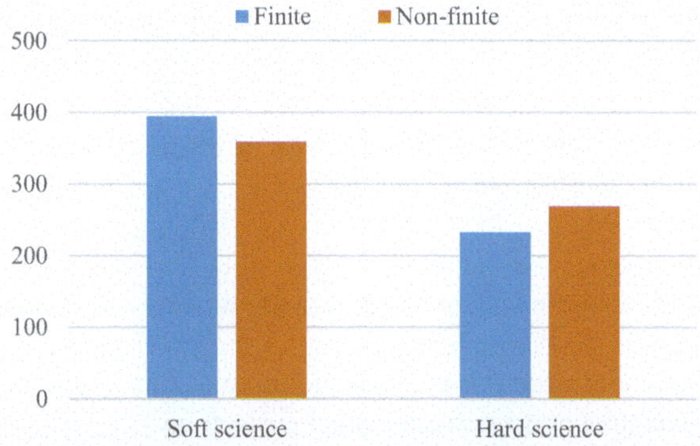


**Table 5.44** Normalized frequencies of finite and non-finite embedded locutions/ideas and facts across disciplines

| | | Soft science | Hard science | Total |
|---|---|---|---|---|
| Nominalization of verbs | Finite | 78.38596 | 26.00707 | 104.393 |
| | Non-finite | 61.19298 | 24.66431 | 85.85729 |
| Nominalization of zero | Finite | 316.6901 | 206.9611 | 523.6512 |
| | Non-finite | 220.7719 | 186.6784 | 407.4504 |

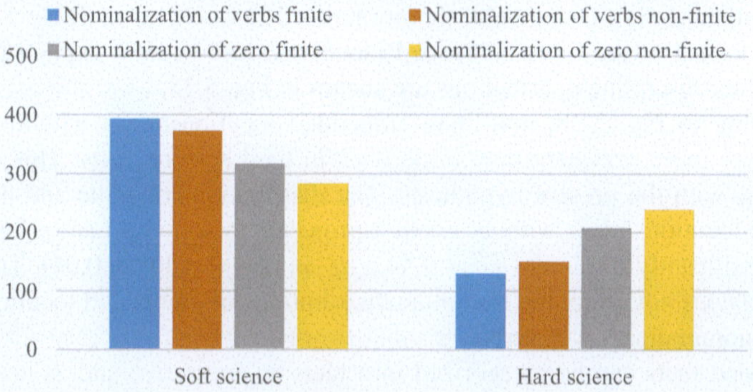


**Fig. 5.37** Discipline distributions of finite and non-finite embedded locutions/ideas and facts

As shown in Fig. 5.37, finite and non-finite embedded locutions/ideas and facts are similarly distributed across disciplines. In soft science texts, finite embedded projections are more prevalent. In hard science texts, non-finite ones are more prevalent. This is not consistent with the present hypothesis. The discipline distributions of finite and non-finite embedded locutions/ideas do not show a significant difference ($\chi^2 = 1.951$, $df = 1$, $p = 0.163 > 0.05$). The discipline distributions of finite and non-finite embedded facts show a significant difference ($\chi^2 = 4.248$, $df = 1$, $p = 0.039 < .05$). Therefore, finiteness can affect the discipline sensitivity of embedded facts.

The genre distribution analysis shows that embedded locutions/ideas, whether being finite or non-finite, tend to occur more in academic texts. Non-finite embedded locutions/ideas with projector are more prevalent in academic texts than finite ones. Finite embedded locutions/ideas without projector are more prevalent in academic texts than non-finite ones. It is hereby hypothesized that non-finite embedded locutions/ideas with explicit projector are more prevalent than finite ones in hard science texts and finite embedded locutions/ideas without explicit projector are more prevalent than non-finite ones in hard science texts. The normalized frequencies of their discipline distributions are shown in Table 5.45.

As shown in Table 5.45, the freqency of embedded locutions/ideas with explicit projector in hard sciences is considerably low. Hence the data is not large enough

**Table 5.45** Normalized frequencies of finite and non-finite embedded locutions/ideas with and without explicit projector across disciplines

| | | Soft science | Hard science | Total |
|---|---|---|---|---|
| Locution/idea with explicit projector | Finite | 17.9883 | 4.946996 | 22.9353 |
| | Non-finite | 18.37427 | 4.240283 | 22.61455 |
| Locution/idea without explicit projector | Finite | 60.39766 | 21.06007 | 81.45773 |
| | Non-finite | 42.81871 | 20.42403 | 63.24274 |

to have statistical significance. All the normalized frequencies in Table 5.45 were converted to that of the finite embedded locutions/ideas without explicit projector (81.46). Their discipline distributions are shown in Fig. 5.38.

According to Fig. 5.38, non-finite embedded locutions/ideas without explicit projector are more prevalent than finite ones in hard science texts. This is not in consistency with the present hypothesis. The distributions of finite and non-finite embedded locutions/ideas without explicit projector in soft and hard science texts are not significantly different ($\chi^2 = 0.441$, $df = 1$, $p = 0.507 > 0.05$). The finiteness hence does not affect the discipline distributions of embedded locutions/ideas involving nominalization of verbs.

Embedded facts can be categorized into facts as appositive and as head. Facts as appositive modify modalized or non-modalized fact nouns. The mode and genre distributions of embedded facts as appositive modifying modalized and non-modalized fact nouns are consistent. Non-finite embedded facts modifying both modalized and non-modalized fact nouns dominate their finite counterparts in written texts with regard to mode distribution and in academic texts with regard to genre distribution. Therefore, it is hypothesized that non-finite facts modifying modalized and non-modalized fact nouns are more prevalent than non-finite ones in hard science texts (Table 5.46).

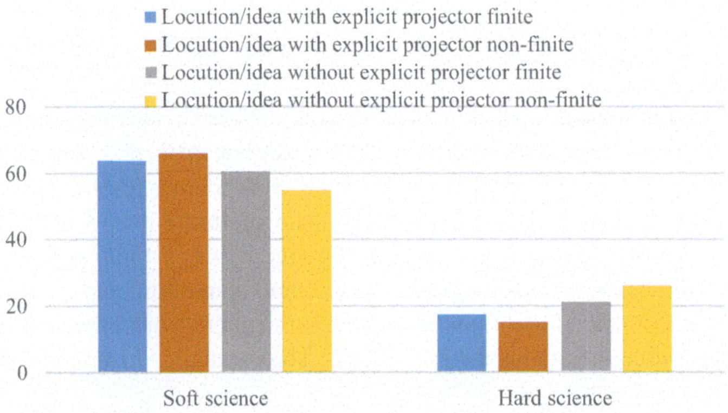


**Fig. 5.38** Discipline distributions of finite and non-finite embedded locutions/ideas with and without projector

**Table 5.46** Normalized frequencies of finite and non-finite embedded facts modifying modalized and non-modalized fact nouns across disciplines

| | | Soft science | Hard science | Total |
|---|---|---|---|---|
| Fact with modality | Finite | 15.16959 | 11.16608 | 26.33567 |
| | Non-finite | 71.1462 | 57.73852 | 128.8847 |
| Fact without modality | Finite | 66.23392 | 29.39929 | 95.63321 |
| | Non-finite | 5.789474 | 3.462898 | 9.252371 |

To facilitate comparison, their total normalized frequencies were converted to that of embedded facts modifying modalized fact nouns (128.88). See Fig. 5.39.

According to Fig. 5.39, facts modifying modalized and non-modalized fact nouns, whether finite or non-finite, prefer to occur in soft science texts. This is opposite to their genre distribution trend. Both embedded facts modifying modalized and those modifying non-modalized fact nouns show similar preference for non-finiteness in hard science texts. However, neither fact clauses modifying modalized fact nouns ($\chi^2 = 0.142$, $df = 1$, $p = 0.707 > 0.05$) nor those modifying non-modalized fact nouns ($\chi^2 = 1.104$, $df = 1$, $p = 0.293 > 0.05$) manifest a significant difference in discipline distribution.

Non-finite cases as appositive are more prevalent in academic texts than finite ones, and finite cases as head are more prevalent in academic texts than non-finite ones. Hence, it can be hypothesized that non-finite cases as appositive and finite cases as head are more prevalent in hard science texts than finite cases as appositive and non-finite cases as head. Their normalized frequencies are shown in Table 5.47.

The total normalized frequencies were converted to that of finite cases as head (401.68). Their discipline distributions are shown in Fig. 5.40.

As shown in Fig. 5.40, the discipline distribution of cases as appositive is in consistency with the hypothesis that non-finite cases as appositive are more technical

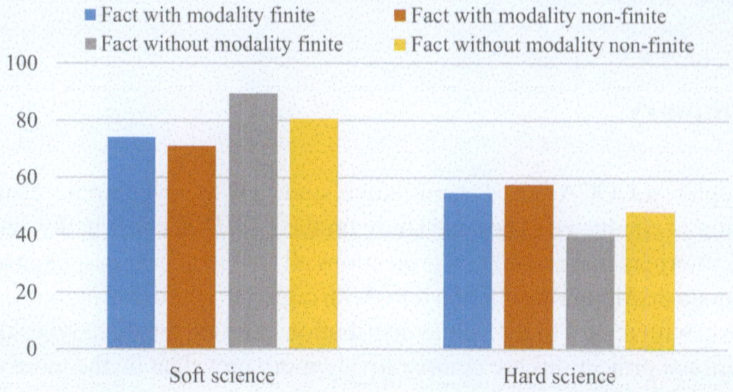


**Fig. 5.39** Discipline distributions of finite and non-finite embedded facts modifying modalized and non-modalized fact nouns

**Table 5.47** Normalized frequencies of finite and non-finite cases as appositive and as head across disciplines

| | | Soft science | Hard science | Total |
|---|---|---|---|---|
| Case as appositive | Finite | 65.22807 | 28.48057 | 93.70864 |
| | Non-finite | 5.695906 | 3.321555 | 9.017461 |
| Case as head | Finite | 235.2865 | 166.3958 | 401.6823 |
| | Non-finite | 143.8363 | 125.477 | 269.3133 |

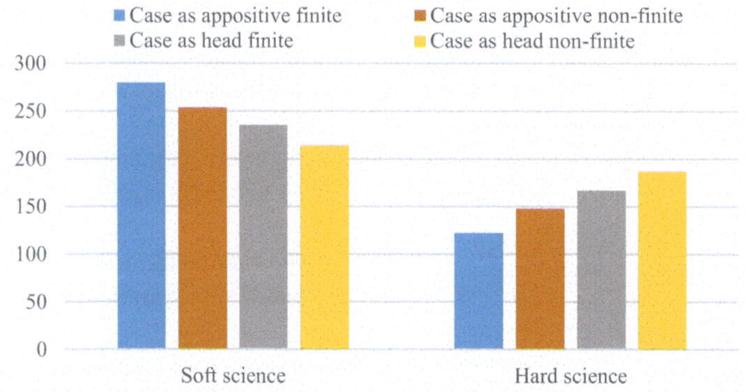


**Fig. 5.40** Discipline distributions of finite and non-finite cases as appositive and as head

than finite ones. The discipline distribution does not show a significant difference ($\chi^2 = 3.77$, $df = 1$, $p = 0.052 > 0.05$).

The discipline distribution of cases as head is not in consistency with the hypothesis that finite cases as head are more technical. Instead, non-finite cases as head are more prevalent in hard science texts. The discipline distribution does not show a significant difference either ($\chi^2 = 2.137$, $df = 1$, $p = 0.144 > 0.05$). Therefore, finiteness does not effect the discipline sensitivity of cases as appositive and as head.

## 5.4 Summary

In this chapter, a COCA-based quantitative study on the synchronic distributions of projection is conducted. The case study on the *I THINK* construction shows that ideational, interpersonal and textual projections all tend to appear in spoken texts with regard to mode distribution, in fiction texts with regard to genre distribution and in soft science texts with regard to discipline distribution. Among the three types of projections, ideational projections are comparatively more prevalent in the more technical texts, followed by interpersonal projections. The lower the grammatical status *I THINK* construction has, the more personal and informal it becomes.

The comparative study on the synchronic distributions of hypotactic clause complexes of projection and clause simplexes with embedded projected clauses shows that the latter are more prevalent in written texts with regard to mode distribution and in academic texts with regard to genre distribution. Projected clauses in hypotactic clause complexes belong to the clause rank and bear logico-semantic relationship with the primary clauses, and projected clauses as fact embedded in mental or verbal process clauses function at the group rank and bear constituent relationship with the matrix clause. The former lead to higher grammatical intricacy and the latter lead to higher lexical density. Hence clause simplexes with embedded projections are more technical than hypotactic clause complexes of projection. What's more, they show no significant difference in their discipline distributions, as both tend to occur in soft sciences texts to indicate the source of quotation and subjective evaluation.

The study on the synchronic distributions of embedded projected clauses explores the mode, genre and discipline sensitivity of embedded projections from three perspectives: level of projection, degree of projection and finiteness of projected clauses. Firstly, embedded projections of locution, idea and fact are not sensitive in mode distribution but they are sensitive in genre and discipline distributions. Among the three levels of projection, embedded facts are the most technical and dominate in academic texts with regard to genre distribution and in hard science texts with regard to discipline distribution. Secondly, embedded projections with different degrees of projection form a cline. The synchronic distribution analysis shows that their mode distributions demonstrate different features from their genre and discipline distributions. As for mode distribution, embedded projections with a higher projection degree are more prevalent in written texts, except for facts of cases. The mode sensitivity of facts of case is affected by the modality construed by the relational process clauses in which they are embedded. Concerning genre and discipline distributions, embedded projections with the lower projection degree are more impersonal and formal, except for the modalized facts as appositive. Modalized facts as appositive are more technical than non-modalized ones because modalized fact nouns can contribute to the impersonality and objectivity of academic writing. Thirdly, the finiteness of projected clauses plays a significant role in determining the mode distribution of embedding projections. Non-finite embedded projections generally dominate in written texts except for cases as head. Finite cases as head are more prevalent in written texts than non-finite ones because finite cases are likely to occur with explicit objective modality occurring more in technical texts. As for genre and discipline distributions, the finiteness of embedded projections does not significantly determine the distribution pattern. Only finite and non-finite cases as head show genre sensitivity, and the finite ones are more academic. The reason for this aligns with their mode distribution pattern. Regarding discipline distribution, finite and non-finite embedded projections with different projection degrees do not exhibit discipline sensitivity.

## References


Biber D, Johansson S, Leech G, Conrad S, Finegan E (1999) Longman grammar of spoken and written English. Longman, London

Cuenca MJ, Crible L (2019) Co-occurrence of discourse markers in English: From juxtaposition to composition. J Pragmat 140:171–184

Dong M, Fang AC, Qiu X (2020) Shell nouns as grammatical metaphor in knowledge construal: Variation across science and engineering discourse. Lingua 248:1–25

Halliday MAK (1989) Spoken and written language. Oxford University Press, Oxford

Halliday MAK, Matthiessen CMIM (2004) An introduction to functional grammar, 3rd edn. Arnold, London

Halliday MAK, Matthiessen CMIM (2014) An introduction to functional grammar, 4th edn. Routledge, London/New York
He Q (2019a) A corpus-based approach to clause combining in English from the systemic functional perspective. Springer, Singapore
He Q (2019b) A corpus-based study of transfers in English nominal groups. Glottotheory 10(1–2):57–84
He Q (2021) A corpus-based study of interpersonal metaphors of modality in English. Stud Neophilol 93(1):50–71
Rose F (2016) On finitization. In: Chamoreau C, Zarina E-F (eds) Finiteness and nominalization. John Benjamins, Amsterdam/Philadelphia, pp 347–372
Charles M (2007) Argument or evidence? Disciplinary variation in the use of the Noun that pattern in stance construction. English for Specific Purposes 26(2):203–218
Chang YY, Swales JM (1999) Informal elements in English academic writing: Threats or opportunities for advanced non-native speakers? In: Candlin CN, Hyland K (eds) Writing: Texts, processes and practices. Longman, London, pp 145–167

# Chapter 6
# Diachronic Study of Projection

In this chapter, the diachronic evolutions of different types of projection and how they relate to each other will be explored. First, a comparison of the overall diachronic distribution patterns of ideational, interpersonal and textual projections will be conducted to provide an overview of the diachronic evolution of projection. Next, the diachronic evolution of ideational projection within the ideational domain will be investigated from the perspective of clause combining and levels of projection. Finally, the diachronic evolution of textual projection will be examined to identify how projecting clauses develop into textual projection and how textual projection relates to ideational and interpersonal projections.

## 6.1 Diachronic Distribution of Overall Frequencies

A total of 844,358 projections were retrieved from the COHA, including 415,186 ideational projections. 315,779 interpersonal projections and 113,399 textual projections. See Table 6.1.

For comparison, all the raw frequencies were converted into normalized frequencies per million words. See their normalized frequencies in Table 6.2.

The overall normalized frequency of interpersonal projections (779.7) and that of textual projections (279.97) were further converted to that of ideational projections (1025.16). Their diachronic distributions from the 1810s to the 2010s are shown in Fig. 6.1.

As shown in Fig. 6.1, the diachronic distributions of all three types of projections demonstrate similar trends of increasing. From the 1820s to the 1870s, all three exhibit a steady increase, and from the 1870s to the 1970s, their distributions continue to rise, albeit with fluctuations. Since the 1970s, the distributions of ideational and interpersonal projections have been decreasing, while that of textual projections initially decreases and then stablizes. A bivariate correlation test shows

 
M. Guo and Q. He, *A Corpus-Based Study of Projection in English from the Systemic Functional Perspective*, The M.A.K. Halliday Library Functional Linguistics Series,
https://doi.org/10.1007/978-981-97-5094-8_6

**Table 6.1** Frequencies of ideational, interpersonal and textual projections in the COHA

| | Ideational projection | | | Interpersonal projection | Textual projection | | | Total |
|---|---|---|---|---|---|---|---|---|
| | Paratactic | Hypotactic | Embedding | | Clause-initial | Clause-medial | Clause-final | |
| 1820s | 846 | 2488 | 611 | 1632 | 91 | 793 | 149 | 6610 |
| 1830s | 1506 | 3998 | 1178 | 3320 | 172 | 1291 | 226 | 11,691 |
| 1840s | 1536 | 4961 | 1394 | 3900 | 162 | 1358 | 329 | 13,640 |
| 1850s | 2604 | 6110 | 1671 | 6088 | 202 | 1707 | 549 | 18,931 |
| 1860s | 2481 | 6987 | 1682 | 7567 | 253 | 1714 | 895 | 21,579 |
| 1870s | 3429 | 9122 | 2086 | 9384 | 251 | 2395 | 1223 | 27,890 |
| 1880s | 4030 | 9755 | 2351 | 11,433 | 282 | 2035 | 1109 | 30,995 |
| 1890s | 4147 | 9892 | 2419 | 10,560 | 235 | 1859 | 962 | 30,074 |
| 1900s | 4492 | 11,599 | 2455 | 11,607 | 219 | 1854 | 1244 | 33,470 |
| 1910s | 4278 | 13,162 | 2761 | 14,315 | 293 | 2106 | 1906 | 38,821 |
| 1920s | 4405 | 14,079 | 3202 | 13,972 | 273 | 1863 | 1558 | 39,352 |
| 1930s | 6570 | 17,307 | 2908 | 19,534 | 1884 | 2064 | 2449 | 52,716 |
| 1940s | 6561 | 17,146 | 2606 | 19,488 | 1579 | 1634 | 2596 | 51,610 |
| 1950s | 7400 | 19,278 | 2703 | 22,477 | 2442 | 2137 | 2966 | 59,403 |
| 1960s | 7317 | 20,181 | 2724 | 26,778 | 3095 | 2297 | 3473 | 65,865 |
| 1970s | 7898 | 19,637 | 2442 | 26,431 | 4545 | 2975 | 3188 | 67,116 |
| 1980s | 6615 | 19,446 | 2563 | 24,608 | 4393 | 2225 | 2765 | 62,615 |
| 1990s | 8019 | 21,587 | 2555 | 27,774 | 4825 | 2886 | 2764 | 70,410 |
| 2000s | 7145 | 21,927 | 2720 | 27,677 | 5337 | 3343 | 2599 | 70,748 |
| 2010s | 6896 | 22,539 | 2779 | 27,234 | 5423 | 3396 | 2555 | 70,822 |
| Total | 98,175 | 271,201 | 45,810 | 315,779 | 35,956 | 41,932 | 35,505 | 844,358 |

**Table 6.2** Normalized frequencies of ideational, interpersonal and textual projections

| Section | Ideational projection | Interpersonal projection | Textual projection |
|---|---|---|---|
| 1820s | 565.08 | 233.77 | 147.98 |
| 1830s | 487.37 | 242.13 | 123.19 |
| 1840s | 499.21 | 246.73 | 116.98 |
| 1850s | 628.03 | 368.17 | 148.64 |
| 1860s | 658.32 | 446.79 | 168.98 |
| 1870s | 779.03 | 499.46 | 205.93 |
| 1880s | 804.13 | 569.74 | 170.72 |
| 1890s | 805.71 | 516.97 | 149.6 |
| 1900s | 843.92 | 528.13 | 150.94 |
| 1910s | 874.41 | 619.62 | 186.34 |
| 1920s | 839.81 | 543.64 | 143.72 |
| 1930s | 963.49 | 705 | 230.88 |
| 1940s | 956.19 | 711.25 | 212 |
| 1950s | 1021.47 | 784.22 | 263.27 |
| 1960s | 1034.92 | 919.48 | 304.41 |
| 1970s | 1037.02 | 916.82 | 371.43 |
| 1980s | 956.79 | 824.34 | 314.32 |
| 1990s | 968.69 | 837.85 | 315.99 |
| 2000s | 911.43 | 794.83 | 323.9 |
| 2010s | 907.12 | 768.16 | 320.82 |
| Overall | 1025.16 | 779.7 | 279.97 |

that three types of projections are significantly positively correlated ($p < 0.01$). The correlation coefficient between ideational projections and interpersonal projections ($r$ 0.962; $p = 0.000 < 0.01$), and that between interpersonal prjoections and textual projections ($r = 0.900$; $p = 0.000 < 0.01$) is much higher than that between ideational projections and textual projections ($r = 0.783$; $p = 0.000 < 0.01$).

Interpersonal projection results from the subjectification of the ideational *I*-projecting clause. Textual projection includes *I*- textual projection and *you*- textual projection, the former resulting from the grammaticalization of interpersonal projection and the latter from grammaticalization of ideational *you*-projecting clauses. The emergence of interpersonal and textual projections does not necessarily lead to the decrease of ideational projection. Therefore, their diachronic distributions do not show a negative correlation. Instead, all the three types show similar diachronic distribution patterns.

Ideational projection can be either realized as clause simplexes with embedding projection or clause complexes of projection. Embedding projection results from the nominalization of projecting verbal groups in clause complexes of projection or from zero (Halliday & Matthiessen 1999). Embedding projections are expected to

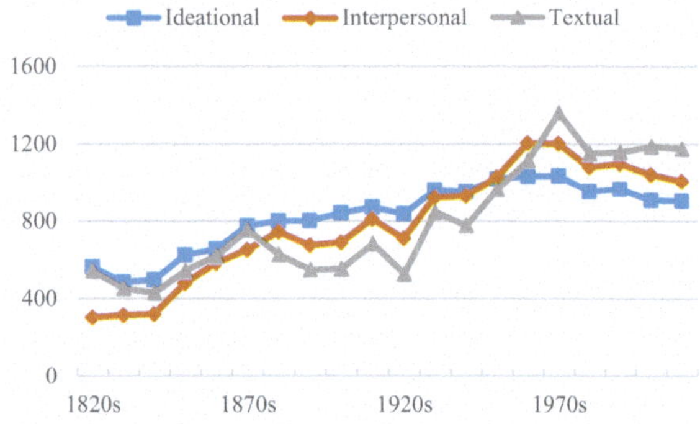


**Fig. 6.1** Overall diachronic distributions of ideational, interpersonal and textual projections

have a negative correlation with clause complexes of projection in diachronic distribution. The diachronic distributions of embedding projections and clause complexes of projection are identified to compare how embedding projections correlate with clause complexes of projection, interpersonal projection and textual projection. To facilitate comparison, the overall frequencies of embedding projections, interpersonal projections and textual projections were all converted to that of ideational projections (912.04). Their diachronic distributions are shown in Fig. 6.2.

According to Fig. 6.2, clause complexes of projection, interpersonal projections and textual projections generally show similar distribution trends. Embedding projections generally shows a similar distribution trend with the other three types of projection before the 1880s and an opposite distribution trend after the 1880s. The correlation test shows that the diachronic distribution of embedding projections is negatively, though not significantly, correlated with those of the other three types of projection (see Table 6.3). The reason for the non-significant correlation between embedding projections and clause complexes of projection is that the frequency of embedding projections calculated in the current research also includes fact projections. Fact projections do not result from the nominalization of projecting verbal groups in clause complexes of projection. The detailed analysis on the correlation between embedding projections as nominalizations and their congruent realizations will be further investigated in the next section.

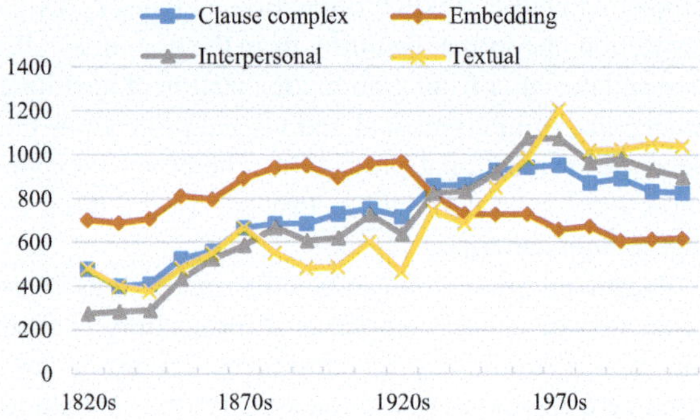


**Fig. 6.2** Diachronic distributions of clause complexes of projection, embedding projections, interpersonal projections and textual projections

**Table 6.3** Correlation test of diachronic distributions of clause complexes, embedding projections, interpersonal projections and textual projections

| | Clause complex | Embedding | Interpersonal | Textual |
|---|---|---|---|---|
| Clause complex | 1 | -0.203 | 0.976** | 0.826** |
| | | 0.391 | 0.000 | 0.000 |
| Embedding | -0.203 | 1 | -0.311 | -0.617** |
| | 0.391 | | 0.181 | 0.004 |
| Interpersonal | 0.976** | -0.311 | 1 | 0.900** |
| | 0.000 | 0.181 | | 0.000 |
| Textual | 0.826** | -0.617** | 0.900** | 1 |
| | 0.000 | 0.004 | 0.000 | |

**Correlation is significant at the 0.01 level (2-tailed)

Diachronically clause complexes of projection evolve in two directions. In one direction, some clause complexes of projection may undergo ideational metaphorization in that the projecting verbal group is nominalized as the projection noun and the projected clause is rank-shifted as the post-modifier of the projection noun. In the other direction, some projecting clauses in the hypotactic clause complexes undergo subjectification and become interpersonal projection that serves as modal adjunct. This is a transfer from the ideational domain to the interpersonal domain. Some interpersonal projections may further undergo grammaticalization and separate from the clause to serve as conjunctive adjuncts that link one independent clause to its preceding clause. This is a transfer from the interpersonal domain to the textual domain. Embedding projections occur within the ideational domain and hence the diachronic distribution of embedding projections has a negative correlation with that of clause complexes. The emergence of interpersonal projections and textual projections involves transcategorization across domains. This means they are not alternative choices to form a system within one semantic domain. Therefore, they do not show a negative correlation.

## 6.2 Diachronic Distribution of Ideational Projections

### 6.2.1 *General Diachronic Distribution of Ideational Projections*

Projection is congruently realized by paratactic and hypotactic clause complexes and metaphorically realized by clause simplexes with embedding projection. Hereby it is hypothesized that the diachronic distribution of embedding projections as a whole is negatively correlated with that of paratactic and hypotactic projections. For congruent realizations of projection, paratactic and hypotactic projections are two alternatives

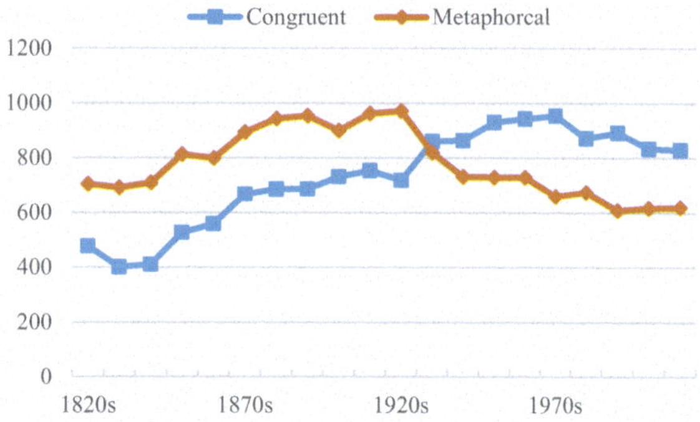


**Fig. 6.3** Diachronic distributions of congruent projections and metaphorical projections

in the system of clause interdependency, hereby it can be hypothesized that paratactic projections and hypotactic projections are negatively correlated in diachronic distribution. The general diachronic distributions of congruent and metaphorical projections will be examined first.

The total normalized frequencies of paratactic projections (242.42) and hypotactic projections (669.62) were added up as the normalized frequency of the congruent realizations of projection (912.04). Embedding locutions and ideas are triggered by the nominalization of projecting verbal groups in paratactic and hypotactic clause complexes and hereby the total normalized frequencies of embedding locutions and ideas are taken as that of the metaphorical realizations of projection. To facilitate comparison, the overall normalized frequencies of the metaphorical realizations of projection (113.12) were converted to that of the total congruent projections (912.04). Their diachronic distributions are shown in Fig. 6.3.

Figure 6.3 shows that the diachronic distributions of both congruent and metaphorical projections rise steadily from the 1830s to the 1890s. Since the 1890s, the two trends demonstrate opposite directions in diachronic change. The trend of congruent projections fluctuates slightly, reaching its peak in the 1980s, and then declines, while the trend of metaphorical projections rises slightly and decreases from the 1920s onward. The bivariate correlation test shows that they are negatively but not significantly correlated ($r = -0.203$; $p = 0.391 > 0.05$). However, their normalized frequencies from the 1890s to the 1990s demonstrate a significantly negative correlation ($r = -0.888$; $p = 0.001 < 0.01$). This is partly consistent with the hypothesis that paratactic and hypotactic projections, as congruent forms, are negatively correlated with embedding projections as the metaphorical forms. They are diachronically complementary and hence form alternatives in a system of choice to some extent. The reason why they are not entirely complementary may be that projections can also be realized as adverbial groups or prepositional phrases (e.g., *admittedly, according to John*).

Then the diachronic distributions of paratactic, hypotactic and embedding projections are compared. The overall normalized frequencies of hypotactic projections (78.97) and embedding projections (113.12) were converted to that of paratactic projections (228.23). Their diachronic distribution trends are shown in Fig. 6.4.

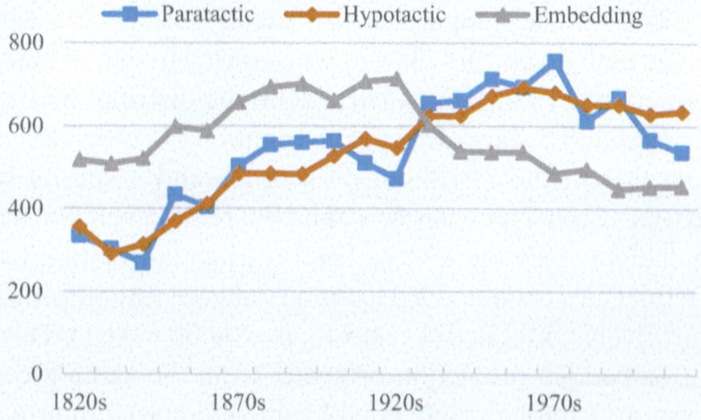


**Fig. 6.4** Diachronic distributions of overall paratactic, hypotactic and embedding projections

According to Fig. 6.4, the diachronic distributions of paratactic and hypotactic projections generally exhibit similar trends. Both types of projection show a consistent increase from the 1820s to the 1970s, followed by a decline following the 1970s. The result of bivariate correlation test indicate a significant positive correlation between the normalized frequency of paratactic projectiobs and that of hypotactic projections($r = 0.924$; $p = 0.000 < 0.01$). This contradicts the hypothesis that paratactic and hypotactic projections are negatively correlated. Paratactic and hypotactic projections do not form a system of choices.

The diachronic distribution of embedding projections mirror that of paratactic and hypotactic projections before the 1890s and then diverges in an opposite direction. Embedding projections are significantly negatively correlated with hypotactic projections from the 1890s to the 2010s ($r = -0.806$; $p = 0.001 < 0.01$). Embedding projections are negatively correlated with paratactic projections from the 1890s to the 2000s ($r = -0.690$; $p = 0.013 < 0.05$). These findings suggest that embedding projections are more associated with hypotactic projections than with paratactic projections.

The nominalization of projecting verbs triggers the projected clause to rank-shift to function as the post-modifier of the projection noun and the projector to serve as the pre-modifier of the projection noun. This metaphorization process may lead to information loss and the projector can be omitted, resulting in embedded locutions/ideas without pre-modifiers. Embedded locutions and ideas with possessive pronouns as pre-modifiers of the projection nouns are semantically closer to the congruent clause complexes of projection because the possessive pronouns can indicate the projectors, and those without possessive pronouns are closer to fact projections. Hereby embedded locutions and ideas with an explicit projector are less metaphorical than those without an explicit projector. It is hypothesized that embedded locutions/ideas with a projector appear earlier than those without a projector, and the former have the potential to further transfer to the latter. The diachronic distributions of embedded locutions/ideas with and without projectors will be compared. A total of 13,207 embedding locutions/ideas with projectors and 32,603 embedding locutions/idea without projectors were retrieved from the COHA. See Table 6.4.

To facilitate comparison, the overall normalized frequency of embedding locution/ideas with projectors (32.63) is converted to that of embedding locution/idea without projectors (74.48). See their diachronic distribution trends in Fig. 6.5.

Figure 6.5 shows that the distribution of embedded locution/ideas with projectors and that of those without projectors exhibit similar trends from the 1820s to the 2010s. Both types show a mild increase over the first ten decades, followed by a decline since the 1920s. The bivariate correlation test shows that the normalized frequencies of embedded locutions/ideas with and without projectors are significantly positively correlated ($r = 0.842; p = 0.000 < 0.01$). This suggests that these two types of embedded projection originate from the same group of data and do not form a system. Although embedded locutions/ideas with projectors are semantically closer to the congruent realizations of projection, their emergence is no earlier than those without projectors. Futhermore, embedded locutions/ideas without projectors are not transferred from those with projectors; rather, both types are transferred from the clause complexes of locutions/ideas.

**Table 6.4** Frequencies of embedding locutions and ideas with and without projectors in the COHA

| | With projector | Without projector |
|---|---|---|
| 1820s | 198 | 413 |
| 1830s | 377 | 801 |
| 1840s | 388 | 1006 |
| 1850s | 467 | 1204 |
| 1860s | 480 | 1202 |
| 1870s | 579 | 1507 |
| 1880s | 612 | 1739 |
| 1890s | 646 | 1773 |
| 1900s | 712 | 1743 |
| 1910s | 753 | 2008 |
| 1920s | 976 | 2226 |
| 1930s | 865 | 2043 |
| 1940s | 819 | 1787 |
| 1950s | 849 | 1854 |
| 1960s | 873 | 1851 |
| 1970s | 738 | 1704 |
| 1980s | 719 | 1844 |
| 1990s | 674 | 1881 |
| 2000s | 745 | 1975 |
| 2010s | 737 | 2042 |
| Total | 13,207 | 32,603 |

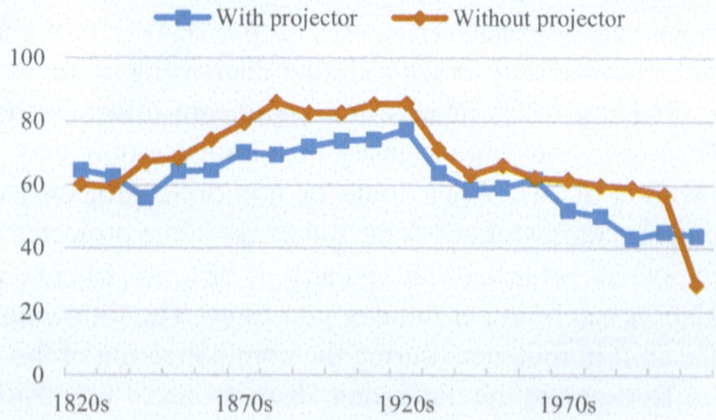


**Fig. 6.5** Diachronic distributions of embedded locution/ideas with and without projectors

### 6.2.2 *Diachronic Distributions of Locutions and Ideas*

#### 6.2.2.1 Diachronic Distribution of Locution Projections

Projection of locutions can be realized either as clause complexes or as nominal groups containing a locution noun modified by an embedded projected clause. Locution nouns are the nominalizations of corresponding verbal verbs. Hereby it is hypothesized that the diachronic distribution of embedding locutions is negatively correlated with that of clause complexes of locution.

The normalized frequency of embedding locutions (17.32) was worked out as the frequency for metaphorical locution and that of hypotactic and paratactic locutions (330.56) was worked out as frequency for congruent locutions. To facilitate comparison, the normalized frequency of metaphorical locutions is converted to that of their congruent counterpart. Their diachronic distributions are displayed in Fig. 6.6.

Figure 6.6 shows that the diachronic distributions of metaphorical and congruent locutions are similar before the 1920s, both exhibiting an upward trend. From the 1920s to the 1970s, the diachronic distributions of metaphoric and congruent locutions demonstrate opposite trends, and their normalized frequencies are significantly

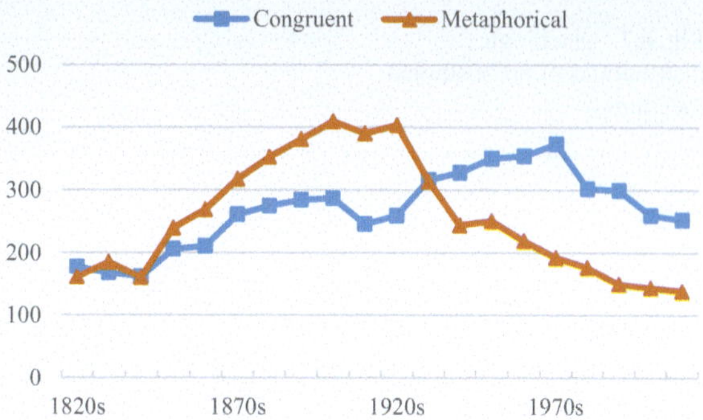


**Fig. 6.6** Diachronic distributions of congruent and metaphorical locutions

negatively correlated ($r = -0.972$; $p = 0.001 < 0.01$). Since the 1970s, the two types of locutions have shown a similar decreasing trend.

The loss of finiteness is a significant effect in the process of nominalization. However, non-finite clauses in nominalization may sometimes regain finiteness (Mithun 2016). When finite or non-finite projected clauses in clause complexes undergo rank-shift, does the finiteness of the projected clause change? Propositional hypotactic projected clauses can only be finite, whereas proposal hypotactic projected clauses can be either finite or non-finite. The following analysis will hereby observe the shift in finiteness during the nominalization of the projection clause complexes.

To examine the diachronic distribution of propositional locutions, some typical projecting verbs that project propositional locution and their corresponding projection nouns were selected, e.g., *state*, *report*, *rumor*, *claim*, *argue*, *insist* and *inquire*. The verbs were used to retrieve propositional hypotactic locutions, and their corresponding projection nouns were used to retrieve propositional embedding locutions. Propositional hypotactic projected clauses can only be finite and propositional embedded projected clauses can be either finite or non-finite. 6269 propositional hypotactic locutions, 7615 finite propositional embedding locutions and 1432 non-finite propositional embedding locutions were retrieved from the COHA. To facilitate comparison, the overall frequencies of finite propositional hypotactic locutions (15.49) and non-finite propositional embedding locutions (3.54) were converted to that of finite propositional embedding locutions (18.8). The diachronic distributions of the three types of propositional locutions are shown in Fig. 6.7.

Figure 6.7 shows that finite hypotactic propositional projections and both finite and non-finite embedding locutions generally exhibit the same diachronic distribution trends. The bivariate correlation test shows that the normalized frequency of finite hypotactic propositional locutions is significantly positively correlated with that of finite embedding propositional locutions ($r = 0.778$; $p = 0.000 < 0.01$) and that of non-finite embedding propositional locutions ($r = 0.583$; $p = 0.007 < 0.01$). This indicates that finite hypotactic propositional locutions are likely to become either finite or non-finite when they undergo downward rank-shift from the clause rank to the word rank. A proposition exchanges information. The subject of the projecting clause and the subject of the projected clause are not necessarily the same within

**Fig. 6.7** Diachronic distributions of propositional locutions

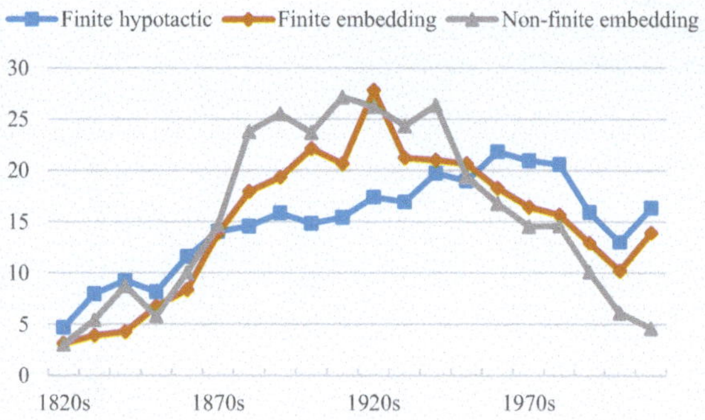

a clause complex of locution projection. Hereby non-finite embedding proposition locutions do not typically assume possessive pronouns serving as pre-modifiers of location nouns as the absent subjects of non-finite embedded clauses. For example:

6.1 a. He argued that the power of evil threatens to overthrow God himself. (COHA_1970)
b. Attar. ney Schenck made much of this affidavit in his argument that Burch is afflicted with paranoia. (COHA_1921)
c. If, however, the argument of being independent on foreign nations is worth any thing, it is on account of the interruptions to which our trade with them may be subjected. (COHA_1975)

In example 6.1a, the subject of the finite projected clause is different from that of the projecting clause. In example 6.1b, the subject in the finite embedding propositional locution is *Burch* which has nothing to do with the projector of the argument. In example 6.1c, the context implies that the subject for the non-finite prejected clause is *our trade,* which can by no means be the projector of *argument*.

What's more, the finite and non-finite embedding propositional locutions are significantly correlated at 0.01 level ($r = 0.888$; $p = 0.000 < 0.01$). This indicates that finite and non-finite propositional embedding locutions do not form a system of choice.

Then the typical verbs that project proposal locutions such as *offer*, *threat*, *promise*, *order*, *require* and *plea* and their corresponding projection nouns such as *offer*, *threat*, *promise*, *order*, *requirement* and *plea* are selected. Proposal hypotactic locutions can be either finite or non-finite. These words were used to retrieve 1282 finite proposal hypotactic locutions, 5863 non-finite proposal hypotactic locutions, 2512 finite proposal embedding locutions, and 4566 non-finite proposal embedding locutions. To facilitate comparison, the overall frequencies of finite proposal hypotactic locution (3.18), finite proposal embedding location (6.2) and non-finite proposal embedding locution (11.27) were converted to that of non-finite proposal hypotactic locution (14.49). Their diachronic distributions are presented in Fig. 6.8.

According to Fig. 6.8, the diachronic distributions of finite hypotactic proposal locutions and finite embedding proposal locutions demonstrate similar trends, and

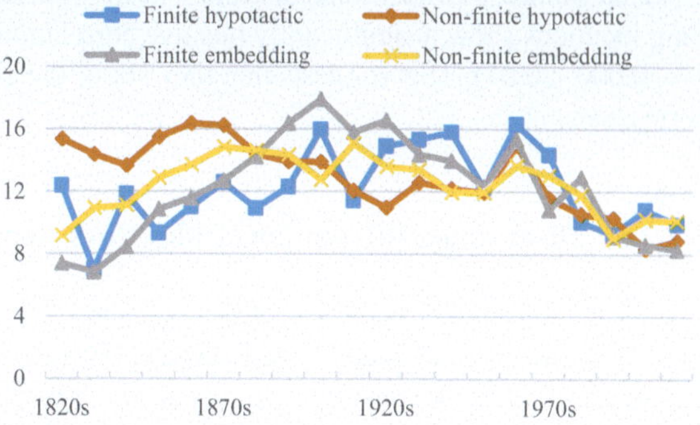


**Fig. 6.8** Diachronic distributions of proposal locutions

those of non-finite hypotactic proposal locutions and non-finite embedding proposal locutions show similar trends. Finite proposal hypotactic locutions are significantly positively correlated with finite proposal embedding locutions ($r = 0.649$; $p = 0.002 < 0.01$), but they are not significantly correlated with non-finite proposal embedding locutions ($r = 0.364$; $p = 0.114 > 0.05$).

Non-finite proposal hypotactic locutions are not significantly correlated with either non-finite proposal embedding locutions ($r = 0.431$; $p = 0.058 > 0.05$) or finite proposal embedding locutions ($r = 0.131$; $p = 0.583 > 0.05$). Proposal exchanges the goods-&-services that the language speaker offers or commands, and non-finite hypotactic proposal clauses usually assume the same subjects as the projecting clauses. In embedding projections of proposal locution, the possessive pronoun serving as the premodifier of the locution/idea noun indicates the projector of the projected clause, and the non-finite embedded locution/idea assumes the pronoun as the subject of the embedded clause. For example:

6.2 a. I promise to love you still. (COHA_1917) (proposal locution of offer)
b. Remember your promise to hold your peace. (COHA_1835) (proposal locution of offer)

As shown in example 6.2a, in the hypotactic clause complex of proposal locution, the non-finite projected clause assumes the same subject *I* as the projecting clause. In 6.2b, the locution noun has the possessive pronoun *your* as modifer to indicate the projector. The non-finite embedded proposal locution in 6.2b assumes the projector indicated by *your* as its subject. Therefore, it is hypothesized that non-finite proposal hypotactic locutions are correlated with embedded proposals with explicit projectors. 1381 Embedding proposal locutions with explicit projector were retrieved and the overall normalized frequencies for finite ones (0.76) and non-finite ones (2.66) were calculated. The bivariate correlation test shows that non-finite proposal hypotactic locutions are significantly positively correlated with non-finite proposal embedding locutions with explicit projector ($r = 0.616$; $p = 0.004 < 0.01$), but they are not significantly correlated with finite proposal embedding locutions with explicit projector ($r = 0.275$; $p = 0.240 > 0.05$). This indicates that the finiteness of proposal hypotactic locutions is more likely to remain the same when shifting from the clause rank to the word rank to modifier locution nouns with explicit projecters.

What's more, the diachronic distributions of finite and non-finite proposal embedding locutions show a significantly positive correlation at the 0.01 level ($r = 0.755$; $p = 0.000 < 0.01$). This suggests that they are of the same group of data and do not form a system.

#### 6.2.2.2 Diachronic Distribution of Idea Projections

The projections of ideas can be realized as paratactic or hypotactic clause complexes or clause simplexes with embedded clauses. Hypotactic ideas and embedding ideas can be either finite or non-finite. Paratactic and hypotactic clause complexes are the congruent forms of projections of idea and embedded clauses modifying idea nouns

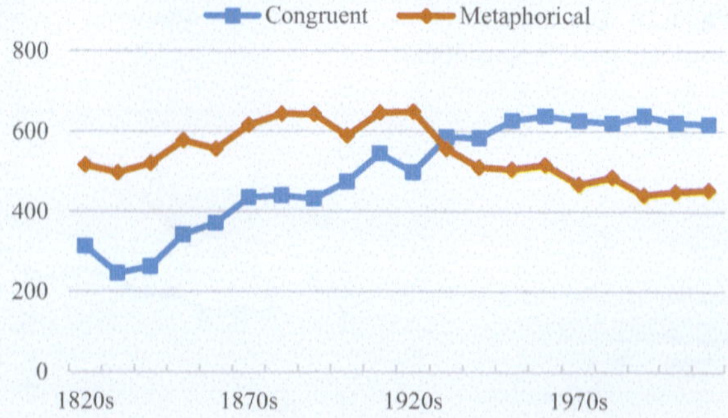


**Fig. 6.9** Diachronic distributions of congruent and metaphorical ideas

are the metaphorical forms. It is hypothesized that the distributions of the congruent and the metaphorical forms are negatively correlated. To facilitate comparison, the normalized frequency of metaphorical ideas (95.8) is converted to that of congruent ideas (629.96). See their diachronic distributions in Fig. 6.9.

Figure 6.9 shows that congruent ideas maintain a steady increasing trend over the past 20 decades. Metaphorical ideas climb from the 1820s to the 1920s and then gradually decline until the 2010s. They demonstrate opposite diachronic distribution trends from the 1870s. The bivariate correlation test shows a significantly negative correlation between them from the 1870s ($r = -0.729$; $p = 0.002 < 0.01$). This finding is partly consistent with the present hypothesis.

Ideas tend to be realized by hypotactic clause complexes rather than paratactic clause complexes. Next, the diachronic distributions of propositional and proposal hypotactic ideas and embedding ideas were compared. Mental verbs *suspect*, *predict*, *assume* and *doubt* were used to represent typical verbs projecting propositional ideas and their corresponding nouns *suspect*, *prediction*, *assumption* and *doubt* were selected to represent propositional idea nouns. The more widely used verb *think* was not selected to avoid retrieving data overlapping with the interpersonal projection *I THINK* which appears in the same form as the hypotactic clause complex of projection. Another widely used mental verb *believe* was not selected because it can project an idea or not. These two meanings cannot be distinguished by automatic retrieving, and hence mental verbs with different interpretations are not included. Accordingly, 4283 propositional hypotactic ideas, 72,055 finite propositional embedding ideas, and only 35 non-finite propositional embedding ideas were retrieved from the COHA. The number of non-finite embedding propositional ideas is significantly smaller than that of finite ones, which indicates that finite hypotactic propositional ideas are not likely to shift to non-finite embedding propositional ideas. The number of non-finite propositional embedding ideas is too small to have statistical significance and hereby they are not included in the following analysis. To facilitate comparison, the normalized frequency of propositional hypotactic ideas (10.57) was converted to that of finite propositional embedding ideas (17.79). See their diachronic distributions in Fig. 6.10.

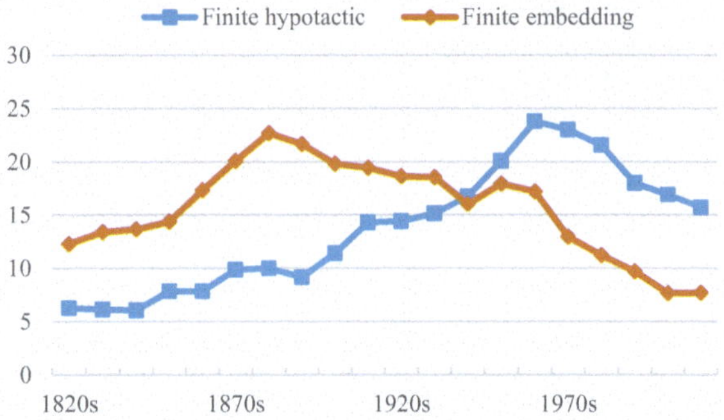


**Fig. 6.10** Diachronic distributions of propositional ideas

Figure 6.10 shows that the diachronic distribution of finite hypotactic propositional ideas shows a general trend of increasing from the 1820s to the 1960s, follwed by a gradual decline until the 2010s. In contrast, the diachronic distribution of finite embedding propositional ideas increases from the 1820s to the 1880s and then steadily decreases until the 2010s. According to the bivariate correlation test, finite propositional hypotactic ideas are not significantly negatively correlated with finite propositional embedding ideas ($r = -0.231$; $p = 0.327 > 0.05$). During the period from the 1890s to the 1960s, the normalized frequencies of hypotactic and embedding finite propositional ideas exhibit a significantly negative correlation trend ($r = -0.914$; $p = 0.002 < 0.01$). This indicates they are, in some way, complementary.

Mental projecting verbs *intent*, *desire*, *hope*, *incline*, *decide*, *resolve* and *wish* and their corresponding projection nouns *intention*, *desire*, *hope*, *inclination*, *decision*, *resolve* and *wish* were selected to retrieve proposal hypotactic and embedding ideas. Accordingly, 7414 finite proposal hypotactic ideas, 32,403 non-finite proposal hypotactic ideas, 6299 finite propositional embedding ideas, and 19,867 non-finite propositional embedding ideas were retrieved from the COHA. To facilitate comparison, the normalized frequencies of finite proposal hypotactic ideas (18.31), finite (15.55) and non-finite (49.05) propositional embedding ideas were converted to that of non-finite proposal hypotactic ideas (80.21). Their diachronic distributions are shown in Fig. 6.11.

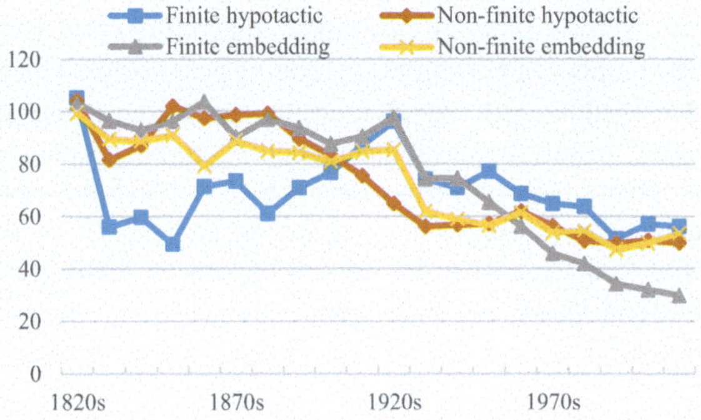


**Fig. 6.11** Diachronic distributions of proposal ideas

According to Fig. 6.11, the four types of proposal ideas show a gradual decrease from the 1830s to the 2010s, except for the finite hypotactic ideas, which fluctuates instead of constantly going down. The normalized frequency of finite proposal hypotactic ideas is significantly positively correlated with that of finite proposal embedding ideas ($r = 0.449$; $p = 0.047 < 0.05$) but not significantly correlated with that of non-finite proposal embedding ideas ($r = 0.39$; $p = 0.089 > 0.05$). Most of the mental words selected can project either the idea of offer or that of command. Usually ideas of offer are realized as non-finite hypotactic clauses and ideas of command as finite hypotactic clauses. For example, *intent* and *incline* can only project ideas of offer and hypotactic finite clauses projected by *intent* are not acceptable. Finite proposal hypotactic clause complexes usually realize the idea of command and have subjects different from the subjects of the projecting clause. For example:

6.3 a. I hope that all my poor human beings don't suffer like this! (COHA_1929)
b. I desire that you will eat this leg of a chicken. (COHA_1895)
c. By the way, I have always cherished a hope that she might yet be found. (COHA_1874)
d. And it is our hope that they may find it here. (COHA_1937)

As shown in 6.3a and 6.3b, the subjects in the projecting clauses are *I* the speaker and the subjects in the projected clauses are *all my poor human beings* and *you*. When the projected clause shifts from the clause rank to the word rank, only the maintainance of finiteness can indicate who is expected to take the command. Finite hypotactic ideas of command cannot be further compressed into non-finite ones because non-finite embedding proposal ideas will automatically assume the projectors of the ideas as the persons to perform the services. This is why finite proposal hypotactic ideas are significantly positively correlated with finite proposal embedding ideas.

Non-finite proposal hypotactic ideas exhibit a significantly positive correlation with both finite proposal embedding ideas ($r = 0.849$; $p = 0.000 < 0.01$) and non-finite proposal embedding ideas ($r = 0.904$; $p = 0.000 < 0.01$). Non-finite hypotactic complexes may realize the proposal of offer or command. For example:

6.4 a. I hope to keep your friendship. (COHA_1901)
b. No, we intend to destroy it for good. (COHA_1970)
c. I wish you to stay here and be Prince Hagen's tutor. (COHA_1912)
d. Frank Frost, I desire you to see that the boys stand at regular distances. (COHA_1864)

6.4a and 6.4b illustrate non-finite proposal hypotactic ideas of offer and 6.4c and 6.4d illustrate non-finite proposal hypotactic ideas of command. In 6.4a and 6.4b, the subjects of the non-finite hypotactic ideas assume the subjects of the projecting clauses. In 6.4c and 6.4d, the subjects of the non-finite hypotactic ideas are different from the subjects of the projecting clauses. Therefore, after undergoing rank-shift, the non-finite hypotactic clauses of offer can remain non-finite and assume the projectors as subjects. However, the non-finite hypotactic clauses of command have to become finite in order to avoid misunderstanding of the subjects of the embedded clauses.

Therefore, non-finite proposal hypotactic ideas exhibit a significant correlation with both finite and non-finite proposal embedding ideas.

Finite and non-finite proposal hypotactic ideas exhibit no significant correlation while finite and non-finite proposal embedding ideas are significantly positively correlated ($r = 0.849$; $p = 0.000 < 0.01$).

### 6.2.3 Diachronic Distribution of Fact Projections

From the COHA, a total of 132,479 embedding projections were retrieved, including 73,289 finite and 59,190 non-finite embedded projections. See Table 6.5.

#### 6.2.3.1 Finite and Non-finite Facts as Appositive

In this section, we will investigate embedded facts as appositives of fact nouns, i.e., chance, need, case and proof.

Finite and non-finite embedding chances and embedding needs were retrieved with typical chance nouns, e.g., *chance*, *likelihood*, *certainty* and *probability*, and need nouns, e.g., *requirement*, *need*, *rule* and *obligation*. Accordingly, 1706 finite facts of chances, 3436 non-finite facts of chances, 1929 finite facts of needs and 3114 non-finite facts of needs were retrieved from the COHA. The normalized frequency of finite chances (4.21) was converted to that of non-finite chances (8.48). Their diachronic distributions are shown in Fig. 6.12.

Figure 6.12 shows that finite chances generally exhibit an increase over the past 20 decades while non-finite chances remain steady, with a slight increase from the 1820s to the 1920s, a sharp decline from the 1920s to the 1940s and fluctuation in the subsequent decades. The bivariate correlation test shows that the normalized frequencies of finite and non-finite chances are significantly negatively correlated ($r = -0.544$; $p = 0.013 < 0.05$). This suggests that finite chances and non-finite chances form a system of choice.

The normalized frequency of finite needs (4.76) was converted into that of non-finite needs (7.69). Their diachronic distributions are shown in Fig. 6.13.

According to Fig. 6.13, the diachronic distributions of finite and non-finite needs demonstrate different trends. Finite needs fluctuate from the 1820s to the 1900s, climb to reach its peak in the 1990s, and decline thereafter. Non-finite needs maintain a fluctuating trend over the past 20 decades. The normalized frequency of finite needs has a significantly negative correlation ($r = -0.629$; $p = 0.003 < 0.05$) with that of non-finite needs. Hereby finite needs and non-finite needs also form a system of choice.

Case nouns such as *fact*, *case*, *point*, *principle* and *accident* were used to retrieve finite and non-finite appositive cases. 21,892 finite appositive cases and 3258 non-finite appositive cases in total are retrieved from the COHA. To facilitate comparison,

**Table 6.5** Frequencies of finite and non-finite embedded projections in the COHA

| | Finite | | | | | | Non-finite | | | | | |
|---|---|---|---|---|---|---|---|---|---|---|---|---|
| | Locution | Idea | Chance | Need | Proof | Case | Locution | Idea | Chance | Need | Proof | Case |
| 1820s | 36 | 249 | 20 | 32 | 9 | 485 | 23 | 303 | 52 | 6 | 0 | 722 |
| 1830s | 75 | 451 | 24 | 43 | 3 | 839 | 58 | 594 | 122 | 24 | 2 | 1056 |
| 1840s | 87 | 594 | 22 | 68 | 12 | 1119 | 46 | 667 | 115 | 34 | 0 | 1101 |
| 1850s | 139 | 675 | 20 | 82 | 6 | 1379 | 69 | 788 | 121 | 35 | 0 | 1333 |
| 1860s | 168 | 768 | 38 | 83 | 10 | 1608 | 71 | 675 | 138 | 24 | 0 | 1329 |
| 1870s | 212 | 936 | 33 | 91 | 14 | 2069 | 101 | 837 | 152 | 36 | 0 | 1587 |
| 1880s | 268 | 1103 | 41 | 119 | 24 | 2453 | 103 | 877 | 151 | 33 | 0 | 1665 |
| 1890s | 305 | 1116 | 58 | 108 | 14 | 2589 | 103 | 895 | 161 | 22 | 0 | 1635 |
| 1900s | 344 | 1098 | 51 | 88 | 18 | 2924 | 128 | 885 | 190 | 28 | 1 | 1800 |
| 1910s | 344 | 1270 | 53 | 112 | 14 | 3151 | 129 | 1018 | 207 | 53 | 1 | 1934 |
| 1920s | 485 | 1471 | 88 | 104 | 23 | 3659 | 162 | 1084 | 253 | 74 | 3 | 1944 |
| 1930s | 366 | 1318 | 86 | 129 | 27 | 3098 | 179 | 1045 | 239 | 110 | 2 | 1918 |
| 1940s | 328 | 1157 | 107 | 90 | 26 | 2776 | 137 | 984 | 176 | 116 | 1 | 1814 |
| 1950s | 337 | 1246 | 124 | 109 | 23 | 2835 | 145 | 975 | 185 | 186 | 0 | 1695 |
| 1960s | 277 | 1239 | 152 | 114 | 21 | 2712 | 141 | 1067 | 191 | 273 | 3 | 1654 |
| 1970s | 237 | 1072 | 149 | 111 | 23 | 2659 | 135 | 998 | 199 | 313 | 0 | 1709 |
| 1980s | 240 | 1094 | 160 | 120 | 15 | 2291 | 100 | 1129 | 221 | 411 | 0 | 1577 |
| 1990s | 215 | 1059 | 147 | 108 | 21 | 2339 | 96 | 1185 | 159 | 467 | 3 | 2194 |
| 2000s | 197 | 1029 | 150 | 99 | 14 | 2617 | 121 | 1373 | 180 | 457 | 1 | 2122 |
| 2010s | 196 | 1040 | 183 | 116 | 23 | 2276 | 117 | 1426 | 224 | 412 | 0 | 833 |
| Total | 4856 | 19,985 | 1706 | 1926 | 340 | 45,878 | 2164 | 18,805 | 3436 | 3114 | 17 | 31,622 |

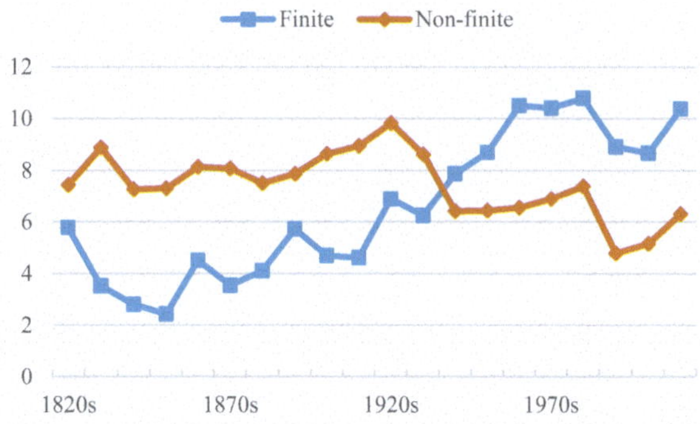


**Fig. 6.12** Diachronic distributions of finite and non-finite embedded chances

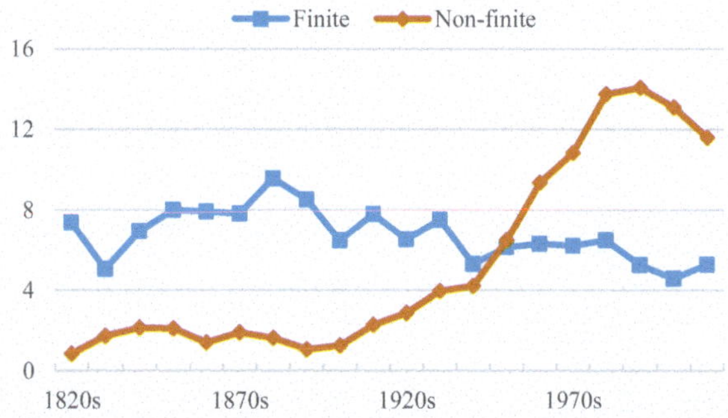


**Fig. 6.13** Diachronic distributions of finite and non-finite embedded needs

the normalized frequency of non-finite appositive cases (8.04) was converted to that of finite ones (54.06). Their diachronic distributions are demonstrated in Fig. 6.14.

As shown in Fig. 6.14, finite appositive cases gradually increase, reaching their peak in the 1920s, and then generally decrease in the following decades, except for the last two decades. Non-finite appositive cases on the whole fluctuate before the 1920s and gradually decline in the subsequent decades. Their normalized frequencies are also significantly negatively correlated ($r = -0.485$; $p = 0.03 < 0.05$), indicating that finite and non-finite appositive cases form a system of choice.

Only 370 finite proofs and 17 non-finite ones were retrieved from the COHA. Both of their normalized frequencies per million words are below 1. The frequencies of finite and non-finite needs are too small to be tested statistically. Therefore, the diachronic distribution of proofs will not be explored in this research.

To sum up, finite appositive chances, needs and cases all demonstrate a negative correlation with their non-finite counterparts. The finite and non-finite appositive clauses modifying fact nouns can form a system of choice. This is different from the diachronic distribution patterns of embedded locutions and ideas in that finite embedding locution and idea clauses do not form a system of choice with their non-finite counterparts.

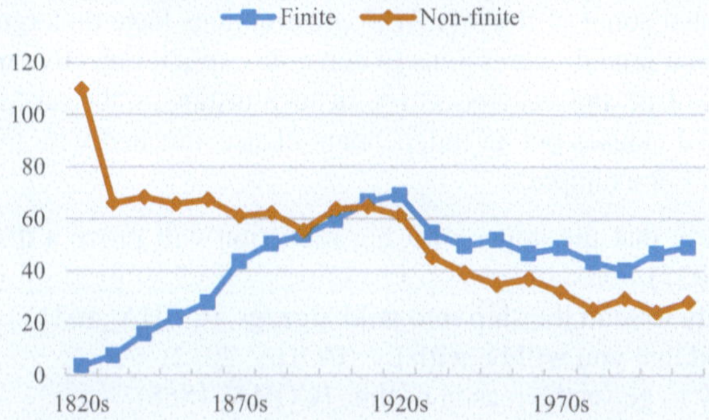


**Fig. 6.14** Diachronic distributions of finite and non-finite appositive cases

#### 6.2.3.2 Finite and Non-finite Facts as Head

Among the four types of facts, only cases can stand on their own as head. To compare the diachronic distributions of finite and non-finite cases as head, the extraposed cases as head that occur in relational clauses were retrieved. The reason is that both finite and non-finite cases as head can appear in such clauses and they can be automatically retrieved by machine in large-sized corpora. Cases as head have no congruent realizations. Hereby it is hypothesized that finite and non-finite cases as head are negatively correlated.

19,921 finite extraposed cases as head and 28,364 non-finite ones were retrieved from the COHA. To facilitate comparison, the normalized frequency of finite cases as head (49.19) was converted to that of non-finite cases as head (70.03). Their diachronic distributions are shown in Fig. 6.15.

Figure 6.15 shows that finite and non-finite cases as head show similar diachronic distributions. Both of them fluctuate from the 1820s to the 1920s and then generally fall down thereafter. Their normalized frequencies are significantly correlated ($r = 0.833$; $p = 0.000 < 0.01$). This is not consistent with the present hypothesis. The

**Fig. 6.15** Diachronic distributions of finite and non-finite cases as head

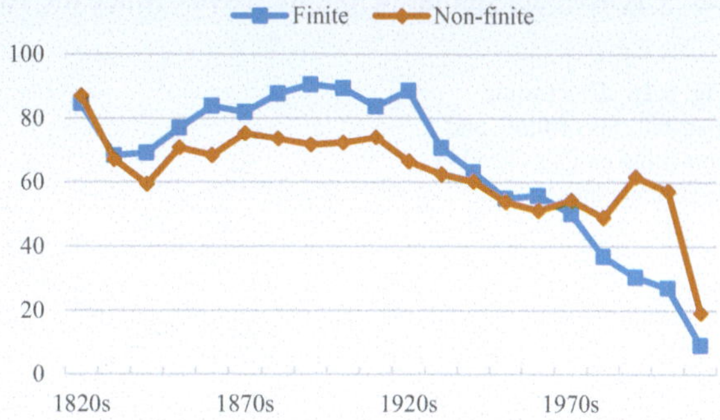

reason may be that some of the *it is ADJ* constructions have undergone subjectification and become modal expressions to construe explicit objective modality, such as *it is likely*, *it is true* and *it is necessary*. In such instances, the succeeding clauses are not embedded clauses but an independent clause attached with modal adjuncts preceding them. For example:

6.5 a. It is likely that the hopes of a big reduction will prove a disappointment. (COHA_1927)
b. It is likely to send the ship into wild zigzags. (COHA_1951)
c. It is good that you will be with us. (COHA_2012)
d. It is easy to guess the reason of this. (COHA_1868)

In 6.5a and 6.5b, *likely* is an epistemic adjective and *it is likely* serves as a modal adjunct to construe the modality of possibility and the clause it is attached to is the proposition being evaluated. In this sense, *that the hopes of a big reduction will prove a disappointment* and *to send the ship into wild zigzags* are not embedded clauses but independent clauses. In 6.5c and 6.5d, *good* and *easy* are attitudinal adjectives and do not involve modality. Hence, *that you will be with us* in 6.5c and *to guess the reason of this* in 6.5d are extraposed subjects and *it* is the subject placeholder in the clauses they are embedded in. Next, the diachronic distributions of constructions involving epistemic and attitudinal adjectives were retrieved. Only those involving attitudinal adjectives can represent the diachronic distributions of extraposed cases as head.

Based on the most typical adjectives collocating with extraposed cases as head in the COCA, two types of adjectives are distinguished: epistemic adjectives and attitudinal adjectives. Modal adjectives include *possible*, *true*, *likely*, *unlikely*, *imperative*, *impossible* and *necessary* and evaluative adjectives include *obvious*, *clear*, *important*, *interesting*, *noteworthy*, *hard*, *difficult*, *easy*, *good* and *better*.

Using the above attitudinal adjectives, 2044 finite extraposed cases and 6774 non-finite extraposed cases as head were retrieved. The normalized frequency of finite ones (5.05) was converted to that of non-finite ones (16.73). Figure 6.16 shows their diachronic distribution trends.

According to Fig. 6.16, the diachronic distribution trends of finite and non-finite cases as head are similar before the 1890s. Since the 1890s, they have been opposite

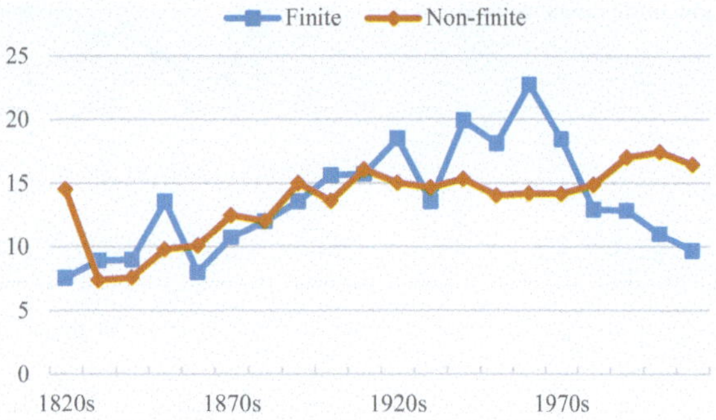


**Fig. 6.16** Diachronic distributions of finite and non-finite cases as head in relational clauses

in most decades. Their normalized frequencies are significantly negatively correlated ($r = -0.616$; $p = 0.025 < 0.05$). This is partly consistent with the present hypothesis. To some extent, the finite and non-finite extraposed cases as head form a system of choice.

As for constructions with modal adjectives serving as modal adjuncts, it can be hypothesized that the corresponding finite and non-finite clauses are positively correlated. 4833 finite and 2345 non-finite clauses attached with explicit objective modality were retrieved. The normalized frequency of finite ones (5.79) was converted to that of non-finite ones (11.93) and their diachronic distribution trends are shown in Fig. 6.17.

The diachronic distributions of finite and non-finite clauses with explicit objective modality demonstrate similar trends from the 1820s to the 2010s. Their normalized frequencies are significantly positively correlated ($r = 0.889$; $p = 0.000 < 0.01$). This is consistent with the present hypothesis.

## 6.3 Diachronic Distribution of Textual Projections

### *6.3.1 General Diachronic Distribution of Textual Projections*

Textual projections are realized as projecting clauses separated from the proposition clauses by a comma. Textual projections have flexible positioning; they can appear in the initial, medial and ending positions of clauses. Among the textual projections in the three possible positions, those appearing in the clause-final position are the most easily identifiable because the order of the pronouns and projecting verbs is different from that of ideational projections. The pronouns in textual projecting clauses usually involve the addresser and the addressee, including *I*, *you* or *we*. Therefore, the following search query was used to search textual projections appearing in the clause-final position from the COHA .

RE 6.1 ., I|you|we [v*].

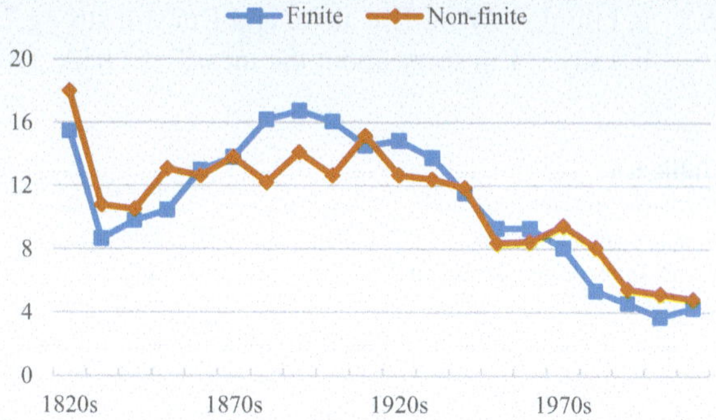


**Fig. 6.17** Diachronic distributions of finite and non-finite clauses attached with explicit objective modality

RE 6.1 can be described as a comma followed by the pronoun *I*, *you* or *me*, a verb, and a period. For example:

6.6 It's only a story, you know. (COHA_1972)

Using RE 6.1, 93 textual projection constructions were retrieved with a total frequency of 58,430. Constructions with non-projecting verbs (e.g., *I do*, *I hear*) were manually removed, resulting in 51 constructions of textual projections appearing at the clause-final position. Their frequencies are presented in Table 6.6.

According to Table 6.6, *I*-projections are more frequent than the other two types. *We*-projections are the least frequent. The only two *we*-projections in the clause-final position are *we know* and *we think*. Among the 51 constructions of textual projections, 40 are realized by pronouns and present-tense verbs and only 9 are realized by pronouns and past-tense verbs. The use of present-tense verbs can indicate that a construction has lost the variety of realization and has become a fixed expression.

The top 10 most frequent textual projections in the clause-final position are presented as follows.

As Table 6.7 shows, the most frequent textual projection in the clause-final position is *you know* and it is far more frequent than any other textual projections. Based on the top 10 most frequent textual projections, the main textual projecting verbs are identified: *know*, *guess*, *think*, *suppose*, *believe*, *mean*, *hope* and *say*.

Based on the main projecting verbs, the following search queries were used to search for textual projections in the clause-initial and clause-medial positions.

RE 6.2. I|you know|guess|think|suppose|believe|mean|hope|say,
RE 6.3. I|you know|guess|think|suppose|believe|mean|hope|say,

RE 6.2 can be described as a period followed by the personal pronoun *I* or *you*, and any one of the projecting verbs (i.e., *know*, *guess*, *think*, *suppose*, *believe*, *mean*, *hope* and *say*). For example:

6.7 You mean, they won't dare refuse. (COHA_1926)

However, some paratactic clause complexes of projection were also retrieved using RE 6.2, such as the following example:

6.8 a. I think, " Wow. I'm alive, and I'm still strong." (COHA_2012)
b. I say, " I'm sorry about the mess." (COHA_1976)

**Table 6.6** Construction numbers and frequencies of textual projections in the clause-final position

| | Number of constructions | | Total frequencies |
|---|---|---|---|
| *I*- | 40 | Present: 33 | 29,217 |
| | | Past: 7 | |
| You- | 9 | Present: 7 | 14,938 |
| | | Past: 2 | |
| *We*- | 2 | | 123 |
| Total | 51 | | 44,278 |

**Table 6.7** Top 10 most frequent textual projections in clause-final position

| | Construction | Frequency |
|---|---|---|
| 1 | *You know* | 13,543 |
| 2 | *I guess* | 4629 |
| 3 | *I know* | 4572 |
| 4 | *I think* | 3833 |
| 5 | *I suppose* | 3050 |
| 6 | *I mean* | 1972 |
| 7 | *I believe* | 1246 |
| 8 | *I thought* | 1218 |
| 9 | *I hope* | 938 |
| 10 | *I say* | 938 |
| | Total | 35,939 |

Hereby RE 6.3 is written to retrieve the paratactic clause complexes with the same pronoun and projecting verbs identified by RE 6.2. RE 6.3 can be described as any period followed by the personal pronoun *I* or *you,* and any one of the projecting verbs (i.e., *know, guess, think, suppose, believe, mean, hope* and *say*). The total frequency of constructions retrieved using RE 6.2, subtracted that retrieved using RE 6.3, yielded the frequency of the most frequent textual projections at the clause-initial position.

As shown in Table 6.8, *you know* is the most frequent textual projection in the clause-initial position. *I mean* is the most frequent *I*-projection in the clause-initial position, which is different from the most frequent *I*- projection in the clause-final position.

In order to retrieve textual projections in the clause-medial position, the following search queries were written:

**Table 6.8** Top 10 most frequent textual projections in clause-initial position

| | Construction | Frequency |
|---|---|---|
| 1 | *You know* | 16,731 |
| 2 | *I mean* | 13,296 |
| 3 | *I know* | 2329 |
| 4 | *I say* | 899 |
| 5 | *You mean* | 677 |
| 6 | *I think* | 615 |
| 7 | *I believe* | 266 |
| 8 | *I suppose* | 223 |
| 9 | *I hope* | 227 |
| 10 | *You say* | 66 |
| Total | | 35,329 |

RE 6.4 ,I|you know|guess|think|suppose|believe|mean|hope|say,
RE 6.5 ",I|you know|guess|think|suppose|believe|mean|hope|say,
RE 6.6 ,I|you know|guess|think|suppose|believe|mean|hope|say,"

RE 6.4 can be described as a comma followed by the personal pronoun *I* or *you*, and any one of the projecting verbs (i.e., *know, guess, think, suppose, believe, mean, hope* and *say*). For example:

6.9 But that money, I think, had better be expended for powder and ball. (COHA_1859)

However, some constructions could involve paratactic projections (e.g., *"The witness will be better heard by the jury where he is, I think," replied Mr. Fay.*) To avoid retrieving data overlapping paratactic projections, RE5 and RE6 are written to retrieve constructions containing the personal pronoun *I* or *you* and any of the projecting verbs (i.e., *know, guess, think, suppose, believe, mean, hope* and *say*) that succeeds or precedes a double quotation mark correspondingly. The frequencies of constructions retrieved using RE 6.4, subtracted those retrieved using RE 6.5 and RE 6.6, yielded the frequencies of the most frequent textual projections in the clause-initial position. The top 10 textual projections are presented in Table.

As shown in Table 6.9, *you know* is the most frequent textual projection in the clause-medial position. The most frequent clause-medial *I*-projection is *I think*, which is different from that in the clause-final and clause-initial positions.

When textual projections of different syntactic positions are taken into consideration, the most frequent textual projections are presented in Table 6.10.

According to Table 6.10, the most frequent textual projection in general is a *you*-projection *you know. You know* can appear in any position. However, very few other *you*-projections rank among the most frequent textual projections. *I*-projections exhibit more variations in realizing textual projection, and their preferred positions also vary. *I mean* is the most frequent among all *I*- textual projections and it prefers to

**Table 6.9** Top 10 most frequent textual projections in clause-medial position

| | Construction | Frequency |
|---|---|---|
| 1 | *You know* | 14,164 |
| 2 | *I think* | 6612 |
| 3 | *I believe* | 3573 |
| 4 | *I suppose* | 3227 |
| 5 | *I know* | 2687 |
| 6 | *I mean* | 2554 |
| 7 | *I say* | 1881 |
| 8 | *I guess* | 1297 |
| 9 | *I hope* | 960 |
| 10 | *You say* | 309 |
| Total | | 37,264 |

appear in the clause-initial position. *I think* prefers to occur most in the clause-medial postion while I guess prefer to appear in the clause-final position.

Textual projections realized by personal pronouns with mental verbs account for 96% of the total textual projections retrieved. Mental verbs are more likely to show language users' attitudes and viewpoints, and hereby they are more likely to undergo subjectification and intersubjectification. The loose relationship between the mental clauses and the projected clauses may contribute to the parenthetical nature of the mental clauses, resulting in the formation of textual projections.

Of the 10 most frequent textual projections, some can construe modality. These constructions may result from the grammaticalization of interpersonal projections. Those that do not construe modality may result from the grammaticalization of corresponding ideational projections. See the categorization of the main textual projections in Table 6.11.

As shown in Table 6.11, more textual projections result from the grammaticalization of interpersonal projections. Those grammaticalized from ideational projections are common makers of fact, such as *you know*. In the following analysis, their diachronic distribution trends will be further compared.

**Table 6.10** Top 10 most frequent textual projections in different syntactic positions

| | Construction | Initial | Medial | Final | Total |
|---|---|---|---|---|---|
| 1 | *You know* | 16,731 | 14,164 | 13,543 | 44,438 |
| 2 | *I mean* | 13,296 | 2554 | 1972 | 17,822 |
| 3 | *I think* | 615 | 6612 | 3833 | 11,060 |
| 4 | *I know* | 2329 | 2687 | 4572 | 9588 |
| 5 | *I suppose* | 223 | 3227 | 3050 | 6500 |
| 6 | *I guess* | 111 | 1297 | 4629 | 6037 |
| 7 | *I believe* | 266 | 3573 | 1246 | 5085 |
| 8 | *I say* | 899 | 1881 | 938 | 3718 |
| 9 | *I hope* | 227 | 960 | 938 | 2125 |
| 10 | *You say* | 66 | 309 | 143 | 518 |
| Total | | 34,763 | 37,264 | 34,864 | 106,891 |

**Table 6.11** Categorization of textual projections

| Source of grammaticalization | Textual projection |
|---|---|
| Interpersonal projection | *I think, I believe, I suppose, I guess, I hope* |
| Ideational projection | *You know, I know, I mean* |

### 6.3.2 Diachronic Distribution of Textual Projections in Different Syntactic Positions

The occupation of textual projections in different syntactic positions is interpreted as different stages in diachronic evolution (Thompson & Mulac 1991). The clause-initial position is regarded as the original position in which textual projections emerge. The clause-medial and clause-final positions are regarded as positions in which textual projections occupy later in their evolution, indicating their positional flexibility and parenthetical nature. In this section, the diachronic distributions of typical textual projections in the three syntactic positions will be compared. It is hypothesized that some clause-initial textual projections gradually move to clause-medial and clause-final positions, and that the normalized frequencies of textual projections in clause-initial position are negatively correlated with those of textual projections in clause-medial and clause-final positions.

The diachronic distributions of the main textual projections in different positions were retrieved from the COHA. See Table 6.12.

**Table 6.12** Frequencies of typical textual projections in initial, medial and final positions

| | Initial | Medial | Final | Total |
|---|---|---|---|---|
| 1820s | 91 | 793 | 149 | 1033 |
| 1830s | 172 | 1291 | 226 | 1689 |
| 1840s | 162 | 1358 | 329 | 1849 |
| 1850s | 202 | 1707 | 549 | 2458 |
| 1860s | 253 | 1714 | 895 | 2862 |
| 1870s | 251 | 2395 | 1223 | 3869 |
| 1880s | 282 | 2035 | 1109 | 3426 |
| 1890s | 235 | 1859 | 962 | 3056 |
| 1900s | 219 | 1854 | 1244 | 3317 |
| 1910s | 293 | 2106 | 1906 | 4305 |
| 1920s | 273 | 1863 | 1558 | 3694 |
| 1930s | 1884 | 2064 | 2449 | 6397 |
| 1940s | 1579 | 1634 | 2596 | 5809 |
| 1950s | 2442 | 2137 | 2966 | 7545 |
| 1960s | 3095 | 2297 | 3473 | 8865 |
| 1970s | 4545 | 2975 | 3188 | 10,708 |
| 1980s | 4393 | 2225 | 2765 | 9383 |
| 1990s | 4825 | 2886 | 2764 | 10,475 |
| 2000s | 5337 | 3344 | 2599 | 11,280 |
| 2010s | 5423 | 3396 | 2555 | 11,374 |
| Total | 35,956 | 41,933 | 35,505 | 113,394 |

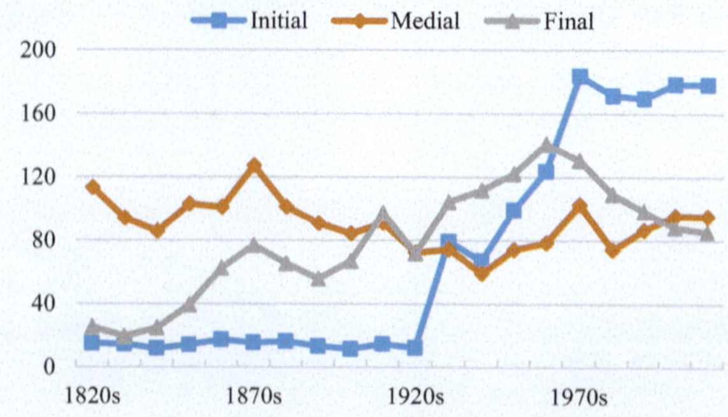


**Fig. 6.18** Diachronic distributions of textual projections in different positions

Their raw frequencies were converted to the normalized frequencies per million words. To facilitate comparison, the total normalized frequencies of clause-initial (88.78) and clause-final (87.67) textual projections were converted to that of clause-medial (103.54) ones. Their diachronic distribution trends are presented in Fig. 6.18.

According to Fig. 6.18, clause-medial textual projections dominate in the 1820s while clause-initial textual projections dominate in the 2010s. Over the past 20 decades, clause-medial textual projections have a slight decrease. Clause-initial textual projections, being the least prevalent in the 1920s, see a sharp increase from the 1920s to the 1970s and have been the most prevalent since the 1960s. Clause-final textual projections increase from the 1820s to the 1960s but have followed a downward trend since then. These diachronic distribution trends indicate that the syntactic positions of textual projections may not initially emerge from the clause-initial position. Besides, appearing in the clause-medial position cannot be directly interpreted as an indicator of the construction's gaining flexibility in position.

The diachronic distribution of clause-initial textual projections is significantly positively correlated with that of clause-final ones ($p = 0.672$, $r = 0.001 < 0.05$). Clause-medial textual projections are negatively but not significantly correlated with clause-initial ($p = -0.199$, $r = 0.399 > 0.05$) or clause-final ($p = -0.425$, $r = 0.061 > 0.05$) textual projections. This indicates that the increasing clause-initial and clause-final textual projections may be compensated by some clause-medial textual projections.

The total normalized frequency of textual projections (279.99) was added up to compare with two other typical lexical discourse makers *in fact* (67.06) and *well* (282.02) to see whether they share the same diachronic distribution trend. Their overall normalized frequencies were converted to that of textual projections (279.99). Their diachronic distributions are shown in Fig. 6.19.

As shown in Fig. 6.19, textual projections and the two discourse markers demonstrate similar diachronic distribution trends, particularly between *in fact* and textual projection. They both fluctuate from the 1820s to the 1920s, increase from the 1920s to the 1970s, and then decrease and stabilize thereafter. The normalized frequency of textual projections is significantly correlated with that of *in fact* ($p = 0.883$; $r = 0.000 < 0.01$) and that of *well* ($p = 0.863$; $r = 0.000 < 0.01$). This indicates that the

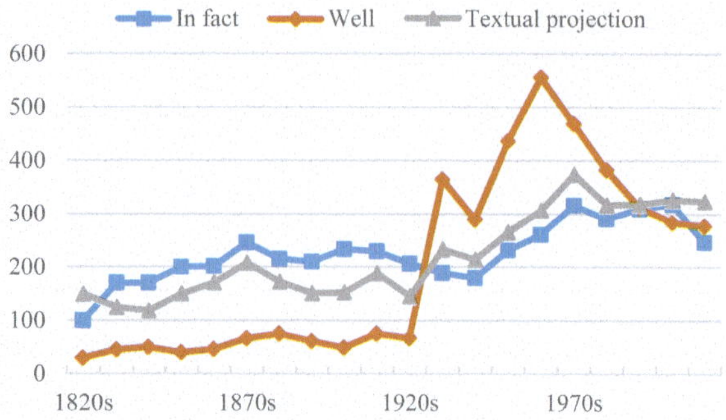


**Fig. 6.19** Diachronic distributions of textual projections, *in fact* and *well*

textual projections retrieved are fully grammaticalized as discourse markers sometime before the 1920s and their diachronic distributions over the past 20 decades do not demonstrate the gradual formation, but rather the diachronic development as well-accepted discourse markers.

The diachronic distributions of some frequently used textual projections in initial, medial and final positions were retrieved. The diachronic distributions of the two discourse markers *well* and *perhaps* are also retrieved to help observe the properties of different categories. See their raw frequencies in Appendix F. Then the SPSS hierarchical cluster analysis is employed, based on the correlation of their diachronic distributions, to identify their categorization. See Fig. 6.20.

According to Fig. 6.20, textual projections can be divided into two types. The first type includes *I think*, *I believe*, *I suppose*, *I guess*, and *I hope*. The second type includes *you mean*, *I mean*, *you know*, and *I know*.

The first type of textual projections is realized by projecting clauses involving modal meanings, such as *I think*, *I believe*, *I suppose*, *I guess* and *I hope*. These constructions are typical interpersonal projections to realize explicit subjective modality. This type of textual projections hereby may be transferred from their corresponding interpersonal projections. The normalized frequencies of these textual projections in different positions were calculated. The overall normalized frequency of textual projections in the clause-initial position (3.12) and that in the clause-final position (30.97) were converted to that in the clause-medial position (34.62). See their diachronic distribution trends in Fig. 6.21.

As shown in Fig. 6.21, the textual projections grammaticalized from interpersonal projections in clause-initial and clause-medial positions show similar trends over the past 20 decades. Both maintain a general trend of decrease and they are significantly positively correlated ($p = 0.825$; $r = 0.000 < 0.01$). In contrast, those in the clause-final position demonstrate an opposite trend of general increase. The diachronic distribution of clause-final ones is negatively correlated with the clause-initial ones ($p = -0.652$; $r = 0.002 < 0.01$) and clause-medial ones ($p = -0.491$; $r = 0.028 < 0.05$). Therefore, over the past 20 decades, textual projections grammaticalized from interpersonal projections have gradually decreased in the clause-initial and clause-medial positions while increasing in the clause-final position. The

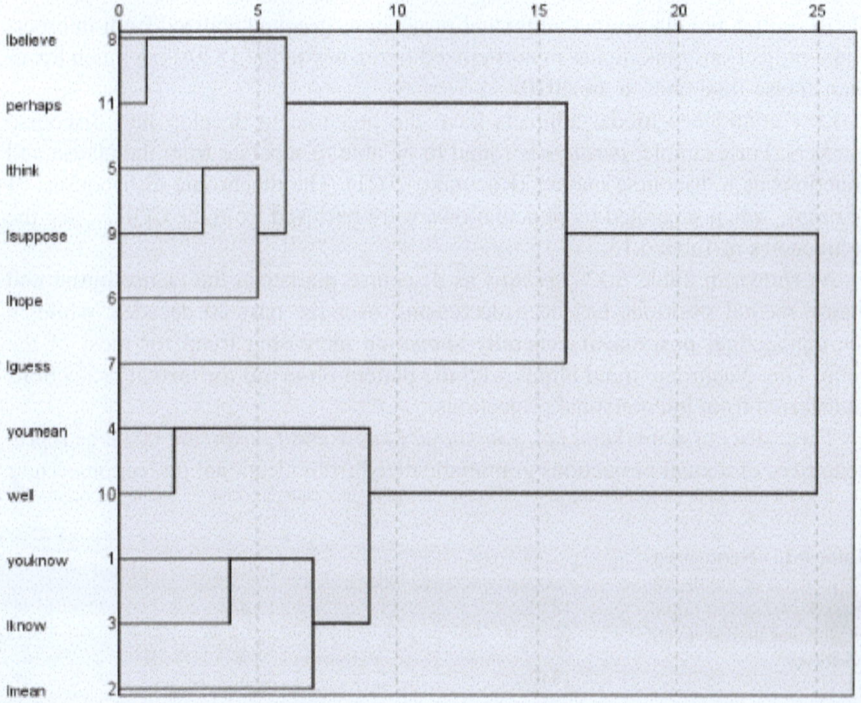


**Fig. 6.20** Hierarchical cluster of typical textual projections and discourse markers

**Fig. 6.21** Diachronic distribution trends of textual projections grammaticalized from interpersonal projection

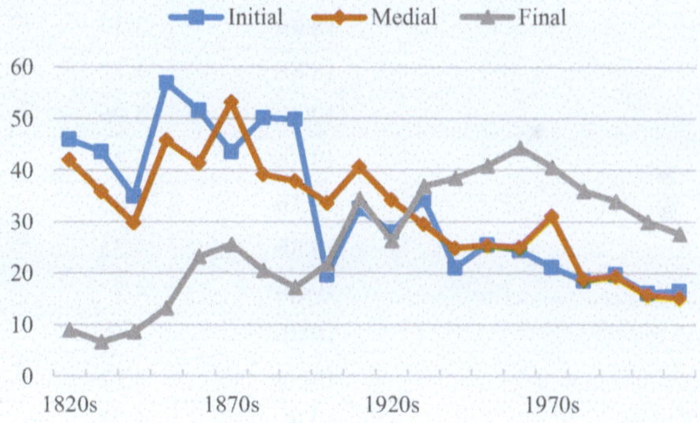


decrease in clause-initial and clause-medial positions is compensated by the increase in clause-final position. This trend may be due to the preference of textual projections to occur in spoken texts. In oral speech, there is no punctuation to formally indicate the parenthetical nature of a construction. Projecting clauses in the clause-initial and clause-medial positions may be interpreted as ideational, interpersonal or textual projeciton. The cognitive burden on the addressee is quite heavy. Occurring in the clause-final position is less likely to lead to misunderstanding. Hereby, clause-initial and clause-medial textual projecitons grammaticalized from interpersonal projections rank higher in normalized frequency in the 1820s, but much lower than clause-final ones in the 2010s.

Low confidence modal adjuncts have the potential to develop into discourse markers. For example, *perhaps* is found to be able to separate from the clause and functions as a discourse marker (Rozumko 2021). The diachronic distributions of *perhaps,* when separated by punctuations, were retrieved from the COHA. See the frequencies in Table 6.13.

As shown in Table 6.13, *perhaps* as discourse marker in the clause-initial and clause-medial positions has been decreasing over the past 20 decades, while in the clause-final position, it generally shows an increasing trend for most of the time. This diachronic trend aligns with the pattern observed for textual projections transferred from interpersonal projections.

Three discourse markers, i.e., *you know, I know* and *I mean,* are taken as representatives of textual projections grammaticalized from ideational projections. Their

**Table 6.13** Normalized frequencies of the discourse marker *perhaps* in initial, medial and final syntactic positions

| | Initial | Medial | Final |
|---|---|---|---|
| 1820s | 9.45 | 113.44 | 1.72 |
| 1830s | 5.18 | 95.18 | 1.6 |
| 1840s | 5.12 | 84.58 | 1.9 |
| 1850s | 6.47 | 90.89 | 2.54 |
| 1860s | 5.43 | 77.11 | 4.9 |
| 1870s | 4.58 | 69.03 | 3.46 |
| 1880s | 3.49 | 58.35 | 3.49 |
| 1890s | 3.72 | 51.79 | 3.43 |
| 1900s | 4.96 | 48.5 | 3.23 |
| 1910s | 5.45 | 43.37 | 5.76 |
| 1920s | 4.86 | 34.82 | 4.01 |
| 1930s | 4.33 | 27.03 | 4.94 |
| 1940s | 4.2 | 20.04 | 5.11 |
| 1950s | 3.66 | 19.47 | 4.85 |
| 1960s | 4.12 | 16.93 | 4.64 |
| 1970s | 3.23 | 17.38 | 4.61 |
| 1980s | 3.08 | 15.91 | 3.45 |
| 1990s | 2.14 | 11.95 | 3.83 |
| 2000s | 1.9 | 10.77 | 2.3 |
| 2010s | 1.89 | 9.08 | 2.45 |
| Total | 87.26 | 915.62 | 72.22 |

**Fig. 6.22** Diachronic distributions of textual projections grammaticalized from ideational projection

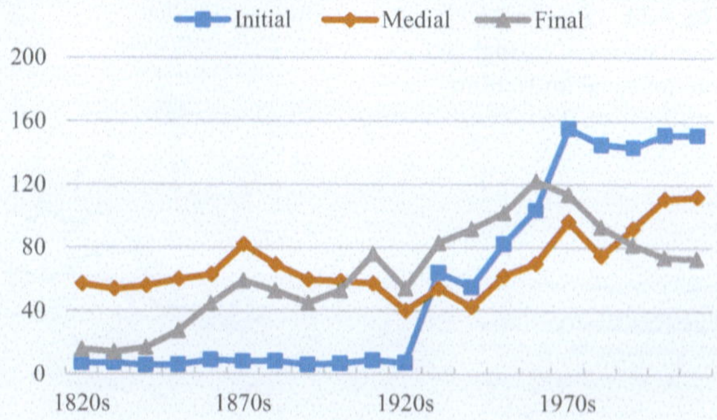


normalized frequencies in the clause-medial (59.15) and the clause-final (53.47) positions were converted to that in the clause-initial (84.78) position. Their diachronic distribution trends are shown in Fig. 6.22.

Figure 6.22 shows that the second type of textual projections in clause-initial, clause-medial and clause-final positions all fluctuate from the 1820s to the 1920s and increase from the 1920s to approximately the 1970s. Since the 1970s, clause-final ones have been decreasing, clause-medial ones have been increasing, and clause-initial ones have maintained a relatively stable level. Among the textual projecitons in the three positions, clause-initial ones have the fast gains, rising from the lowest in the 1820s to the highest in the 2010s. Generally speaking, the diachronic distribution trends of the textual projections grammaticalized from ideational projections in different positions show a similar trend. The bivariate correlation test shows that the normalized frequency of clause-initial ones is significantly negatively correlated with those of clause-medial ($p = 0.757$; $r = 0.000 < 0.01$) and clause-final ones ($p = 0.715$; $r = 0.000 < 0.01$). This indicates that textual projections, e.g., *you know*, *I know*, increase in all the three positions and are increasingly preferred in the clause-initial position. This is different from the diachronic development of textual projections grammaticalized from interpersonal projections which increasingly tend to occur in the clause-final position.

### *6.3.3 Diachronic Distribution of Textual Projections Grammaticalized from Interpersonal Projection*

In this section, the diachronic development of textual projections grammaticalized from interpersonal projections will be explored.

The matrix clause hypothesis (Thompson & Mulac 1991) holds that constructions such as *I think* and *I see* are originally the matrix clauses followed by the *that* complementizer introducing complement clauses. Later the *that-* deletion leads to

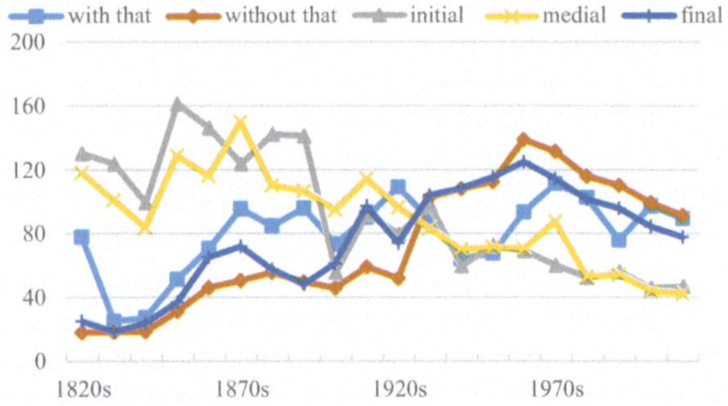


**Fig. 6.23** Diachronic distributions of textual and interpersonal projections

structural indeterminacy. Ultimately, the constructions gradually become parenthetical units and are able to appear in different positions in the clause. It is hereby hypothesized that clause-initial textual projections are negatively correlated with corresponding hypotactic clause complexes without *that* complementizer. The normalized frequencies of hypotactic clause complexes with *that* (5.39) and without *that* (97.9) were worked out and then those of clause-initial, clause-medial and clause-final textual projections and hypotactic clause complexes with *that* were converted to that of hypotactic clause complexes without *that* (97.9). See Fig. 6.23.

According to Fig. 6.23, hypotactic clause complexes with and without *that* complementizer and clause-final textual projections show similar diachronic distribution trends and their distribution trends are opposite to the corresponding clause-initial and clause-medial textual projections. The bivariate correlation test shows that the normalized frequency of clause-initial textual projections is significantly negatively correlated with that of hypotactic clause complexes without *that* ($p = -0.705$; $r = 0.001 < 0.01$) and is not significantly but negatively correlated with that of hypotactic clause complexes with *that* ($p = -0.334$; $r = 0.15 > 0.05$). The normalized frequencies of clause-medial textual projections and hypotactic clause complexes without *that* are also significantly negatively correlated ($p = -0.676$; $r = 0.001 < 0.01$), and are not significantly but negatively correlated with hypotactic clause complexes with *that* ($p = -0.135$; $r = 0.570 > 0.05$). This shows that clause-initial and clause-medial textual projections are complementary with corresponding hypotactic clause complexes without *that*.

### *6.3.4 Diachronic Distribution of Textual Projections Grammaticalized from Ideational Projection*

The normalized frequencies of the corresponding hypotactic projections with *that* complementizer (10.74) and without *that* complementizer (40.12) were calculated. Then the above normalized frequencies and those of textual projections were converted to that of the clause-initial textual projections (84.78) to compare their diachronic distribution trends. See Fig. 6.24.

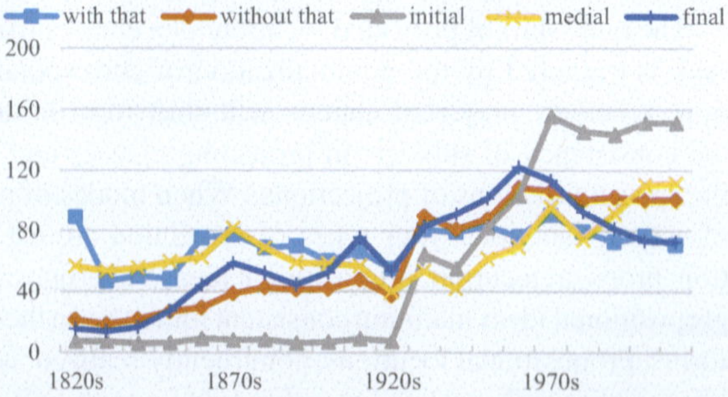


**Fig. 6.24** Diachronic distributions of textual and ideational projections

Figure 6.24 shows that all five diachronic distribution trends manifest similarity, particularly in the period between the 1830s and the 1970s. The normalized frequency of hypotactic clause complexes without *that* is significantly positively correlated with clause-initial ($p = 0.929$; $r = 0.000 < 0.01$), clause-medial ($p = 0.588$; $r = 0.006 < 0.01$) and clause-final ($p = 0.894$; $r = 0.000 < 0.01$) textual projections. This means that the emergence of textual projections like *you know* and *I know* in all the positions do not lead to the decrease in the the number of corresponding projecting clauses in hypotactic clause complexes of projection.

## 6.4 Summary

This chapter conducts a COHA-based quantitative research on the diachronic distributions of projections.

The overall diachronic distributions of ideational, interpersonal and textual projections show similar increasing trends and are significantly positively correlated with each other. Embedding projections, on the other hand, show an opposite diachronic distribution trend to ideational projections, interpersonal projection and textual projection. In the transfer of projection from the ideational domain to the interpersonal domain, and from the interpersonal domain to the textual domain, the relations arising in the new domain coexist with those in the original domain and they do not form the system of choice. Within the ideational domain, clause simplexes with embedding projections and clause complexes of projection are complementary.

The diachronic distribution analysis of paratactic hypotactic and embedding projections of locutions /ideas shows that paratactic projections and hypotactic projections are positively correlated, and both of them are negatively correlated with embedding projections. Therefore, the congruent realization and the metaphorical realization of locution/idea projections form a system of choice. A further comparison between the diachronic distributions of embedding locutions/ideas with and without projector shows that their diachronic distribution trends are similar. Thus, they are of the same group of data and do not form a system of choice.

The rank-shift of projected locution/idea clauses from the clause rank to the word rank is triggered by the nominalization of corresponding verbal groups of projection. Whether projected clauses will shift from finite to non-finite is affected by the consistency of subjects in projecting clauses and projected clauses, as well as the speech functions of projections. When modes of projection intersect with types of speech functions, four types of projection are categorized: propositional locution, proposal locution, propositional idea, and proposal idea. Proposal locutions and propositional ideas maintain consistent finiteness in their congruent and metaphorical forms. Propositional locutions, congruently realized as finite dependent clauses, can be metaphorically realized as either finite or non-finite embedded clauses. Proposal ideas can be congruently realized as either finite or non-finite dependent clauses, the former remaining finite while the latter becoming finite after undergoing rank-shift.

The diachronic distribution analysis shows that the finite and non-finite embedding locutions/ideas are not complementarily distributed. Therefore, finite and non-finite embedding locutions and ideas do not form a system of choice. The finite and non-finite embedding facts as appositives of fact nouns, i.e., chance, need, proof and case, are complementary and the corresponding finite and non-finite embedding fact clauses form a system of choice. Finite and non-finite embedding facts as heads do not form a system of choice because they are affected by the subjectification of the relational process matrix clauses.

The diachronic distributions of textual projections indicate that the typical textual projections retrieved may have been fully grammaticalized before the 1820s. Their distribution trends are similar to those of other typical non-clausal discourse markers, such as *well* and *in fact*. Two types of textual projections is identified. The first type of textual projections is grammaticalized from interpersonal projections and it tends to transfer from the clause-initial and clause-medial positions to the clause-final position. The second type of textual projections is not grammaticalized from interpersonal projections, and its frequencies in clause-initial, clause-medial and clause-final positions all increase over the past 20 decades, with the frequency in the clause-initial position increasing the fastest. The evolution of textual projections is further analyzed by comparing the diachronic distributions of textual projections and the corresponding interpersonal projections or ideational projections. For textual projections grammaticalized from interpersonal projections, the clause-initial and clause-medial textual projections are complementary with the corresponding hypotactic clause complexes without *that* complementizer. For textual projections not grammaticalized from interpersonal projections, their distributions do not complement with corresponding clause complexes without *that* complementizer. Textual projections of this type, in all positions, show similar diachronic distribution trends to the corresponding hypotactic clause complexes of projection without *that* complementizer.

## References


Halliday MAK, Matthiessen CMIM (1999) Construing experience through meaning: A language-based approach to cognition. Cassell, London/New York

Mithun M (2016) Shifting finiteness in nominalization: From definitization to refinitization. In: Chamoreau C, Estrada-Fernández Z (eds) Finiteness and nominalization. John Benjamins, Amsterdam, pp 297–322

Rozumko A (2021) Textual functions of low confidence adverbs: The case of perhaps. Lingua 268:1–11

Thompson SA, Mulac AA (1991) Quantitative perspective on the grammaticization of epistemic parentheticals in English. Approaches to Grammaticalization 2:313–32

# Chapter 7
# Discussion

In Chap. 5, a COCA-based quantitative research has been conducted to explore the synchronic distributions of projections. In Chap. 6, a COHA-based quantitative research has been conducted to explore the diachronic distributions of projections. This chapter will discuss the research findings.

## 7.1 Projection and Text Technicality

### *7.1.1 Text Technicality of Projection*

The COCA-based study of the synchronic distributions of ideational, interpersonal, and textual projection *I THINK* finds that all the three functions prefer to occur in spoken texts with regard to mode distribution, in non-academic texts with regard to genre distribution and in soft science texts with regard to discipline distribution. Among the three types of projections, textual projections are the most prevalent in spoken texts, followed by interpersonal projections and ideational projections. The transfer from ideational projection to interpersonal projection is cross-metafunctional transcategorization. Ideational projection primarily functions to construe the projection process while interpersonal projection primarily functions to construe explicit subjective modality. The transfer embodies the process that "an objective relationship fades away, leaving behind a subjective relationship that was originally immanent in it" (Langacker 1998: 75–76). Interpersonal projection corresponds to what Biber et al. (1999) identify as stance markers and what Quirk et al. (1985) identify as style and content disjuncts. It can be a source to express the speaker's view on the given proposition and hence can contribute to interactive conversational texts. The higher frequency in spoken texts is consistent with Biber et al.'s (1999) in that conversation has the highest frequency of the most common stance adverbial and



M. Guo and Q. He, *A Corpus-Based Study of Projection in English from the Systemic Functional Perspective*, The M.A.K. Halliday Library Functional Linguistics Series,
https://doi.org/10.1007/978-981-97-5094-8_7

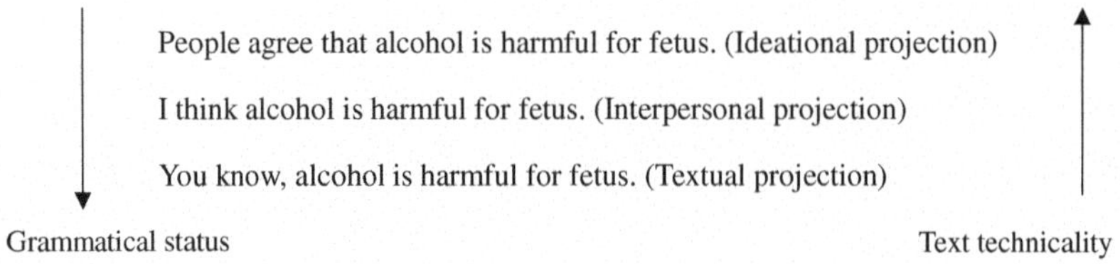


**Fig. 7.1** Projecting clause and text technicality

He's (2021) finding that explicit subjective modality tend to occur in non-technical language. Spoken language allows more personal involvement, and hereby interpersonal projections that explicitly realize modal assessment are more suitable in spoken texts instead of written texts. Textual projections do not construe verbal or mental processes nor realize modality. Textual projections do not integrate into the proposition in information exchange. Halliday and Hasan (1976) and Martin (1992) regard such constructions as internal conjunctions. Conjunctive adverbs function as cohesive ties at the textual domain, and hence textual projections are the results of the grammaticalization of the open-set category to the closed-set category. They are more prevalent in spoken texts because they function as "reaction signal and initiator" (Quirk et al. 1985: 444). Written texts prefer conjunctions that mainly indicate grammatical relations between language units (e.g., subordination and coordination) and logico-argumentative meanings (e.g., exemplification, definition, addition).

The text technicality of ideational, interpersonal, and textual projections can be demonstrated in Fig. 7.1.

In summary, projecting clauses with more referential meanings are more technical. It is subjectification and grammaticalization that weaken the technicality of the corresponding projecting clauses. Subjectification imbues the clause with interpersonal meaning. Grammaticalization further weaken the original referential meaning and transforms the construction into a dispensable parenthetical marker outside the main proposition.

### 7.1.2 *Text Technicality of Projected Clauses*

The grammatical status of projected clauses belongs to the clause rank in hypotactic clause complexes of projection or the group rank in clause simplexes of embedding projection. They manifest mode and genre sensitivity but not discipline sensitivity. The former are found to be more prevalent in non-technical texts. See Fig. 7.2.

Clause complexes are higher in grammatical intricacy and hereby are more prevalent in spoken texts with regard to mode distribution and in non-academic texts with regard to genre distribution because spoken texts are "more complex in terms of grammatical intricacy" (Halliday & Matthiessen 2004: 655). Projected clauses functioning at the group rank can be viewed as nominalizations serving as participants in verbal or mental process clauses. Nominalization leads to higher lexical density

He said that John was a teacher. (Hypotacitc locution/ idea: clause)

I thought that Brandon Ross had a good day. (Hypotactic locution/ idea: clause)

I believe that John is a teacher. (Hypotactic locution/idea: clause)

I believe (the fact) that John is a teacher. (embedded fact: group)

I admit (the fact) that John is a teacher. (embedded fact: group)

Grammatical status ↓ Text technicality ↓

**Fig. 7.2** Projected clause and text technicality

and tends to be more prevalent in written texts with regard to mode distribution and in academic texts with regard to genre distribution because written texts are "more complex in terms of lexical density" (Halliday & Matthiessen 2004: 655). Both the hypotactic clause complexes of projection and clause simplexes of embedding projection tend to occur more in soft science texts with regard to discipline distribution. The reason is that soft science texts integrate more voices (Charles 2007). Projecting clauses in hypotactic clause complexes of projection can indicate the source of quotation so the writer can give credit to other researchers and use their work in the cumulative construction of knowledge (Charles 2006). A lot of clause simplexes with embedded facts contain emotive mental verbs such as *worry*, *fear*, and *rejoice*, which do not fit into the objectiveness of hard science texts.

### *7.1.3 Text Technicality of Embedding Projection*

According to Halliday and Matthiessen (1999, 2004), the rank-shift of projected clauses is triggered by the nominalization of projecting verbs or the nominalization of zero. Therefore, embedding projection is a metaphorical realization of what is congruently realized as clause complex of projection. Nominalization is the most powerful source for creating ideational metaphor (Halliday & Matthiessen 1999). The synchronic analysis of embedding projections at different levels shows that embedding projections of locution, idea, and fact manifest genre and discipline sensitivity. They are more prevalent in academic texts than in fiction texts with regard to genre distribution. The reason is that embedded clauses of projection can enhance the complexity of nominal groups and increase the lexical density of texts. This is consistent with the features of academic writing. Another reason is that using a head noun instead of a projecting clause to indicate the source of the projected proposition can avoid presenting the personal projector and this can contribute to the objectiveness of academic texts. Embedding facts are found to be the most prevalent in academic texts, followed by locutions and ideas. The reason may be that locutions and ideas can be construed by clause complexes of projection while facts can only be construed as already packaged information in nominal groups. Embedding locutions, ideas and facts all occur more in soft science texts. Embedding locutions and ideas are more prevalent in soft science texts than facts, while embedding facts are the most prevalent in hard science texts. The reason is that soft science texts, on the whole, involve more personal views than hard science texts. The construction of knowledge in soft science texts relies more on the examination of others' views and integration of different arguments, while that in hard science texts relies more on experimental evidence (Charles 2007; Becher & Trowler 2001). Embedding locutions and ideas can be used as effective devices to represent arguments, thus they dominate in soft science texts. Embedding facts construe the meaning of higher semantic abstraction in a more impersonal way, hence they dominate in hard science texts.

The synchronic distribution analysis of the embedding projections with different degrees of projection shows that they manifest both genre and discipline sensitivity. The embedding projection with a lower degree of projection and higher degree of metaphorization are more prevalent in academic texts with regard to genre distribution and in hard science texts with regard to discipline distribution, except for modal facts. The relationship between the degree of projection in embedding projection and text technicality can be demonstrated in Fig. 7.3.

As shown in Fig. 7.3, a lower degree of projection means lower visibility of the projector. Embedding fact projections demonstrate the lowest degree of projection because facts are not created by projectors and they seem to be ready-made meanings from nowhere. This can contribute to the higher abstraction and objectification of texts (Halliday & Matthiessen 1999). Facts modifying modalized fact nouns are more technical than those modifying non-modalized fact nouns. One reason is that modalized fact nouns are semantically richer than non-modalized fact nouns. This fits into the higher semantic richness of academic texts. Another reason is that modalized fact nouns can construe modality in an objective way without showing the person making the evaluation. This fits into the objectiveness of academic texts.

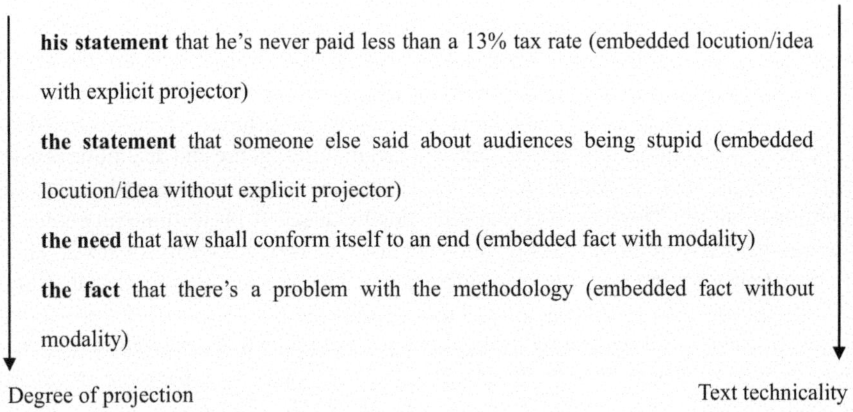


**Fig. 7.3** Embedding projection and text technicality

It is found that finiteness can contribute to the mode sensitivity of embedding projection, but it does not significantly affect the genre and discipline distributions. There are two reasons that can account for the prevalence of non-finite embedded clauses in written texts. One is that non-finite embedded clauses can contribute to the conciseness of language. The other is that the absence of a finite element in a non-finite clause makes it less likely to be challenged, and this can contribute to the objectiveness of language. The mode and genre distributions of the embedded cases as heads manifest opposite preference in finiteness with other embedded projections. Finite cases as head are more prevalent in written texts with regard to mode distribution and in academic texts with regard to genre distribution. The reason is that finite cases as head tend to occur in clauses of relational process, mental process and existential process. Such matrix clauses as *it seems*, *it is said that* and *it is possible that* involve explicit objective modality. The effect is that the matrix clauses realize the modality and the finite case as head realizes the modalized proposition. Non-finite cases as head are more likely to occur in clauses of relational process that construe attitudinal evaluation instead of modal evaluation and hence the distribution is not affected by explicit objective modality.

The findings on the text technicality of projection have significant pedagogical implications for developing EFL learners' awareness of mode, genre, and discipline variations in projection use, and for enhancing their capability to apply suitable projection resources in specific contexts, particularly in academic settings. For example, in academic writing, embedded projection can contribute to the conciseness of wording by concealing the projector. Therefore, students can be instructed to integrate projected clauses into nominal groups when citing information from different sources. Additionally, students should be guided to apply non-finite embedded projected clauses to increase the text technicality in academic writing.

The synchronic findings also offer a new perspective on viewing projections with different grammatical statuses. This contributes to a deeper understanding of the nature of projecting clauses in their roles as modal adjuncts and conjunctive adjuncts. When serving as modal adjuncts, projecting clauses are more subjective than conventional modal adverbs and are less technical. When serving as conjunctive adjuncts, projecting clauses do not indicate logical relationships but rather function as attention gainers or turn initiators, and they are hereby colloquial, interactive, and dialogic. The delicate classification enriches the literature on projection in SFL.

The findings of the study on the synchronic distributions of projection also shed light on the study of grammatical metaphor in SFL. Projection nouns of locution and idea are nominalizations of projecting verbs, and nominalization creates grammatical metaphor (Halliday & Matthiessen 2004). The observed variations in the use of embedding projections contribute to the growing body of evidence of how grammatical metaphor relates to text technicality. Embedding projections, as ideational metaphor, are more technical, and the degree of metaphorization generally increases the corresponding text technicality. The findings on the use variation of three types of projection also provides insights into the study of interpersonal and textual grammatical metaphors. Interpersonal projections, as interpersonal metaphor, realize explicit subjective modal assessment and hence are not preferred in technical texts. Textual projections, as textual metaphor, are not favored in technical texts either.

Moreover, the findings of the study on the distribution of embedded facts as heads serving as extraposed subjects indicate that the interaction of ideational metaphor and interpersonal metaphor plays a role in determining the text technicality of corresponding lexico-grammatical forms. Such indications raise an intriguing question of how interpersonal metaphor interacts with ideational metaphor in achieving text technicality.

## 7.2 Evolution Patterns of Projection

### *7.2.1 Overall Evolution Patterns of Projection*

The overall diachronic distribution analysis of ideational, interpersonal, and textual projections shows that all the three types of projections increase over the past 20 decades. Their diachronic frequencies are significantly and positively correlated. They do not form a system of choice. This means that the emergence of interpersonal projections does not lead to a decrease of corresponding ideational projections, and the emergence of textual projections does not lead to the decrease of corresponding ideational or interpersonal projections. Grammaticalization features divergence (Hopper 1991), i.e., the original lexical meaning of the construction continues to exist. Therefore, as the frequency of textual projections increases, those of ideational and interpersonal projections also increase with similar distribution trends. The overall diachronic distributions of congruent and metaphorical ideational projections show that embedding projections, as metaphorical realizations, result from the evolution of ideational projections realized congruently by clause complexes within the ideational domain.

Two directions of language evolution are observed in the diachronic distribution analysis. The first is the metaphorization within the ideational domain through the nominalization of projecting verbs or zero which triggers the rank-shift of projected clauses. The second is the leftward cross-metafunctional transcategorization of projecting clauses. The subjectification of projecting clauses from the ideational domain to the interpersonal domain results in interpersonal projection, and the grammaticalization from the ideational or interpersonal domain to the textual domain results in textual projection. The dynamic evolution dimensions can be illustrated in Fig. 7.4.

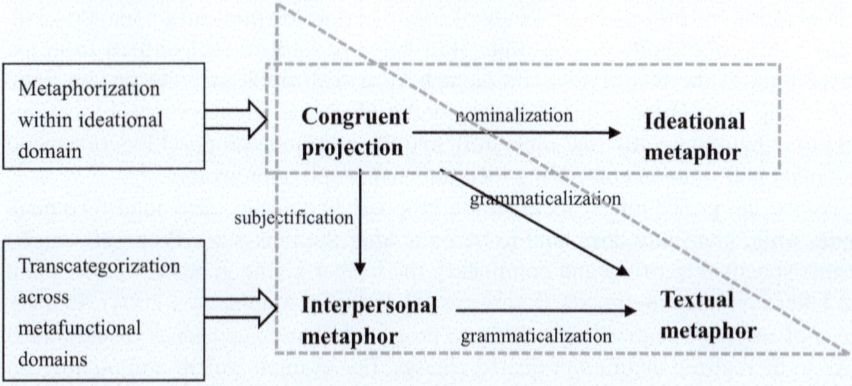


**Fig. 7.4** Evolution dimensions of projection relations

### 7.2.2 *Evolution Pattern of Ideational Projection*

Within the ideational domain, the diachronic distribution of embedding projections demonstrates different trends from those of clause complexes of projection. The negative correlation between embedding projections and clause complexes of projection indicates that they are complementary and form a system of choice. This finding confirms Halliday and Matthiessen's (1999, 2004) idea that embedding projection involves nominalization and is a metaphorical realization of projection.

The diachronic distribution analysis of ideational projections shows that paratactic and hypotactic projections are complementary to embedding projections. Embedding locutions/ideas with explicit projectors are regarded closer to their congruent realizations because the nouns construing projectors in projecting clauses are adjectivized as pre-modifiers of corresponding locution/idea nouns. The diachronic distributions of embedding locutions and ideas show similar trends, both being transferred from clause complexes of projection. Embedding locutions/ideas with projector take place no earlier than those without projector. That is to say, embedding locutions/ideas without projector are not transferred from those with projector.

Does the finiteness of the projected clauses in hypotactic clause complexes of projection shift during the nominalization process? Does the non-finite embedding projection result from the further compression of information from the corresponding finite embedding projection? Propositional locutions and ideas are realized as finite hypotactic clause complexes, while proposal locutions and ideas are realized as either finite or non-finite hypotactic clause complexes. The evolutions of proposition and proposal projections are further examined respectively.

Regarding the projection of locutions, finite hypotactic proposition locutions are likely to be either finite or non-finite after being downward rank-shifted from the clause rank to the word rank. The metaphorical realization as finite or non-finite embedding proposition projections is a matter of choice. Finite proposal locutions tend to remain finite after the rank-shift, and the non-finite proposal locutions tend to remain non-finite in embedding locutions with explicit projectors.

As for the projection of ideas, finite proposal hypotactic ideas tend to remain finite, while non-finite ones tend to be finite after the rank-shift. Proposals can be further specified as offers and commands, the former giving goods-&-services and the latter commanding goods-&-services (Halliday & Matthiessen 2004). Usually ideas of offer are realized as non-finite projected clauses and ideas of command have to be realized as finite projected clauses. For example, *intent* and *incline* can only project ideas of offer and no finite clauses projected by *intent* have been found. The finite proposal hypotactic clauses of idea usually realize ideas of command, and the subject in the finite projected clause is usually different from that of the projecting clause. For example:

7.1 a. I hope that all my poor human beings don't suffer like this! (COHA_1929).
b. I desire that you will eat this leg of a chicken. (COHA_1895).
c. By the way, I have always cherished a hope that she might yet be found. (COHA_1874).
d. And it is our hope that they may find it here. (COHA_1937)

As illustrated in 7.1a and 7.1b, the subjects in the projecting clauses are both *I* and the subjects in the projected clauses are *all my poor human beings* and *you*. The subjects in the projecting and projected clauses are different. When the projected clauses rank-shift from the clause rank to the word rank, only being finite can indicate who is expected to take the command. Finite hypotactic ideas of command cannot be further compressed into non-finite ones because non-finite embedding ideas of proposal will automatically assume the projector of the idea as the subject of the embedding proposal idea. This is why finite hypotactic ideas of proposal are significantly positively correlated with finite embedding ideas of proposal. Non-finite hypotactic clauses of idea may realize proposals of offer or command. For example:

7.2 a. I hope to keep your friendship. (COHA_1901)
b. No, we intend to destroy it for good. (COHA_1970)
c. I wish you to stay here and be Prince Hagen's tutor. (COHA_1912)
d. Frank Frost, I desire you to see that the boys stand at regular distances. (COHA_1864)

7.2a and 7.2b illustrate non-finite proposal hypotactic ideas of offer and 7.2c and 7.2d illustrate non-finite proposal hypotactic ideas of command. In 7.2a and 7.2b, the subjects of the non-finite hypotactic clauses of ideas assume the subjects in the projecting clauses. In 7.2c and 7.2d, the subjects of the non-finite hypotactic ideas are different from the subjects in the projecting clauses. Therefore, after undergoing rank-shift, the non-finite hypotactic clauses realizing the idea of offer can remain non-finite in the embedding ideas and assume the projectors as subjects. However, the non-finite hypotactic clause realizing idea of command has to become finite in order to avoid misunderstanding of the subject of the embedding clause. Therefore, non-finite hypotactic clauses realizing the ideas of proposal are significantly correlated with both finite and non-finite embedding clauses realizing the idea of proposal. The shift from being finite to non-finite is usually believed to mark a downward rank-shift from the clause rank to the group rank (Rose 2016). The nominalization involving proposal idea projection indicates a scenario for the "refinitization" in downward rank-shift (Mithun 2016).

Fact projections are nominalizations of zero and they do not have a congruent form. Finite and non-finite facts as appositives of fact nouns are complementary and form a system of choice. Facts as heads typically enter relational process clauses to function as participants (Halliday & Matthiessen 2004: 472). Most of the facts as head serving as subjects are extraposed to the final position and replaced by a dummy *it* as subject placeholder in the initial position. In the current study, extraposed facts as head were retrieved to represent facts as head. Their diachronic distribution trend is not complementary with that of facts as appositive. The reason is that their diachronic distributions are affected by factors from the interpersonal domain. Some of the *it is ADJ* constructions have undergone subjectification and become modal expressions to construe explicit objective modality, e.g., *it is likely*, *it is true* and *it is necessary*. In such cases, the succeeding clause is not an embedding fact clause but an independent clause attached with a modal adjunct in the initial position. The comparative study is further narrowed down to focus on the finite and non-finite embedding facts as head in relational clauses and it is found that their diachronic distributions over the past 12 decades are complementary.

The findings of the study on the diachronic distribution of ideational projections support the idea that embedded locutions and ideas have undergone the nominalization of projecting verbs. The research on how embedding projections develop in history reveals the process of nominalization of projecting verbs, especially the corresponding syndromes of rank-shift and information compression. The findings contribute to a more delicate depiction of embedding projections.

### 7.2.3 Evolution Pattern of Textual Projection

The diachronic analysis of textual projections identified two major types of projecting clauses that tend to develop into textual projections. One contains the subject *I* and a cognitive mental verb that can project personal idea. Such constructions are suitable for subjectification that semanticizes meaning that expresses the speaker's attitude and viewpoint (Taverniers 2008). Subjectification results in a loose connection between the projecting clause and the given proposition clause. Other subjectivized constructions are also found to shift to peripheral positions such as *actually* in a clause (Traugott & Dasher 2002) or *lovely* in a nominal group (Adamson 2000). Getting loosely connected with the succeeding proposition prepares the construction to be further grammaticalized into textual projections.

The second type of textual projection does not involve interpersonal meaning. It can be further specified as constructions grammaticalized from verbal process clauses and mental clauses. Constructions grammaticalized from projecting clauses contain subjects *I* or *you* and projecting verbs without low-value/confidence lexical meaning, such as *mean*. The lexical meaning of such projecting clauses, e.g., *I mean*, manifests high confidence. They belong to what Hudson (1972) defines as factive clauses that assumes the succeeding proposition as well-accepted information. This type of textual projection serves as what Brinton (2008) describes as a neutral marker that does not involve truth value. Constructions grammaticalized from mental/verbal process clauses take projected facts as complement. Such constructions contain the subject *I* or *you* and a perceptive mental verb such as *notice*. Perceptive verbs take projected facts as complement. Projected fact clauses pre-exists before the mental clauses. Since it is not brought into existence by the mental process, facts as complement succeeding perceptive mental verbs are quite semantically independent. This may prepare the subjects and mental verbs to structurally separate from the proposition. Subject *I* and *you* occur in this type of construction because they can contribute to the speaker-hearer interaction. Subject *I* is speaker-oriented and contributes to the indication of turn-taking. Subject *you* is listener-oriented and contributes to attention managing in dialogic discourses.

The clause-initial position is regarded as the position where textual projections emerge. Moving to clause-medial and clause-final positions can indicate their positional flexibility (Thompson & Mulac 1991). In the data retrieved from the 1820s, the raw frequency of textual projections in the clause-medial position ranks the highest, followed by those in the clause-final and clause-initial positions. Over the past 20 decades, the overall diachronic distribution of the typical textual projections shows similar trends to other typical discourse markers such as *well*, indicating that they are well-developed textual projections serving as discourse markers. This also confirms the idea that arising markers coexist with older markers (Hopper 1991). Over the past 20 decades, textual projections grammaticalized from interpersonal projections and those from ideational projections show different tendencies in their distributions across different clausal positions.

The clausal positions of textual projections grammaticalized from interpersonal projections tend to move rightward from the clause-initial and clause-medial positions to the clause-final position. The reason may be that occurring in the clause-initial and clause-medial positions may lead to misinterpretation of the construction as an interpersonal projection that expresses modal assessment. Another possible reason is that such constructions have several possible pragmatic roles to play when they are syntactically separated from the proposition clause, e.g., commitment modifier (Holmes 1984), hedging modifier (Myer 1989), and discourse initiator (Quirk et al. 1985). If the epistemic meaning is involved (e.g., hedging modifier), the construction can be interpreted as a modal adjunct and it is a constituent of the proposition clause. It is not yet fully grammaticalized. Clause-initial and clause-medial positions are common positions for modal adjuncts (e.g., *probably*). When no epistemic meaning is involved, it merely functions as a discourse marker. This marks the final separation from the proposition clause, indicating full transfer from the interpersonal domain to the textual domain. Positioning in the clause-final position indicates its function as a neutral marker. In this sense, the clause-initial and clause-medial textual projections grammaticalized from interpersonal projections are still undergoing an intermediate stage of the grammaticalization process, and the clause-final ones can be viewed as fully grammaticalized as discourse markers. For example:

7.3 a. I think that Conkey was a coward for not going farther. (COHA_1930)
b. I think Conkey was a coward for not going farther.
c. I think, Conkey was a coward for not going farther.
d. Conkey, I think, was a coward for not going farther.
e. Conkey was a coward for not going farther, I think.

In 7.3a and 7.3b, *I think* is interpersonal projection expressing the speaker's judgment on the given proposition. 7.3c and 7.3d illustrate the separation in form, which is marked by punctuation in written form. However, clause-initial and clause-medial positions are possible positions for interpersonal meaning. Cases in 7.3c and 7.3d can be viewed as the intermediate stage to interpret the construction as a discourse marker. In the intermediate stage, the interpretation of the subject-mental verb construction as interpersonal projection or ideational projection has competitive tension. Such a tension lies in between interpersonal projection without successor *that* (e.g., 7.3b) and textual projection in clause-initial (e.g., 7.3c) or clause-medial (e.g., 7.3d) positions. In 7.3e, when *I think* appears in the final position, it functions as an indicator of additive or adversative relation between the proposition and the context.

The diachronic distributions of interpersonal projections with and without *that* and textual projections in the three positions show that only clause-initial and clause-medial textual projections grammaticalized from interpersonal projections are complementary with corresponding interpersonal projections not being succeeded by *that*. This confirms that appearing in clause-initial and clause-medial positions can be viewed as an intermediate stage during the grammaticalization of subject-projecting verb constructions. Some low-confidence modal adverbs, e.g., *perhaps*, also manifest a tendency to be grammaticalized as discourse markers (Rozumko 2021). Such emerging one-word or phrasal discourse markers that lexically express modal meaning, e.g., *perhaps*, also show similar increasing prevalence in the clause-final position.

The textual projections directly grammaticalized from ideational projections increase in all three positions, with the frequency in the clause-initial position increasing the fastest and ranking overwhelmingly the highest in the 2010s. Their referential meaning does not involve epistemic meaning, and the roles they play as discourse markers are similar to conjunctive adjuncts. Textual projections mainly function as "reaction signal and initiator" (Quirk et al. 1985) to "signal transitions in the interactive development of discourse" (Biber et al. 1999) regardless of the positions they appear in. The clause-initial position is the best position to initiate a new clause, and that is why the frequency of textual projections grammaticalized from ideational projections soared in the clause-initial position. Their diachronic distributions of textual projections in the three positions show similar trends to those of the hypotactic clause complexes without the *that* complementizer. Hereby, this type of textual projections, having no potential to realize modal meanings and serving merely as neutral discourse markers, do not undergo the intermediate stage to compete for occupying the clause-initial and clause-medial positions, at least over the past 20 decades. Other single-word discourse markers do not express modal assessment, e.g., *well* and *now*, also show similar diachronic distribution trends in the three clausal positions.

The findings on the diachronic evolution of textual projections identify projecting clauses with the potential to develop into textual projections and help predict the future development of similar constructions in the English language. The discovery of the two pathways that projecting clauses may follow to develop into textual projections enriches the existing knowledge on metaphorization in SFL, particularly the transcategorization across semantic domains.

## References


Adamson S (2000) A lovely little example: Word order options and category shift in the premodifying string. In Fischer O, Rosenbach A, Steind D (eds.), Pathways of change: Grammaticalization in English. John Benjamins, Amsterdam, pp 39–66

Becher T, Trowler PR (2001) Academic tribes and territories: Intellectual enquiry and the culture of disciplines. SRHE & Open University Press, Buckingham

Biber D, Johansson S, Leech G, Conrad S, Finegan E (1999) Longman grammar of spoken and written English. Longman, London

Brinton LJ (2008) The comment clause in English. Cambridge University Press, Cambridge

Charles M (2006) Phraseological patterns in reporting clauses used in citation: A corpus-based study of these in two discipline. J English Spec Purposes 25:310–331

Charles M (2007) Argument or evidence? Disciplinary variation in the use of the Noun that pattern in stance construction. J English Spec Purposes 26(2):203–218

Halliday MAK, Hasan R (1976) Cohesion in English. Longman, London

Halliday MAK, Matthiessen CMIM (1999) Construing experience through meaning: A language-based approach to cognition. Cassell, London/New York

Halliday MAK, Matthiessen CMIM (2004) An introduction to functional grammar, 3rd edn. Arnold, London

He Q (2021) A corpus-based study of interpersonal metaphors of modality in English. Stud Neophilol 93(1):50–71

Holmes J (1984) Modifying illocutionary force. J Pragmat 8(3):345–365

Hopper PJ (1991) On some principles of grammaticization. Approaches Gramm 1:17–35

Hudson RA (1972) English complex sentences: An introduction to systemic grammar. North-Holland, Amsterdam

Langacker RW (1998) On subjectification and grammaticization. In Koenig JP (ed) Discourse and cognition: Bridging the gap. CSLI Publications, Stanford, pp 71–89

Martin JR (1992) English text: System and structure. John Benjamins, Philadelphia/Amsterdam

Mithun M (2016) Shifting finiteness in nominalization: From definitization to refinitization. In: Chamoreau C, Estrada-Fernández Z (eds) Finiteness and nominalization. John Benjamins, Amsterdam, pp 297–322

Myers G (1989) The pragmatics of politeness in scientific articles. Appl Linguis 10(1):1–35

Quirk R, Sidney G, Geoffrey L, Svartvik J (1985) A comprehensive grammar of the English language. Longman, London

Rose F (2016) On finitization. In Chamoreau C, Zarina EF (eds) Finiteness and nominalization. John Benjamins, Amsterdam/Philadelphia, pp 347–372

Rozumko A (2021) Textual functions of low confidence adverbs: The case of perhaps. Lingua 268:1–11

Taverniers M (2008) Interpersonal grammatical metaphor as double scoping and double grounding. Word 59(1–2):83–109

Thompson SA, Mulac AA (1991) Quantitative perspective on the grammaticization of epistemic parentheticals in English. Approaches Gramm 2:313–329

Traugott EC, Dasher RB (2002) Regularity in semantic change (Cambridge Studies in Linguistics 96). Cambridge University Press, Cambridge

# Chapter 8
# Conclusion

## 8.1 Major Findings

The first research question is what mode, genre, and discipline distribution features projections have. Within the ideational domain, the metaphorical realization of projection follows the general synchronic distribution of nominalization. The more metaphorical the embedding projection is, the more obscure the projector is. The invisibility of the projector enables the projected information to be less specific and more generic. In this way, more metaphorical embedding projection approaches the nature of thing more closely and tends to occur in more technical texts. What's more, the non-finite embedding projection is more compressed in information. Being non-finite allows less room for negotiation. Hereby, non-finite embedding projections generally occur more in the more technical texts than finite ones. When certain embedding projections involve expressions of modal meaning, the mode, genre and discipline distributions will be affected. One case is the modal fact. Facts as the appositive of modal fact nouns are more technical than those as the appositive of non-modal fact nouns. This is affected by the implicit objective modality realized by modal fact nouns. Another case is the fact as head. Finite cases as head are more technical than non-finite ones because finite facts as head are more likely to occur in relational process clauses in which the *it is ADJ* construction serves as explicit objective modality. In this sense, the degree of compression in information in the ideational domain interacts with the modality expression in the interpersonal domain to determine the synchronic distribution of fact projections.

Projecting clauses across different domains also demonstrate features of synchronic distribution. Only some ideational projections have the potential to be subjectified as interpersonal projections and further grammaticalized as textual projections. Such projecting constructions tends to occur in non-technical texts. The reason is that such projecting clauses construe the verbal process of giving personal opinion with low/median confidence in the ideational domain and the explicit subjective modality in the interpersonal domain and serve as discourse markers in the textual



M. Guo and Q. He, *A Corpus-Based Study of Projection in English from the Systemic Functional Perspective*, The M.A.K. Halliday Library Functional Linguistics Series,
https://doi.org/10.1007/978-981-97-5094-8_8

domain. The semantic nature leads to their prevalence in non-technical texts instead of technical texts.

The second research question is what diachronic evolution trends projection relations have. Two directions of evolution are identified. The first direction involves the evolution within the ideational domain. Projection clause complexes undergo metaphorization and result in embedding projections. The distribution of projection clause complexes is complementary to that of embedding projections; hereby, they form a system of choice. In the process of nominalization, the congruent realization of the projector as a nominal group can be realized metaphorically as a pre-modifier of the locution/idea noun. Embedding locutions and ideas with and without a pre-modifier indicating the projectors are found to be of the same group of data. In the diachronic evolution, embedding locutions/ideas with projector do not precede those without projector. The finite and non-finite embedding locutions/ideas are not diachronically complementary. That means finite embedding locutions/ideas are not further compressed into non-finite clauses. The finiteness of the projected clause in the hypotactic clause complex usually remains the same after the rank-shift from the clause rank to the word rank. The finiteness change of embedding clauses are determined by the speech function fulfilled and the subject consistency of the projecting clause and the projected clause. For example, the non-finite proposal idea of command tends to be finite after the rank-shift because the projector and the subject of the projected clause are different.

Embedding fact projections have no congruent realizations. In their diachronic evolution, the finite and non-finite facts as appositives to modify fact nouns are complementarily distributed. Therefore, finite and non-finite facts as appositive form a system of choice. The diachronic evolution of finite and non-finite facts standing on their own is affected by the explicit objective modality realized in the interpersonal domain. Facts as head can serve as extraposed subjects in the relational clauses. However, in the interpersonal domain, the impersonal projection *it is ADJ* (when the value is epistemic) realizes explicit objective modality, and it may be transferred from an implicit objective modality (e.g., *probably*). Such a transcategorization also affects the diachronic distribution of facts as head. The diachronic distribution of facts as head manifests the interaction of the ideational domain and the interpersonal domain.

The second direction of diachronic change is a leftward across-domain transcategorization of projection constructions. Two types of constructions that have the potential to transfer across semantic domains are identified. What they share in common is their potential to get separated from the proposition in the projected clause. Their pathways to transfer across different semantic domains are different. The first type is projecting construction containing subject *I* and a cognitive verb, e.g., *I think* and *I guess*. Such a projecting clause construes the process of the speaker giving a personal attitude with low/median confidence. With this nature, it has the potential to undergo subjectification, resulting in interpersonal projection serving as a modal adjunct. The information focus lies in its succeeding proposition. This paves the way for further leftward transfer to a more peripheral position. In the grammaticalization process, the interpersonal projection serving as a modal adjunct further moves leftward from the interpersonal domain to the textual domain, resulting in textual projection serving as an internal conjunction. Being clause-initial and clause-medial textual projections can be viewed as an intermediate stage because they may still function either as epistemic markers or neutral discourse markers. Being able to appear in a clause-final position is the indicator of their full grammaticalization.

The second type of constructions includes projecting clauses containing projecting verbs with high confidence (e.g., *I mean*) or mental clauses containing subjects *I* or *you* and mental verbs that take fact clauses as complement (e.g., *I know, you know*). In the latter ones, the verbs do not project the fact clauses. The projected clauses are facts standing on their own. Such a projected clause demonstrates the lowest degree of projection. The fact clauses pre-exist before the mental clauses, and they are relatively independent from the mental process clauses. Hereby, constructions of this type also have the potential to be separated from their complements. Once separated from the succeeding clauses, they serve as internal conjunctions in clause-initial, clause-medial, and clause-final positions. The transfer from mental clause construction to discourse marker does not have to undergo subjectification before grammaticalization.

## 8.2 Research Limitations

The synchronic and diachronic distribution analysis in the current research is exploratory, and some limitations should be acknowledged.

Firstly, the data collection is constrained by the retrieval of only typical constructions. Although typical constructions can represent the language phenomenon under research, the data retrieved is occasionally insufficient to yield statistically significant results, particularly in the disciplinary distribution analysis.

Secondly, the nominalizations of projecting clauses are challenging to retrieve because some locution and idea nouns do not have corresponding lexical verbs. For instance, the noun *view* can be the nominalization of verbs like *think* or *believe*. The noun *wish* is not necessarily nominalized from the verb *wish* but may be nominalized from verbs like *want* or *hope*. Only nominalizations with corresponding lexical verbs can be retrieved. This limitation prevents a comprehensive representation of the language phenomena and affects the validity of the general distribution analysis.

Thirdly, the data in the COCA include American English in use since the 1820s. The absence of data prior to the 1820s limits the investigation of how projection relations emerged in earlier historical phases. That is why the initial separation of *I*-cognitive mental verb construction and the *I*/*you*-perceptive mental verb construction from the respective propositions is not directly and explicitly addressed in the current study.

Fourthly, the transfer across different semantic domains is not necessarily marked by form and has to be analyzed from meaning interpretation. This presents obstacles for large-scale corpus-based studies because automatic retrieval can manage form identification only. For example, constructions undergoing the transfer from the ideational domain to the interpersonal domain exhibit no explicit changes in lexicogrammatical forms. They both appear in the form of a hypotactic projection clause. Whether the same projecting clause should be interpreted as ideational or interpersonal projection relies on both explicit factors (e.g., first-person projector and tense) and implicit factors (e.g., genre, cohesion, and cultural background). In the current research, large-scale automatic data retrieval can only identify data based on explicit factors. *I THINK* is chosen as the representative construction. It is one of the most grammatical realizations and receives a more independent status, but it is inevitable that some of them are primary clauses in clause complexes to construe. In the current research, considering all the instances of *I THINK* in clause complexes as interpersonal projections realizing explicit subject modality is somewhat overgeneralized.

## 8.3 Suggestions for Future Research

In light of the limitations in the present research, some suggestions are presented for future research as follows.

Firstly, data prior to the 1820s can be examined in future studies to facilitate quantitative research on the generation of interpersonal and textual projections. Automatic data retrieval can be combined with manual processing to have more accurate identification of relevant constructions. What's more, constructions that are not yet fully subjectivized or grammaticalized can be identified and examined to observe the earlier evolution of cross-domain language changes.

Secondly, in the present research, the search queries for retrieving textual projections only identify subject + mental verb constructions. In authentic language use, there are many other projection-related constructions that are highly grammaticalized, such as *regarding, as is known to all,* and *generally speaking*. These constructions may also have undergone transfer across semantic domains. Examining other projection-related constructions can expand our understanding of the evolution of projection. The grammaticalization of the verb-to-verb construction is also worth attention in future research. A projection clause complex can have either a finite or non-finite projected clause. Non-finite projected clauses in the hypotactic projection clause complexes have no complementizer. Therefore, the verb-to-verb construction containing a projecting verb and a non-finite clause can exhibit a diachronic change in information focus. The referent meaning of the projecting verb may get vaguer. Gradually, the projecting clause loses the grammatical status of a primary clause and the verb-to-verb construction receives the status of a hypotactic verbal group. Typical examples of this are constructions such as *want to* and *intend to*.

Thirdly, the current research focuses only on projection in the English language. What about other languages? For example, in the Chinese language, projection is realized as paratactic and hypotactic projection clause complexes. Does fact projection resulting from the nominalization of projecting verbs or zero also exist in Chinese?

Does the diachronic evolution of projection in different languages demonstrate similarities or differences? Exploring projection in different languages and comparing cross-language projections can provide deeper insights into the nature of projection.

# Appendix A
# System Network of Clause Relation in English

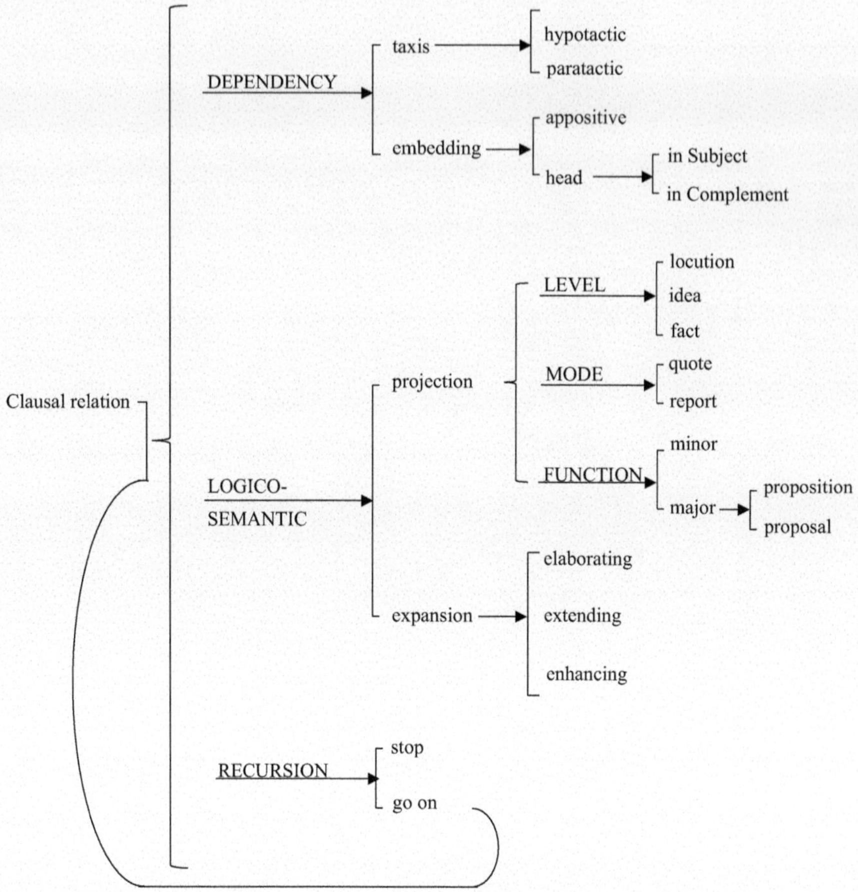




M. Guo and Q. He, *A Corpus-Based Study of Projection in English from the Systemic Functional Perspective*, The M.A.K. Halliday Library Functional Linguistics Series,
https://doi.org/10.1007/978-981-97-5094-8

# Appendix B
# CLAWS7 Tagset

APPGE possessive pronoun, pre-nominal (e.g., *my*, *your*, *our*)

AT article (e.g., *the*, *no*)

AT1 singular article (e.g., *a*, *an*, *every*)

BCL before-clause marker (e.g., *in order* (*that*),in order (*to*))

CC coordinating conjunction (e.g., and, or)

CCB adversative coordinating conjunction (e.g., *but*)

CS subordinating conjunction (e.g., *if*, *because*, *unless*, *so*, *for*)

CSA *as* (as conjunction)

CSN *than* (as conjunction)

CST *that* (as conjunction)

CSW *whether* (as conjunction)

DA after-determiner or post-determiner capable of pronominal function (e.g., *such*, *former*, *same*)

DA1 singular after-determiner (e.g., *little*, *much*)

DA2 plural after-determiner (e.g., *few*, *several*, *many*)

DAR comparative after-determiner (e.g., *more*, *less*, *fewer*)

DAT superlative after-determiner (e.g., *most*, *least*, *fewest*)



M. Guo and Q. He, *A Corpus-Based Study of Projection in English from the Systemic Functional Perspective*, The M.A.K. Halliday Library Functional Linguistics Series,
https://doi.org/10.1007/978-981-97-5094-8

DB before determiner or pre-determiner capable of pronominal function (*all*, *half*)

DB2 plural before-determiner (*both*)

DD determiner (capable of pronominal function) (e.g., *any*, *some*)

DD1 singular determiner (e.g., *this*, *that*, *another*)

DD2 plural determiner (*these*, *those*)

DDQ wh-determiner (*which*, *what*)

DDQGE wh-determiner, genitive (*whose*)

DDQV wh-ever determiner, (*whichever*, *whatever*)

EX existential *there*

FO formula

FU unclassified word

FW foreign word

GE Germanic genitive marker—(' or *'s*)

IF *for* (as preposition)

II general preposition

IO *of* (as preposition)

IW *with*, *without* (as prepositions)

JJ general adjective

JJR general comparative adjective (e.g., *older*, *better*, *stronger*)

JJT general superlative adjective (e.g., *oldest*, *best*, *strongest*)

JK catenative adjective (*able* in *be able to*, *willing* in *be willing to*)

MC cardinal number, neutral for number (e.g., *two*, *three*)

MC1 singular cardinal number (*one*)

MC2 plural cardinal number (e.g., s*ixes*, *sevens*)

MCGE genitive cardinal number, neutral for number (*two's*, *100s*)

MCMC hyphenated number (*40–50*, *1770–1827*)

MD ordinal number (e.g., *first*, *second*, *next*, *last*)

MF fraction, neutral for number (e.g., *quarters*, *two-thirds*)

ND1 singular noun of direction (e.g., *north*, *southeast*)

NN common noun, neutral for number (e.g., *sheep*, *cod*, *headquarters*)

NN1 singular common noun (e.g., *book*, *girl*)

NN2 plural common noun (e.g., *books*, *girls*)

NNA following noun of title (e.g., *M.A.*)

NNB preceding noun of title (e.g., *Mr.*, *Prof.*)

NNL1 singular locative noun (e.g., *Island*, *Street*)

NNL2 plural locative noun (e.g., *Islands*, *Streets*)

NNO numeral noun, neutral for number (e.g., *dozen*, *hundred*)

NNO2 numeral noun, plural (e.g., *hundreds*, *thousands*)

NNT1 temporal noun, singular (e.g., *day*, *week*, *year*)

NNT2 temporal noun, plural (e.g., *days*, *weeks*, *years*)

NNU unit of measurement, neutral for number (e.g., *in*, *cc*)

NNU1 singular unit of measurement (e.g., *inch*, *centimetre*)

NNU2 plural unit of measurement (e.g., *ins.*, *feet*)

NP proper noun, neutral for number (e.g., *IBM*, *Andes*)

NP1 singular proper noun (e.g., *London*, *Jane*, *Frederick*)

NP2 plural proper noun (e.g., *Browns*, *Reagans*, *Koreas*)

NPD1 singular weekday noun (e.g., *Sunday*)

NPD2 plural weekday noun (e.g., *Sundays*)

NPM1 singular month noun (e.g., *October*)

NPM2 plural month noun (e.g., *Octobers*)

PN indefinite pronoun, neutral for number (*none*)

PN1 indefinite pronoun, singular (e.g., *anyone*, *everything*, *nobody*, *one*)

PNQO objective wh-pronoun (*whom*)

PNQS subjective wh-pronoun (*who*)

PNQV wh-ever pronoun (*whoever*)

PNX1 reflexive indefinite pronoun (*oneself*)

PPGE nominal possessive personal pronoun (e.g., *mine*, *your*)

PPH1 3rd person sing. neuter personal pronoun (*it*)

PPHO1 3rd person sing. objective personal pronoun (*him*, *her*)

PPHO2 3rd person plural objective personal pronoun (*them*)

PPHS1 3rd person sing. subjective personal pronoun (*he*, *she*)

PPHS2 3rd person plural subjective personal pronoun (*they*)

PPIO1 1st person sing. objective personal pronoun (*me*)

PPIO2 1st person plural objective personal pronoun (*us*)

PPIS1 1st person sing. subjective personal pronoun (*I*)

PPIS2 1st person plural subjective personal pronoun (*we*)

PPX1 singular reflexive personal pronoun (e.g., *yourself*, *itself*)

PPX2 plural reflexive personal pronoun (e.g., *yourselves*, *themselves*)

PPY 2nd person personal pronoun (*you*)

RA adverb, after nominal head (e.g., *else*, *galore*)

REX adverb introducing appositional constructions (e.g., *namely*, *viz.*, *e.g.*)

RG degree adverb (*very*, *so*, *too*)

RGQ wh-degree adverb (*how*)

RGQV wh-ever degree adverb (*however*)

RGR comparative degree adverb (*more*, *less*)

RGT superlative degree adverb (*most*, *least*)

RL locative adverb (e.g., *alongside*, *forward*)

RP prep. adverb, particle (e.g., *about*, *in*)

RPK prep. adv., catenative (*about* in *be about to*)

RR general adverb

RRQ wh- general adverb (*where*, *when*, *why*, *how*)

RRQV wh-ever general adverb (*wherever*, *whenever*)

RRR comparative general adverb (e.g., *better*, *longer*)

RRT superlative general adverb (e.g., *best*, *longest*)

RT quasi-nominal adverb of time (e.g., *now*, *tomorrow*)

TO infinitive marker (*to*)

UH interjection (e.g., *oh*, *yes*, *um*)

VB0 *be*, base form (finite, i.e., imperative, subjunctive)

VBDR *were*

VBDZ *was*

VBG being

VBI *be*, infinitive (To be or not… It will be..)

VBM *am*

VBN *been*

VBR *are*

VBZ *is*

VD0 *do*, base form (finite)

VDD *did*

VDG *doing*

VDI *do*, infinitive (I may do… To do…)

VDN *done*

VDZ *does*

VH0 *have*, base form (finite)

VHD *had* (past tense)

VHG *having*

VHI *have*, infinitive

VHN *had* (past participle)

VHZ *has*

VM modal auxiliary (*can*, *will*, *would*, etc.)

VMK modal catenative (*ought*, *used*)

VV0 base form of lexical verb (e.g., *give*, *work*)

VVD past tense of lexical verb (e.g., *gave*, *worked*)

VVG -ing participle of lexical verb (e.g., *giving*, *working*)

VVGK -ing participle catenative (*going* in *be going to*)

VVI infinitive (e.g., *to give… It will work…*)

VVN past participle of lexical verb (e.g., *given*, *worked*)

VVNK past participle catenative (e.g., *bound* in *be bound to*)

VVZ -s form of lexical verb (e.g., *gives*, *works*)

XX not, n't

ZZ1 singular letter of the alphabet (e.g., *a*, *b*)

ZZ2 plural letter of the alphabet (e.g., *a's*, *b's*)

# Appendix C
# POS List

| | | | |
|---|---|---|---|
| [nn*] | noun.all | [v?d*] | verb.ED |
| [v*] | verb.all | [v?n*] | verb.EN |
| [j*] | adj.all | [v?g*] | verb.ING |
| [r*] | adv.all | [vv*] | verb.[LEX] |
| [xx*] | neg.all | [vb*] | verb.[BE] |
| [at*] | art.all | [vd*] | verb.[DO] |
| [d*] | det.all | [vh*] | verb.[HAVE] |
| [p*] | pron.all | [jjr*] | adj.CMP |
| [app*] | poss.all | [jjt*] | adj.SPRL |
| [i*] | prep.all | [rp*] | adv.PRTCL |
| [c*] | conj.all | [rrq*] | adv.WH |
| [n*] | noun.all + | [pn1*] | pron.INDF |
| [*nn1*] | noun.SG | [pp*] | pron.PERS |
| [*nn2*] | noun.PL | [pnq*] | pron.WH |
| [*nn0*] | noun.CMN | [ppx*] | pron.REFL |
| [np*] | noun. + PROP | [mc*] | num.CARD |
| [nn*] | noun.-PROP | [md*] | num.ORD |
| [vv0*] | verb.BASE | [cc*] | conj.CRD |
| [v?i*] | verb.INF | [cs*] | conj.SUB |
| [vvi*] | verb.INF/LEX | [uh*] | interj |
| [vm*] | verb.MODAL | [y*] | PUNC |
| [v?z*] | verb.3SG | | |



M. Guo and Q. He, *A Corpus-Based Study of Projection in English from the Systemic Functional Perspective*, The M.A.K. Halliday Library Functional Linguistics Series,
https://doi.org/10.1007/978-981-97-5094-8

# Appendix D
# Query Syntax

<table>
<tr><th colspan="4">Simple slot</th></tr>
<tr><th>Syntax</th><th>Meaning</th><th>Examples</th><th>Sample matches</th></tr>
<tr><td>Word</td><td>One exact word</td><td>Mysterious</td><td>Mysterious</td></tr>
<tr><td>[pos]</td><td>Part of speech (exact)</td><td>[v?g*]</td><td>Going, using</td></tr>
<tr><td>[pos*]</td><td>Part of speech (wildcard)</td><td>[v*]</td><td>Find, does, keeping, started</td></tr>
<tr><td rowspan="2">[lemma]</td><td rowspan="2">Lemmas (all forms of a word)</td><td>[sing]</td><td>Sing, singing, sang</td></tr>
<tr><td>[tall]</td><td>Tall, taller, tallest</td></tr>
<tr><td>[=word]</td><td>Synonyms [[=strong]</td><td>Formidable, muscular, fervent</td><td></td></tr>
<tr><td>[user:list]</td><td>Customized lists</td><td>[mark_davies@byu.edu:clothes]</td><td>Tie, shirt, blouse</td></tr>
<tr><td>Word|word</td><td>Any of these words</td><td>stunning|gorgeous|charming</td><td>Stunning, charming, gorgeous</td></tr>
<tr><td>*xx</td><td>Wildcard: * = any # letters</td><td>un*ly</td><td>Unlikely, unusually</td></tr>
<tr><td>X?xx</td><td rowspan="2">Wildcard: ? = one letter</td><td>s?ng</td><td>Sing, sang, song</td></tr>
<tr><td>X?xx*</td><td>s?ng*</td><td>Song, singer, songbirds</td></tr>
<tr><td>-word</td><td>NOT (followed by PoS, lemma, word, etc.)</td><td>-[nn*]</td><td>The, in, is</td></tr>
<tr><td>word.[pos]</td><td>Exact word and part of speech</td><td>strike.[v*]</td><td>Strike (only as a verb)</td></tr>
<tr><td>word*.[pos]</td><td>Substring and part of speech</td><td>dis*.[vvd]</td><td>Discovered, disappeared, discussed</td></tr>
</table>

(continued)



M. Guo and Q. He, *A Corpus-Based Study of Projection in English from the Systemic Functional Perspective*, The M.A.K. Halliday Library Functional Linguistics Series,
https://doi.org/10.1007/978-981-97-5094-8

(continued)

Simple slot

| Syntax | Meaning | Examples | Sample matches |
|---|---|---|---|
| [lemma].[pos] | Lemma and part of speech | [strike].[v*] | Strike, struck, striking |
| [=word].[pos] | Synonym and part of speech | [=beat].[v*] | Hit, strike, defeat (but not nouns, like *rhythm* or *drumming*) |
| [[=word]] | Synonym and lemma | [[=publish]] | Announced, circulating, publishes, issue (no part of speech specified, so some noun uses) |
| [[user:list]] | Customized list and lemma | [[mark_davies@byu.edu:clothes]] | Tie, tying, socks, socked, shirt, blouses (no part of speech specified, hence tying) |
| [[=word]].[pos] | Synonym and lemma and part of speech | [[=clean]].[v*] | Mop, scrubs, polishing |
| [[user:list]].[pos] | Customized list and lemma and part of speech | [[mark_davies@byu.edu:clothes]].[n*] | Tie, ties, sock, socks (i.e., just nouns) |

Multiple slots

<table>
<tr><th>Syntax</th><th>Examples</th></tr>
<tr><td>fast|quick|rapid [nn*]</td><td>Fast food, rapid transit</td></tr>
<tr><td>Pretty -[nn*]</td><td>Pretty smart' pretty as (but not pretty girl, pretty picture, etc.)</td></tr>
<tr><td>[get] her to [v*]</td><td>Get her to stay, got her to sleep</td></tr>
<tr><td>.|,|; nevertheless [p*] [v*]</td><td>. Nevertheless it is<br>; nevertheless he said</td></tr>
<tr><td>[break] the [nn*]</td><td>Break the law, broke the story</td></tr>
<tr><td>[[beat]].[v*] * [nn*]</td><td>Beat the Yankees, beaten to death</td></tr>
<tr><td>[=gorgeous] [nn*]</td><td>Beautiful woman, attractive wife</td></tr>
<tr><td>[put] on [ap*] [mark_davies@byu.edu:clothes].[n*]</td><td>Put on her hat, putting on my pants</td></tr>
</table>

# Appendix E
# Typical Projection Nouns

| Level of projection | Speech function | Nouns |
|---|---|---|
| Locution | Statement | Statement, report, news, rumor, claim, assertion, argument, insistence, proposition, assurance, intimation |
| | Question | Question, query, inquiry, argument, dispute |
| | Offer | Offer, suggestion, proposal, threat, promise |
| | Command | Order, command, instruction, demand, request, plea |
| Idea | Statement | Thought, belief, knowledge, feeling, notion, suspicion, sense, idea, expectation, view, opinion, prediction, assumption, conviction, discovery |
| | Question | Doubt, question |
| | Offer | Intention, desire, hope, inclination, decision, resolve |
| | Command | Wish, desire, hope, fear |
| Fact | Case | Fact, case, point, principle, accident, lesson, grounds |
| | Chance | Chance, possibility, likelihood, probability, certainty, offchance, impossibility |
| | Proof | Proof, indication, implication, confirmation, demonstration, evidence, disproof |
| | Need | Requirement, need, rule, obligation, necessity, onus, expectation, duty |



M. Guo and Q. He, *A Corpus-Based Study of Projection in English from the Systemic Functional Perspective*, The M.A.K. Halliday Library Functional Linguistics Series,
https://doi.org/10.1007/978-981-97-5094-8

# Appendix F
# Raw Frequency of Diachronic Distributions of Typical Textual Projections in Different Syntactic Positions


M. Guo and Q. He, *A Corpus-Based Study of Projection in English from the Systemic Functional Perspective*, The M.A.K. Halliday Library Functional Linguistics Series, https://doi.org/10.1007/978-981-97-5094-8

| Position | Decade | *You know* | *I mean* | *I know* | *You mean* | *I think* | *I hope* | *I guess* | *I believe* | *I suppose* | *Well* | *Perhaps* |
|---|---|---|---|---|---|---|---|---|---|---|---|---|
| Initial | 1820s | 12 | 3 | 11 | 0 | 9 | 14 | 1 | 10 | 5 | 145 | 66 |
| | 1830s | 33 | 8 | 24 | 0 | 19 | 17 | 2 | 18 | 16 | 516 | 71 |
| | 1840s | 27 | 3 | 10 | 0 | 16 | 24 | 1 | 18 | 9 | 628 | 81 |
| | 1850s | 28 | 10 | 17 | 0 | 39 | 22 | 1 | 14 | 23 | 534 | 107 |
| | 1860s | 42 | 22 | 33 | 0 | 42 | 20 | 3 | 17 | 14 | 605 | 92 |
| | 1870s | 37 | 12 | 21 | 0 | 39 | 12 | 0 | 19 | 23 | 1004 | 86 |
| | 1880s | 45 | 23 | 21 | 1 | 47 | 20 | 0 | 16 | 24 | 1265 | 70 |
| | 1890s | 35 | 13 | 20 | 2 | 50 | 22 | 3 | 13 | 17 | 1000 | 76 |
| | 1900s | 59 | 12 | 43 | 1 | 17 | 13 | 4 | 21 | 5 | 850 | 109 |
| | 1910s | 111 | 11 | 43 | 3 | 35 | 9 | 8 | 15 | 16 | 1420 | 126 |
| | 1920s | 103 | 28 | 23 | 3 | 34 | 13 | 5 | 19 | 13 | 1456 | 125 |
| | 1930s | 1175 | 246 | 208 | 59 | 45 | 14 | 5 | 17 | 22 | 8951 | 120 |
| | 1940s | 950 | 283 | 149 | 67 | 30 | 7 | 7 | 15 | 8 | 7125 | 115 |
| | 1950s | 1487 | 466 | 211 | 128 | 35 | 9 | 7 | 12 | 15 | 11,226 | 105 |
| | 1960s | 1654 | 921 | 224 | 154 | 42 | 5 | 11 | 12 | 6 | 14,204 | 120 |
| | 1970s | 2041 | 2059 | 227 | 85 | 33 | 6 | 7 | 9 | 9 | 11,606 | 93 |
| | 1980s | 2072 | 1951 | 198 | 65 | 26 | 3 | 7 | 5 | 14 | 9633 | 92 |
| | 1990s | 2273 | 2084 | 251 | 58 | 36 | 4 | 13 | 11 | 6 | 8354 | 71 |
| | 2000s | 2354 | 2543 | 273 | 36 | 23 | 7 | 16 | 13 | 5 | 7815 | 66 |
| | 2010s | 2305 | 2631 | 356 | 25 | 36 | 3 | 10 | 2 | 4 | 7589 | 67 |
| Medial | 1820s | 139 | 23 | 34 | 6 | 114 | 102 | 9 | 211 | 69 | 65 | 792 |
| | 1830s | 221 | 32 | 71 | 8 | 261 | 76 | 31 | 276 | 125 | 129 | 1305 |

(continued)

(continued)

| Position | Decade | *You know* | *I mean* | *I know* | *You mean* | *I think* | *I hope* | *I guess* | *I believe* | *I suppose* | *Well* | *Perhaps* |
|---|---|---|---|---|---|---|---|---|---|---|---|---|
| | 1840s | 212 | 69 | 65 | 11 | 233 | 56 | 34 | 265 | 150 | 178 | 1337 |
| | 1850s | 340 | 35 | 111 | 11 | 333 | 104 | 39 | 246 | 283 | 153 | 1503 |
| | 1860s | 424 | 37 | 136 | 16 | 357 | 77 | 41 | 262 | 227 | 191 | 1306 |
| | 1870s | 704 | 41 | 147 | 14 | 482 | 110 | 39 | 309 | 371 | 266 | 1297 |
| | 1880s | 566 | 49 | 165 | 16 | 427 | 75 | 37 | 268 | 250 | 276 | 1171 |
| | 1890s | 477 | 45 | 152 | 11 | 458 | 69 | 37 | 227 | 213 | 280 | 1058 |
| | 1900s | 584 | 38 | 143 | 12 | 387 | 57 | 60 | 205 | 238 | 271 | 1066 |
| | 1910s | 574 | 51 | 181 | 7 | 454 | 57 | 171 | 235 | 260 | 355 | 1002 |
| | 1920s | 419 | 48 | 149 | 11 | 438 | 51 | 85 | 256 | 308 | 302 | 895 |
| | 1930s | 637 | 90 | 219 | 13 | 450 | 46 | 113 | 194 | 212 | 1059 | 749 |
| | 1940s | 453 | 97 | 202 | 11 | 326 | 49 | 138 | 130 | 171 | 762 | 549 |
| | 1950s | 770 | 133 | 252 | 21 | 345 | 47 | 139 | 154 | 199 | 1242 | 558 |
| | 1960s | 845 | 195 | 262 | 22 | 361 | 37 | 132 | 141 | 201 | 1816 | 493 |
| | 1970s | 1376 | 281 | 201 | 15 | 542 | 41 | 139 | 127 | 177 | 1789 | 501 |
| | 1980s | 1057 | 225 | 183 | 15 | 308 | 29 | 110 | 95 | 117 | 1674 | 475 |
| | 1990s | 1555 | 303 | 185 | 11 | 337 | 20 | 167 | 89 | 121 | 1865 | 396 |
| | 2000s | 1970 | 394 | 238 | 19 | 270 | 26 | 144 | 82 | 112 | 1981 | 375 |
| | 2010s | 1960 | 469 | 257 | 16 | 297 | 14 | 140 | 60 | 91 | 2175 | 322 |
| Final | 1820s | 23 | 20 | 11 | 0 | 11 | 17 | 6 | 23 | 22 | 10 | 12 |
| | 1830s | 64 | 10 | 24 | 6 | 27 | 10 | 16 | 22 | 28 | 4 | 22 |
| | 1840s | 79 | 14 | 10 | 4 | 33 | 20 | 21 | 40 | 47 | 9 | 30 |
| | 1850s | 171 | 24 | 17 | 12 | 64 | 18 | 38 | 66 | 75 | 5 | 42 |

(continued)

(continued)

| Position | Decade | *You know* | *I mean* | *I know* | *You mean* | *I think* | *I hope* | *I guess* | *I believe* | *I suppose* | *Well* | *Perhaps* |
|---|---|---|---|---|---|---|---|---|---|---|---|---|
| | 1860s | 331 | 34 | 33 | 13 | 127 | 42 | 39 | 63 | 143 | 9 | 83 |
| | 1870s | 537 | 39 | 21 | 15 | 137 | 48 | 52 | 91 | 192 | 12 | 65 |
| | 1880s | 503 | 35 | 21 | 8 | 123 | 36 | 55 | 76 | 153 | 6 | 70 |
| | 1890s | 417 | 50 | 20 | 11 | 132 | 24 | 42 | 66 | 116 | 11 | 70 |
| | 1900s | 532 | 53 | 43 | 21 | 144 | 39 | 99 | 82 | 146 | 5 | 71 |
| | 1910s | 811 | 92 | 43 | 15 | 189 | 49 | 258 | 89 | 216 | 13 | 133 |
| | 1920s | 596 | 86 | 23 | 17 | 145 | 40 | 198 | 77 | 221 | 15 | 103 |
| | 1930s | 856 | 161 | 208 | 17 | 254 | 66 | 371 | 80 | 224 | 143 | 137 |
| | 1940s | 971 | 181 | 149 | 27 | 228 | 84 | 418 | 72 | 213 | 100 | 140 |
| | 1950s | 1145 | 218 | 211 | 26 | 267 | 84 | 480 | 72 | 218 | 99 | 139 |
| | 1960s | 1316 | 195 | 224 | 24 | 285 | 77 | 525 | 75 | 267 | 213 | 135 |
| | 1970s | 1421 | 167 | 227 | 33 | 356 | 70 | 396 | 74 | 225 | 177 | 133 |
| | 1980s | 1056 | 133 | 198 | 31 | 355 | 56 | 386 | 60 | 163 | 170 | 103 |
| | 1990s | 1028 | 170 | 251 | 25 | 324 | 68 | 464 | 43 | 151 | 192 | 127 |
| | 2000s | 874 | 147 | 273 | 29 | 325 | 55 | 431 | 46 | 121 | 152 | 80 |
| | 2010s | 845 | 166 | 356 | 23 | 342 | 46 | 357 | 38 | 131 | 123 | 87 |

The manufacturer's authorised representative in the EU is Springer Nature Customer Service Centre GmbH, Europaplatz 3, 69115 Heidelberg, Germany. If you have any concerns regarding our products, please contact ProductSafety@springernature.com

Printed and bound by CPI Group (UK) Ltd, Croydon, CR0 4YY
01/10/2026
02225926-0001